Be

"Nouev...   3

2016

Os Melhores "Novos" Poeta...   3

2016

Compiled and edited by
Tendai R. Mwanaka & Daniel Da Purificação

Langaa Research & Publishing CIG

Publisher:
Langaa RPCIG
Langaa Research & Publishing Common Initiative Group
P.O. Box 902 Mankon
Bamenda
North West Region
Cameroon
Langaagrp@gmail.com
www.langaa-rpcig.net

Distributed in and outside N. America by African Books Collective
orders@africanbookscollective.com
www.africanbookscollective.com

ISBN-10: 9956-764-89-2

ISBN-13: 978-9956-764-89-1

About the editors

Tendai Rinos Mwanaka is a multi-disciplinary artist who lives in Chitungwiza, Zimbabwe. Books published include among others, *Zimbabwe: The Urgency of Now (creative nonfiction), Finding a Way Home (stories novel), Revolution (poems), Playing To Love's Gallery(poetry), Pearls of Awareness (poetry)*. Curator and editor of the following anthologies, *Democracy, Good Governacne and Development in Africa, Best New African Poets Anthologies, Zimbolicious Poetry Anthology, Experimental Writing African Vs Latin America Anthology*. He is also a published and exhibited visual artist (photography, painting, drawing, collage, video.) represented by Arna Gallery, Sweden. A sound/musical artist, mentor, translator, scholar, theorist, reviewer, critic... Work has been published in over 400 journals in over 27 countries, translated into French, Germany and Spanish.

Daniel da Purificação, was born in 1983 in some place called Angola. Has a Bachelor diplome and Masters Degree. He likes to speak and read, is always thinking and writing all the time. Since 2002 he has lived out of the place where he was born. He is a Honour invited at Hispanamerican Writers summit HORAS DE JUNIO that happens every year in Sonora (México). He also works as a journalist on rádio and a freelancer, teacher at university, is a public policy consultant... He is also a recommended facilitator and he talks about society, philosophy, politics, education, democracy... He has two collections of poems (THE ANGOPOEMS and INTERMITENCIAS) that he hopes will be postdeath publications... Now he lives between México and Angola.

Contributor's Bio Notes

Ajise Vincent is an economist and social researcher based in Sokoto, Nigeria. His works have appeared or are forthcoming at *The Bond Street Review, Indiana Voice Journal, Jawline Review, Jalada, Ink, Sweat & Tears, Chiron Review, Asian Signature, Ann Arbor Review, Yellow Chair Review, Bombay Review, Birmingham Arts Journal, Best New African Poets 2015 Anthology, Snapdragon: a journal of art & healing, The Cadaverine, Souvenir literary journal, Elsewhere, Sentinel Quarterly* & various literary outlets. He is a recipient of the *Eriata Oribhabor poetry prize 2015*. He loves coffee, blondes & turtles.

Asiko Joan is a Kenyan Stage and Screenwriter, Poet, a budding author of short African stories and a performing artist. She is a graduate of Theatre Arts and Film Technology from Kenyatta University. She draws her passion from the world around her. Her works mostly tackle social and economic issues.

Atukunda Rogers is a journalist, filmmaker, writer, researcher and educator.
He was born in Mbarara hospital on 27th March 1987. He got a government scholarship and joined Makerere University, Kampala where he graduated with an Honours BA Education in Literature and English Language studies in 2011.

Awendit Marial is a South Sudanese poet and essayist, born Dec, 1989. His poems have appeared in the *Brittle Paper* and the *Kalahari Review*. He resides in his hometown Yerul.

Ballard Chaun was raised in both Missouri and California. He has lived with his wife in Ghana, West Africa, where they taught at a local area school. He writes, "For the past five years, we have travelled and taught throughout various countries, and we are currently preparing for our new relocation to Saudi Arabia." He has had poems recently published and accepted by *shufPoetry, Grist, Sukoon,* and *The Caribbean Writer.*

Ballot Mari: I am an Author and Poet living in Stellenbosch, South Africa at present. I have been passionate about Poetry and Nature from an early age. I wrote my first poem at age of 5. Here we encountered atrocious political injustices and the complexities of corruption as well as more than 11 official different languages in one country?

Baptista Britos Adriano nasceu em 1992, Zambézia (Moçambique), é estudante finalista do curso de Tradução Francês-Português na Universidade Eduardo Mondlane, é poeta, residente na cidade de Maputo.

Benfiquista Fabious é o psiodónimo literário de Fábio Audora Pedro, nascido em Saurimo, Lunda Sul a 31 de Março de 1994. Frequentou os estudos primários e secundários na mesma cidade, onde actualmente frequenta o curso de Gestão de Recurso Humanos, no Instituto Superior Politécnico Lusíada da Lunda Sul e exerce a função de repórter na empresa Arte Visual Lda. Para além de coordenador do Secretariado Arquidiocesano da Juventude, na Arquidiocese de Saurimo. É membro do núcleo Lev'Arte Lunda Sul, onde descobre a veia poética e participou da primeira Antologia do núcleo, intitulada "As sementes do Nordeste". Conta apenas com obras em prelo.

Bismarck Mimi Brako: I am originally from Ghana. In the last 18 years, I have lived in the United States of America. After taking off from my teaching career to raise my children, I decided to work on some writing (something that I have always been passionate about). I plan on publishing an anthology in the next year. The premise of my anthology is nostalgia. It captures various themes, events, foods, and memories of things that I remember as a child in Ghana. The 3 poems in this anthology are samples from the collection.

Botha Ernestu: I am a 20 year-old aspiring poet from South Africa, Richards Bay. I have been writing poetry since I was very young and write in my two home languages Afrikaans and English.

Canhanga Mohamed, *Mociano dos Santos,* nasceu em Luanda, em Junho de 1997. Filho do jornalista e escritor Luciano (Soberano) Canhanga, cedo foi influenciado para Letras e Ciências Sociais, mas é na Arquitectura, outra arte, que mais se revê, frequentando o II ano da Licenciatura em Urbanismo e Paisagismo. O gosto pela composição textual já leva tempo. Porém, a queda para o texto conotativo é recente e encontra nos livros escritos e outros colecionados pelo pai a fonte de conhecimento artístico, lendo desde Saramago a Pepetela. A observação, sempre presente entre os artistas da palavra, dá força aos seus textos que descrevem vivências, sentimentos e anseios.

Canhanga Soberano nasceu no Libolo, Angola, em 1976. Licenciado em Comunicação Social e mestrando em Ciências Empresariais. Trabalhou em diversos media nacionais e estrangeiros. Leccionou na Universidade Lweji A Nkonde e no Instituto Superior Politécnico Lusíada da Lunda Sul. Foi assessor de comunicação da diamantífera Catoca e dirige o Gabinete de Recursos Humanos do Ministério da Geologia e Minas.Publicou: "O Sonho de Kaúia" (romance-2010), "Manongo-Nongo" (contos-2012), "10encantos (poesia -2013), "O Relógio do Velho Trinta" (romance-2014), "O coleccionador de pirilampos" (Contos-2014) e "Canções ao vento" (poesia 2015). No prelo: "Amor sem Pudor" (poesia).

Cassoma Cláudia is an emerging writer from Luanda, the capital of Angola. Her passion for writing has followed her since her early seasons, being ameliorated each day. Besides the act of creating written works, Cláudia devotes her life to social work deeply believing in a better world.

Chafaki Fayssal is a Moroccan Arab poet, whose poetic style still preserves the norms and conventions of Classical Poetry in Arabic, English, Russian, and Spanish, in form and content, but delivers conventionally and conveys faithfully modern and contemporary messages to a multi-cultural literary audience. Fayssal Chafaki is a simple farmer, poet, and writer, and lives now in the Western country-side of the Kingdom of Morocco, where he has devoted himself to revive poetry and literature which, seemingly, have ceased to play their important and great universal role.

Chambule Márcia Rosel,de nacionalidade Moçambicana,Nascida a 10 de Setembro de 1994,escreve poemas desde os 12 anos.
Tem feito declamações dos seus poemas em vários saraus que tem acontecido na cidade e província de Maputo.

Charles Tembi is a Zimbabwean-born writer and poet who has recently attained a Masters Degree in English Studies from Stellenbosch University, South Africa, where she currently resides.

Chikowore Handsen: I am a poet who writes to inform, entertain and engage. I believe in the power of words to draw attention and also to incite deep thinking. I like poetry and believe that poems are good therapy. I have been published in a few magazines and read my poems at events.

Chikowore Tafadzwa: After completing my A Level studies, I started writing poems. Poetry helps me to express my feelings in a unique and exciting way. I also use poems as tools for informing people. I was inspired to write poems by my uncle *Handsen* who is an established poet.

Chilaule Virgílio Henrique, nascido a 15 de Dezembro de 1990 em Maputo, fez o Curso de Psiquiatria e Saúde Mental. Actualmente trabalha como Técnico de Psiquiatria e Saúde Mental. Iniciou sua careira na poesia em 2009, fazendo parte de um grupo cultural chamado aldeia literária, do qual nasceu uma antologia poética, com a participação dos seus 3 poemas com títulos: "Rio Incomáti", "O preço do Saber" e "Casar-te-ei". Desde então, tem pulicado em jornais, dando como menção o jornal Xitende e tem participado em várias obras literárias, tendo seu textos publicados em antologias internacionais tais como Galiza-Moçambique "Numa Linguagem e Numa Sinfonia" e "Caravelas em Viagem" editadas em suiça.

Chipandambira Phumulani was born in Mhondoro Ngezi, he currently stays with his family in Norton (Zimbabwe). He is a freelance writer who likes reading and writing poems and short stories.

Chirasha Mbizo was born in Zvishavane district in 1978. He is an internationally acclaimed performance poet, writer and creative projects facilitator and live literature producer. In 2003 he was the New Generation Poetry Delegate at The Gothenburg International Book Fair, Nordic African Institute Writers Seminar, and Swedish Writers Union reading night in Sweden. He co-authored a poetry anthology titled, Whispering Woes of Ganges and Zambezi with Sweta Vikram, an Indian born-New York based poet.

Chumo Gideon (Mr. Roundsquare) is a dark humour monger, tramedist, and fictioneer of maximalist prose, poetry and short story. He studied English Language, Linguistics and Literature in college, and taught for long in the Horn of Africa before retiring back home to HR practice. You can catch up with him @Chumolet or in http://www.myroundsquare.blogspot.com and http://www.abortedpoet.wordpress.com

Coates Christine is a poet and writer from Cape Town. She has an MA in Creative Writing from the University of Cape Town. Her poems and stories have been published in various literary journals. Her debut collection *Homegrown*, published in 2014, by Modjaji Books, received an honourable mention from the Glenna Luschei Prize. Her poems have been selected for the EU Sol Plaatje Poetry anthologies every year since inception: 2011 – 2016, and *Best "New" African Poets 2015 Anthology*.

Correia Cátia Regina, 26 anos, nascida e residente no Rio de Janeiro (Brasil) região da Baixada fluminense , mulher preta,nascida em diáspora,que busco constantemente referências e inspiração (de vida e poesia) em reminiscências africanas,que acabam se misturando, supostamente com essa tal brasilidade. Estudante de Letras na Universidade Federal rural do Rio de Janeiro Integrante de grupos de luta e resistência da juventude negra local, desenvolvo o tom de alguns versos, nos amores, lutas, angustias,e "achismos" de quem transita por discursos e vozes múltiplas dentro de minha (pseudo) realidade .

David Stephen Temitope is a Nigerian poet currently studying for a Ph.D in South Africa. His poems explore the quotidian experiences of Africans.

Dlamini Ndumiso: I am a 20 years old. My writing journey started at the age of 15 when I was visiting a psychologist that my school had recommended I go see, since I was being a very troublesome teen. In the doctor's waiting room, I picked up a book by Khalil Gibran, a compilation of his poetry and some of his short stories. Immediately I was taken up and since then, I have been writing and writing.

His poetry is famed for its Pan-African eloquence and profundity, therefore **Dzonze Edward** is a Zimbabwean born writer who appreciates life with a poetic bias, spoken word artist "NRS", Edward has 2 poetry collections to his name, *Many Truths Told at Once* (Royalty Publishing USA, 2015) and *Wisdom Speaks* (Royalty Publishing USA, 2016). Co-editor of *Zimbolicious Poetry Anthology*

Domingos Magno, António D. S. Domingos de nome completo, 39 anos de idade. Estudante universitário de economia e gestão. Vivo em Luanda para onde me mudei com a família no tempo de guerra, sou da Gabela, kwanza Sul. Pai, filho, activista cívico e acérrimo defensor dos direitos humanos o que me condena a ser um eterno poeta da vida.

Armel Fernand Mbida Ebo'o est né le 19 mars 1981 au Cameroun. Il a découvert la poésie grâce aux écrivains français Victor Hugo et Baudelaire, ainsi qu'à travers l'écrivain espagnol Federico García Lorca. Il a étudié le Commerce International ce qui lui a permis de connaître d'autres cultures. Pour écrire, il s'inspire de l'histoire des villages dominés par les nations impérialistes. Il se définit lui-même comme "amoureux des gens et de la nature".

Ezeigwe Kelechi is a queer feminist and poet. He has been published in anthologies and journals, including *The Muse Journal*, reputed to be the longest surviving student journal in West Africa (since 1963). He has won the first prize for poetry at The Muse Literary Arts festival 2015, and won the third prize for the same category the following year, 2016. His work was published in the *Best New African Poets 2015 Anthology* edited by Tendai R.Mwanaka and Daniel da Purifacacao. He believes in Individualism.

Farinha Ismael, poeta, declamador, escritor e contabilista, nasceu em Angola província de Luanda aos 27.08.1981. Começou a escrever poesia por influência do movimento Hip Hop (RAP) foi a sua primeira manifestação artística, tem participado em declamações de poesia em Luanda nas actividades culturais, é membro no movimento Lev´Arte, Chá de Caxinde.
Participou em algumas antologias, em Angola e Brasil.

Fernandes Joel: Escritor e poeta estudante do curso de engenharia informática pela universidade. Técnica de Angola utanga nasceu em luanda aos,07,10,1981 no município do cazenga

Fernando Evaristo de 22 anos, escrevo a 4 anos. Meu gosto pela escrita começa na altura em que transito para o segundo ciclo do ensino secundário e porque química era a das piores disciplinas para mim decido seguir as letras e lá tive oportunidade de estudar a literatura e a arte de escrever entrou em mim. Sou vencedor do concurso "desenha-me a tua liberdade" da CCFM/ICMA (Centro Cultural Franca Moçambique/ Instituto Cultural Alemanha Moçambique) e de mais concursos. Meu maior foco é a poesia e contos.

Cris Poetisa é o pseudônimo de **Ferreira Cristina**, nascida aos 23 de Abril de 1975 na Província de Cabinda/Angola, onde cresceu e viveu muitos anos. Tem 4 meninas que são a sua maior alegria. Tem uma grande paixão pela escrita desde os tempos de adolescência e é através desta linda arte que é a poesia que consegue exprimir todos os seus sentimentos. Participei em uma Antologia denominada Elos-No Verso.Também é uma apaixonada pela estética.

Garcia Antonio has served in the SA Army as an officer and senior officer for 16 years. His experience includes two UN deployments in the DRC and in Sudan as well as various national and regional deployments. Among several degrees he holds an MA in History (Cum Laude), Garcia writes and researches on topics ranging from the First World War, Anglo-Boer War, Korean War, military geography, Peacekeeping and future war. Furthermore, the author teaches as an adjunct lecturer at *Unisa* and will be a visiting scholar at Columbia University during 2017.

George Abigail is a South African diarist, writer and poet, aspirant young adult novelist and playwright. Her prose *Wash Away My Sins* was nominated for the Pushcart Prize. She has received grants from ECPACC, the National Arts Council in Johannesburg, and the Centre for the Book in Cape Town.

Gombera Charmaine: I champion the defending of human rights driven by the strong desire and thirsty to be free mentally, socially, and economically. Poetry uncoils the umbilical cords of being dependent and oils the spheres of freedom. A pen is sharp razor to bring freedom.

Sheril Guzha is a 24 year old Zimbabwean writer who can sweep you off your feet, take you down memory lane and back to the present, all the way to endless imaginations of what the future holds with passion inked on paper. She is an enthusiastic writer who is driven by the whole spectrum of emotions, from hurt, pain, melancholy and despair to hope, joy and love

Al Hassanein Rana: Rana is a young revolutionary female with a cutting gift for writing. Daughter of an Egyptian writer. She does not hesitate to express herself and she often does not care about political correctness. She breaks the clichés about the Egyptian women or about religion in Muslim countries. Rana was awarded in HAMSA annual *Dream deferred essay contest*. Lately, she contributed with a collective of her writings in *Graffiti Baladi book project* that was published in France by *Omniscience Editions.*, a *BNAP 2015* contributor!

Hayward Michelle: I am a 24 year old female living in Cape Town. I have travelled all over Africa – Zimbabwe, Mozambique, Malawi, Swaziland, Tanzania and Egypt. Besides travelling, I also love kite surfing and of course I love reading and writing poetry but I have never had a poem published.

Hurley Niall: In a country where it's easy to hold on to old hangups, Niall seeks to add something new to the conversation. Previously he's done so as a teacher, blogger and advertising copywriter. But he believes nothing can be more powerful than sharing South Africa's new narrative than poetry and prose.

Ibrahim Nureni was born in Lagos, Nigeria. He is an essayist, poet, analyst, playwright and activist. His poems have been published (and sent for publication) both in local and international journals and magazines.

My name is **Agu Raphael Gift Ihuoma**. I am from Abia State, Nigeria. I am 19 years old. I am a student and a young writer.

Ijalusi Tola is a Nigerian poet and writer who writes from Ibadan and whose works have appeared on various online Literary Journals and Magazines such as *PAROUSIA Magazine, PIN Quarterly Journal, Bravearts Magazine, Kalahari Review, Kreative Diadem, Duane's Poe Tree, WRR, The Poet Community etc*

Jaison Lisa is budding poet and writer born and raised in the city of Gweru in Zimbabwe. She studied at the Midlands State University before relocating to SA. She has also been active in writing social development proposals for RathoAfrica, an NGO she founded in 2016 to focus on programs that advance gender equality and conduct social research on social and humanitarian issues.

Jorge Augusta é uma jovem angolana que nasceu a 10 de Maio de 1995, no Huambo, mas residente em Saurimo, onde frequentou os seus estudos primários e secundários em Saurimo, Lunda Sul. Cidade em que frequenta actualmente o 2º ano do Curso de Geologia na Escola Superior Politécnica da Lunda Sul, afecta a Universidade Lueji

A'nkonde. Apesar de não ter nenhuma obra publicada, reúne já alguns inscritos e é membro do Núcleo Le'Arte Lunda Sul. É actriz e também intérprete de surdos.

Juma Brenda is a Kenyan Poet, Stage and Screenwriter, Actress and a Filmmaker and a Graduate of Theatre Arts and Film Technology from Kenyatta University. She derives her passion from any form of art be it Literary, Performing or Visual Arts. Her works revolve around social, political and economic commentaries.

Kapp Beula, born in the city of Johannesburg, matriculated from the school Noordelig, where after working mostly in sales, discovered the love of teaching. Currently resides in Jozi enjoying teaching; loves writing, reading and making jewelry.

Khoza Tralone Lindiwe holds a BA Communications degree from the University of Johannesburg (RAU) and a Post graduate Diploma in Marketing. She is a qualified Marketing Specialist. She regularly writes for *All4Women* and *Bizcommunity* in South Africa and internationally her work includes writing for *MUMRU* a United Kingdom's online magazine for single mothers, as well as for a South Australian Woman's Fashion Magazine.

Kudyahakudadirwe Christopher 'Voice' is a Zimbabwean freelance writer, poet and teacher living and working in South Africa. He holds a Masters of Creative Writing from the University of the Western Cape. His short stories appear in *Ghost-Eater and Other Stories* and *New Contrast*. Two of his poems were recently published in *Best "New" African Poets 2015 Anthology*. Eight of his poems have appeared in *Harvest: The University of the Western Cape Masters in Creative Writing Poetry Anthology 2016*. His novel, *You Are Not Alone,* is currently with publishers.

Kunguru Dennis Brad is a graduate of Makerere University and currently teaching English at Kitengela International School in Kenya. His passion for writing began during his studies in Uganda and he has never looked back ever since. He is also a part time actor and a script writer.

"Poeta das Calças rasgada", pseudónimo literário de **Kunsevi Tony**, nascido aos 08 de Dezembro de 1980, na província do Zaire, Nzeto. É um jovem portador de vários talentos capazes de darem vida as letras, imagens e outras obras artísticas, Poeta, declamador, membro do Movimento Lev´Arte desde 2009.

Khwela Nelisa Khethokuhle is a 20 year-old from a small town in Kwa-Zulu Natal, South Africa. She is an introvert and enjoys spending her time reading and reflecting. Her interests include languages, astronomy, literature, art and gothic calligraphy. Her poetry is inspired by poets such as *Sara Teasdale* and *Emily Dickinson*.

Lobadias Obedes – Escritor, declamador, compositor musical e activista moçambicano. 22 anos de idade. É um dos autores de Leveza da Alma, Entre o Samba o Fado e a Poesia e Em todos os Ritmos da Poesia (Brasil, 2014, 2015 e 2016 respectivamente). Já foi jornalista e animador de rádio. É estudante universitário.

Meu nome é **Luciano Ngonga Salvador**, sou angolano de 26 anos de idade e sou formado em engenharia civil. Desde pequeno que gosto de artes e literatura é uma paixão que tenho. Comecei a escrever poemas com 13 anos, e fui mostrando as pessoas quando completei 16, e desde então tenho buscado melhorar dia após dia. Não tenho livro publicado ainda, mas estou em fase de conclusão de 3 livros que venho escrevendo desde os 18. Um de poemas já constituído mas sem patrocínio a espera de uma oportunidade. Os livros são projectos não oficiais que faço nos meus tempos livres e espero um dia poder lança-los .

Mabungu Eliza is a Film and Television graduate from the University of Johannesburg; she is a daughter of two Mozambican parents. She is a writer, versatile in writing. She would like to establish her own Production company in the future which will be derived from her short stories.

I am **Mangwende Kelvin**, I have published two Shona plays namely *Chaminuka,* and *Chimurenga (War)* An Anthology of poems called *The* *madman in Heaven*. I have featured in several anthologies and I have published a collection of short stories called *An axe with a Blood*.

Masikonte Monicah: a 24 year old Kenyan girl. She graduated from Daystar University with a bachelor of communication. She started writing professionally in 2015 and is currently working on her first poetry collection book. She lives in Nairobi Kenya

Masilela Sibusiso Ernest is a 34 year old male born in a town called Emalahleni in Mpumalanga, he is a metaphysical poet who loves creative writing and spends most of his time reading and travelling. He believes that poetry can free the mind and bring enlightenment…

My name is **Mavolwane Mandla Ashley**, aged 18years. I live in Chitungwiza a town just outside the capital city of Zimbabwe. I was doing my Advanced Level, studying History, Divinity & Literature In English at Zengeza 1 High School.

Maziba Dime is originally from Democratic Republic of Congo. He considers himself as pan-Africanist and a disciple of Marcus Garvey. He is a poet, writer and activist. He is also a financial accountng student from Durban University of Technology in the Republic of South Africa, the country where he is currently living. He is taking part in the Florence Foundation, an NGO which protests against women abuse and children illiteracy mainly in the eastern part of Congo. He is working on his poetry book.

Mbambo Mikateko E. is a qualified journalist and a Media Relations Officer by profession. She is an aspiring poet and novelist. She collects and enjoys African literary works. Apart from writing she is a pastel drawer and crafts woman. Mikateko has poems and stories on Africa waiting to heard and read.

McKeown James is an 11 year old from Grahamstown, South Africa, who attends St Andrew's Senior Prep. He writes poetry and short stories, and is about halfway through his first novel, a sci-fi epic. James is also mad about football, and spends a lot of time practicing to be a better keeper for his team.

Mhondera Chenjerai is a Writer (novelist, author, poet, playwright, song-writer) an Actor and Performing Poet, published in *Best New African Poets 2015 Anthology, Zimbolicious Poetry Anthology*, and several online journals. He is a Patron and Founder of International Writers Association (IWA), formerly Young Writers Club. Helps to nurture talents and publishes upcoming writers through his literary Organisation. He is a Citizen of the World.

Mitra Amitabh is a South African poet based at East London, South Africa. He is a visual artist, having exhibited his acrylic works in major galleries of South Africa, India and the Europe. Amitabh heads the Department of Emergency Medicine and Trauma at Cecilia Makiwane Hospital, Mdantsane, Eastern Cape.

Mmeka Chuma (Born June 21, 1975) is a unique and multi-talented Nigerian. He is a new-generation performance artist and author of several books; he is a movie actor, altruist and activist with a chain of laudable activities. Married with children, Chuma a.k.a. "T-char" takes life one step at a time

Hello. My name is **Moagi Marumo**. I am 22 years old. Born and raised in South Africa. I have always had a love of writing. I suffer from bipolar and most of my poems reflect intense emotion or a lack thereof.

I am **Mojolaoluwa Mof'Oluwawo**, a young and inspired African who holds poetry as a sublime form of self expression. As to handiwork, a jeweler, a photographer by hobby and a writer by lifestyle. I blog on sundry issues on
oluwapelumimojolaoluwalivingstone.wordpress.com

Mucha Pasomi is an educationist. She has published educational and creative works in Kenya and the UK. Her days and interests are occupied by her three sons, extended family, reading, learning, teaching, writing, charity work, church, friendships and, generally, the business of living fruitfully. "Sycophanta" was inspired by, well, sycophants.

Nabasa Linda is a prolific poet, short story writer and playwright. As she writes from the heart, she is passionate about writing from page to stage to give women and children a holistic voice in theatre. She is also a creative consultant for *Mango Tree Uganda*.

Naicker Ravi is a Teacher at Kwahluzingqondo High School in KwaZulu-Natal, South Africa. His interests are reading, writing and watching movies. He was responsible for researching his family history since 1891.

The poet, **Naidoo Myron Menon** was born and raised in Durban. He is a High School Mathematics Teacher in Durban. He plays cricket and is deeply involved in spiritual activities of *The Sai Organization of South Africa*. Myron travels yearly to Prishanti, India to assist with charity work.

Nawa Khanyisile writes that, "The act of writing poems helps me tap into parts of myself that often don't make sense until they're down on paper. Poetry is food. We either share, compare, or learn a piece, then we nibble with the anticipation of becoming full after being openly expressive and heard." He is a 13 year old poet from Johannesburg, South Africa.

Ndanzi Tunu is a Tanzanian student taking doctor of medicine at Kilimanjaro Christian medical college, located in Moshi a region in the northern of Tanzania, writer of poetry, published some of her poems at *All poetry* a public exchange forum. She lives in Mbeya,Tanzania

Negrouche Samira est une poète algérienne de langue française auteure d'une dizaine de recueils de poésie, d'anthologies et de traductions; également traductrice de poètes contemporains de l'arabe et de l'anglais vers le français. Ses livres sont principalement publiés en Algérie et en France. Traduite dans une vingtaine de langues, elle est publiée dans de nombreux pays en volume ou en collectifs. Parmi ses publications: L'opéra cosmique (2003) Le Jazz des oliviers (2010) et Six arbres de fortune autour de ma baignoire

(2017). Médecin de formation, elle se consacre exclusivement à l'écriture.

Neto Levita Estanislau: Fiz a publicação dos dois em um so Mas apenas em formato digital em Maio de 2016 e recepção do público foi boa agora estou a escrever o 4 livro intitulado O meu encontro com Deus A par doa artigos e compilações que gosto de fazer a parte... No campo literário acho que a biografia é essa mano...

Nieuwenhuis Bianca: I am a young South African currently in my final year studying English Literature and Creative Writing through UNISA. I have always had a passion for literature. My mother instilled a love of reading in me. Reading and writing became my escape from worldly problems, my solitude.

My name is **Nieuwoudt Jacobus Gideon Louis**. I'm 26 years old. Born in 1990. 2nd of February 1990. That's what I'd call a double whammy. I'm South-African and Afrikaans. I'm a philosophizing humorist. An Outlaw Romantic. A Boere Romantiek.

Ngobale Eric: His poem in this anthology was inspired by the xenophobic attacks that took place within the Republic of South Africa during 2015. It is a reflection of his frustrations as well as his fears and concerns with regards to xenophobia.

Nonso Charles ORJI: An avid lover of art in literary form, I see that the fabrics of the world are sewn on the diligent hands of words thus the realization of this leads ultimately to the soul awakening. I yearn that all will come to love poetry.

Ntensibe Joseph: I am passionate when it comes to writing poetry although I embrace other genres. Being a high school teacher of Literature and English, I work with young people with writing. I am finalising the publication of my anthology of over one hundred poems.

Nxomani Refilwe Khanya writes, "Being black and unable to speak a vernacular language, I grew up in a childhood littered with ridicule.

It was through mastering the only language in my arsenal, English, that I gained my sense of self-worth and through writing poetry that I learned what it *really* meant to communicate.

Nyamu Kariuki is a highly artistic Kenyan poet, radio playwright, editor and high school teacher. He graduated from Makerere University with honours in English, Literature and Education. He is published widely both in print and online, such as in *A Thousand Voices Rising, Best New African Poets 2015 Anthology,* and also forthcoming in *Multi-verse: Kenyan Poetry in English Since 2003, Experimental Writing: Volume 1, Africa Vs Latin America Anthology,* among others.

Ochoki Michael 'Wudz' is a Kenyan poet and memoirist residing in Sudan. He co-founded *Eldoret Poets Association, One-Night Stand Poetry* and editor of EPA annual anthology. Winner of *KOLA: African Street Writers Awards,* his poems have appeared in *BN Poetry Award, StoryMoja Hay Festival,* several anthologies, magazines and blogs. His muse is mysticism, the absurdity of human nature and philosophy. He's currently working as a journalist and educator in war-torn Northern Sudan state.

Omuna Andrew H is a teacher by profession, with love for writing and film. He is currently pursuing a Master's degree in Literature at Makerere University. He is still compiling his first poetry anthology as well as aspiring on making films.

Ojok James Onono: I am an upcoming Poet from Gulu, Northern Uganda. In 2008, one of my poems *Lamunu, My Mother,* won the second prize in the poetry poster project competition organized by Uganda Women's Writers Association *Femrite.* In 2015 I published a poetry book with *Nissi Publisher* Kampala entitled *But My Heart.* I am a freelance Journalist attached to *102, Mega Fm Gulu* and *Acholi-Times* an online media.

Osei Anthony Akoto Jr: Though seeking a doctorial degree in Public Health Law and Psychological Counseling in Northern California, Anthony has had a love of artistic expression ranging from dancing, to music and of course poetry. Since moving to the states in 2005 for undergraduate studies, Anthony has been blessed with many different opportunities to express his artistic side which have allowed him growth as a writer and poet for both peer-reviewed medical articles and fictional/descriptive poetry as well.

The inaugural Poet Laureate for Cheshire, UK , **Owen Harry** came to South Africa in 2008. He has published six poetry collections, including *Small Stones for Bromley* (Lapwing Publications, 2014). He edited *I Write Who I Am: an anthology of Upstart poetry*, featuring the work of nineteen young poets from township schools in the Eastern Cape; and the international anthology *For Rhino in a Shrinking World*, in support of efforts to save this iconic animal from extinction. Harry lives in Grahamstown, South Africa.

Owoyemi Ayomide is a medical doctor who moonlights as a poet, he is an art enthusiast and has had one of his poems published on www.sarabamag.org

Oyeku Ayo's works have appeared in various anthologies across the globe, including, *Illuminations* (Celestial Arts, 2006); *Fingernails across the Chalkboard* (Third World Press, 2007); *Stand Our Ground* (Freedomseed Press, 2013); *The Sky is Our Earth* (Sankofa, 2015). He also appeared as a Guest Contributor in *According to Sources* (Writers Project of Ghana, 2015). *VINYL, Kalahari Review & Brittle Paper* are places to visit for his most recent poems.

Palaia Fernando Paciencia Luteiro: Estudiante Angolano Residente no exterior do País (Cuba)

Pedro Marcelo Bernardo Maluarte, filho de Bernado Pedro Teresa e Maria Isabel Joaquim Malaurte, de nacionalidade moçambicana, nascido aos 21 de dezembro de 1986 na provincia de Inhambane, cidade de inhambane, licenciado em geografia pela universidade Eduardo Mondlane e actualmente, estudante no curso de mestrado em população e desenvolvimento, é autor dos poemas que a seguir são expostos.

Pephel Marvel Chukwudi grew up in Abia State, and studied at Nnamdi Azikiwe University, Nigeria. His works have appeared or are forthcoming in *High Coupe, Praxis Magazine for Arts and Literature, The Kalahari, Peeking Cat Poetry, Poetry Tree on the Charles,* amongst others.

p'Khisa Wafula is a poet, writer, essayist and teacher from Kenya. He studied English, Literature and Education at Moi University. His poetry has been published in *Best "New" African Poets 2015 Anthology, Aubade Magazine* (Issue 1), *Emanations* (issue 2), *African writer, Antarctica Review, NYSAI Press* and several other online literary journals.

Eu sou **Polá Carmona,** Nascido aos 22/03/1997, natural da Cidade de Quelimane, Província da Zambézia – Moçambique. Estudante do 2º Ano do curso de Relações Internacionais e Diplomacia, no Instituto Superior de Relações Internacionais, em Maputo. A arte é a única língua que falo. Eu gosto da poesia e nela vejo uma oportunidade de trazer à vida as palavras e sentimentos mortos que jazem dentro de mim.

Purdon Bradley is a young poet and writer from East London. The poems focus on themes of nature, depression (and recovery from depression), love, soul-searching, and various themes based on the fantasy genre. Their affinity to nature and philosophy is what greatly inspires their poetry.

Ribeiro Rosa, é uma poetisa Lusoangolana nascida no Huambo (Angola), actualmente vive na Inglaterra. Escreve desde pequenina.

Robalo Sónia Sousa, nasceu a 04 de Maio de 1974, na Ilha Terceira-Açores. O seu trajecto de vida foi algo muito singular (com um percurso um pouco sinuoso que a fez evoluir e tornar-se numa mulher decidida, com raízes e convicções fortes). Filha de pai e família paterna Angolana e mãe e família materna Portuguesa. Regressou a Portugal com 26 anos. A sua filha nasceu, quando frequentava o 4º ano do seu curso e para poder concluir a formação, esta acompanhava-a para a faculdade e estágio. Dois anos depois de ter terminado a sua licenciatura e com uma criança de dois anos nos braços voltou para o Fundão Dedicou-

Saxingo Guilson Silvano é angolano, nasceu a 1 de Agosto de 1994. É licenciando em Direito, no Instituto Superior Politécnico Lusíada da Lunda Sul. Autor do livro "Aurora Jubilosa" publicado em 2016, co-autor da Antologia Poética "Entre o sono e o sonho" VI volume, pela Chiado Editora, em 2015. Coordena o Núcleo Lev´Arte Lunda Sul e colabora como repórter na Arte Visual, Comunicação e Prestação.

Sehloho Abel is a journalist, blogger, short story author and a photographer. He majors in English and Literature. With the nature of his qualification, he has volunteered at a local community newspaper. He is currently studying his Degree in Creative Writing at the University of South Africa.

Shea Thandiwe is a 26 year old Mosotho girl. She lives in Maseru, Lesotho. She holds a BA degree in English Language and French from National University of Lesotho. She started as a Spoken Word poet, performing for local radio stations and high school talent shows.

Simbad Hélder é pseudónimo de Helder Silvestre Simba André, filho de Pompílio Mateus André e de Albertina Simba, nasceu aos 13 de Agosto de 1987, na província de Cabinda, em Angola. É estudante do 4ª ano do curso de Línguas, Tradução e Administração da Universidade Católica de Angola; professor de Língua Portuguesa e de Literatura Africana. Começou a sua actividade artística entre 1997 e 1998, escrevendo poesia. É Coordenador Geral e membro co-fundador do Movimento Litteragris. Tem poemas, contos e artigos publicados na revista Agris Magazine, no Jornal Cultura Angolana e no Blogg brasileiro *poemario-prosaeverso.blogspot.com*.

Sombra Edgar Ginga ou simplesmente Poeta Sombra, é Angolano, Natural de Luanda, aos 17/09 e Casado com Tânia Ginga. É Escritor, Compositor e Poeta, formado em Gestão de Recursos Humanos. É membro do Movimento Berço Literário (Coordenador do Núcleo de

Belas), é simpatizante da brigada Jovem de Literatura, é amigo do Lev´árte. É um escritor que tem como fonte de inspiração, tudo o que nos cerca…a vida, a natureza humana etc.

Yeshni Sookraj: I am an aspiring poet of Indian heritage from Durban, South Africa. I hold a BA in Communication Science from the University of South Africa with 8 years of all round experience in media, communication and marketing. In 2005 my poem *"Reality"* was published by the Poetry Institute of Africa - *An Anthology of Africa Verse* – titled *Transcending Moments*.

Swanson Archie is a 60 year old Capetonian poet and surfer. His poems appear in the 2016 *English Alive Anthology* of 50 years of South African high school poetry, the *2014 McGregor Poetry Festival Anthology* and the *Best New African Poets 2015 Anthology* as well as in the South African quarterly poetry publications - *New Contrast* and *Stanzas*. In 2016 three of his poems in *Best New African Poets 2015 Anthology,* were translated into Spanish by Martín López-Vega and published in the Spanish National newspaper, El Mundo. A poem also appears in the anthology - *Experimental writing: Africa vs. Latin America*.

Taiye Ojo is a young Nigerian who uses poetry as a handy tool to hide his frustration with the society. "I'm a twenty- three-year-old microbiology graduate from Tansian University. I love books and Anime in that order." Taiye, has some of his muddled thoughts published and forthcoming in a few e-magazines such as *Kalahari Review, Tuck magazine, Lunaris Review, Elsewhere, whispersinthewind33* and so on.

L'écrivain **Tchak Sami** est né en 1960 au Togo. Il y a fait des études de philosophie avant de s'installer depuis 1986 en France pour ses études où il a obtenu un doctorat de sociologie. Depuis plusieurs années il se consacre à l'écriture. Il a publié à ce jour huit romans (dont Place des Fêtes et Hermina aux éditions Gallimard, Le paradis des chiots et Al Capone le Malien aux éditions du Mercure de France) et cinq essais (dont La sexualité féminine en Afrique aux éditions L'Harmattan et La couleur de l'écrivain aux éditions La Cheminante).

Thompson Jarred is an English graduate of Alabama State University. He currently lives in Johannesburg, South Africa and is seeking to study his Master's in Creative Writing.

Tokwe Hosea is Chief Library Assistant at Midlands State University, Zimbabwe, His first short story, *The Carcass* appeared in the *Munyori Online Journal*. Hosea Tokwe delivered his performance poetry at the Poetry Slam in 2012 organised by Pamberi Trust. He is among the poetry contributors in the *Best New African Poets 2015 Anthology*, and *Zimbolicious poetry anthology*

Tshukudu Thato: I am a 17-year-old male that stumbled upon a great interest in poetry at the age of 14. I began writing short poems then after a year of maturing I learned to write from the heart without any restrictions. I am passionate about Poetry and wish to inspire potential young writers.

Tsiwah Abeiku "Nana" Arhin, author and co-author of *Dead Epistles* and *Palm Leaves* (both poetry collections) edits Poetry for *Lunaris Review*, Nigeria. Tsiwah writes and performs with the Afro-poetry movement, *The Village Thinkers*, from his fatherland, Cape Coast, Ghana.

Ussaque Orlando Jaoquim, nascido aos 15 de Outubro de 1992. Quanto a sua inserção na literatura, há muito que se desvendar ainda, pois não se sabe com exactidão quando começa a escrever, segundo ele, afirma com algumas dúvidas que descobriu o domínio pela escrita em meados do ano de 2009. Para além do mundo das letras, estuda actualmente engenharia electrónica e telecomunicações na Escola Superior de Ciências Náuticas.

Venketsamy Roy, born in a small Indian village called Illovo in South Africa. I am a lecturer of Mathematics and Life Skills at the University of Pretoria. My inspiration for poetry began in 1975 at primary school. I write poetry as a hobby and enjoy oil paintings.

de Viriato Victor "Vitória certa daquele que tem muita sorte". Apareci num momento de liberdade espiritual do meu criador no ano

de 2008. Vivi preso no papel dentro da gaveta até a criação da página do facebook em 2013 e aqui estou:
www.facebook.com/-otairivedrotciv

Wilcox Afua is a female architect based in Johannesburg. She was born to a Ghanaian mother, English father and was raised in the sleepy town of Mbabane, Swaziland. She holds a postgraduate MArch at the University of Witwatersrand. She is also currently a design lecturer at the University of Johannesburg. Afua is the founder of the *Poetic Seed Poetry festival* in Swaziland that was started in 2009-2012 in order to educate underprivileged youths about the performance art of slam poetry.

Williams Athol is a South African poet and social philosopher. He was awarded the *Sol Plaatje European Union Poetry Award* in 2015 and 2016. Athol has published three poetry collections, the most recent being *Bumper Cars*. He holds five degrees and is currently studying political philosophy at Oxford University.

Chamo-me **Zita Lorna Telma** natural de xai-xai de nacionalidade Moçambicana, nascida aos 12 de janeiro de 1993.

Znaidi Ali (b.1977) lives in Redeyef, Tunisia. He is the author of several chapbooks, including *Experimental Ruminations* (Fowlpox Press, 2012), *Moon's Cloth Embroidered with Poems* (Origami Poems Project, 2012), *Bye, Donna Summer!* (Fowlpox Press, 2014), *Taste of the Edge* (Kind of a Hurricane Press, 2014), and *Mathemaku x5* (Spacecraft Press, 2015). For more, visit *aliznaidi.blogspot.com*.

Zvoushe Vupenyu is a father of three beautiful girls, Zvoushe is a Zimbabwean poet based in Gweru. He started writing when he was at high school. He has appeared in a number of anthologies and is currently working on publishing his own volume.

Zulu Lucas is a South African contemporary poet, a student at university of Johannesburg. He lives in Kwa-guqa Emalahleni, his work is recently published in *Stand There Shining a recovery anthology* (USA) 2016

Table of Contents/Table des Matières/Tabela de Conteúdos

Introduction/La presentation/Introdução.................... xxxvii

Part 1: Place, Heritage and Identity.......................1-36

Chenjerai Mhondera (Zimbabwe): I want that Africa Go!
Roy Venketsamy (South Africa): African Sunrise
Chaun Ballard (USA): Field Notes
Nonso Charles Orji (Nigeria): Lagos
Amitabh Mitra (South Africa): Mdantsane, East London
Handsen Chikowore (Zimbabwe): Victoria Falls
Niall R Hurley (South Africa): Shelley Point
Harry Owen (South Africa): Hadeda
Archie Swanson (South Africa): wind pump
Michael 'Wudz' Ochoki (Kenya/Sudan): Ka
Mbizo Chirasha (Zimbabwe): Identity Apples
Cláudia Cassoma (Angola): The Africa I know
Mimi Brako Bismarck (Ghana/USA): How We Ate Fufu
Chaun Ballard (USA): Lessons
Roy Venketsamy (South Africa): Unsung Heroes (a tribute to my dad)
Yeshni Sookraj (South Africa): The Spirit of its Searcher
Ravi Naicker (South Africa): The Naicker Patriarch
Chaun Ballard (USA): Twelve ways of Looking at Darkness
Edward Dzonze (Zimbabwe): The black African
Bianca Nieuwenhuis (South Africa): I too am an African
Athol Williams (South Africa): Echoes
Ojo Taiye (Nigeria): Untitled
Harry Owen (South Africa): Questions to ask in South Africa

Part 2: Language, Writing, Poetry and Art................. 37-50

Mbizo Chirasha (Zimbabwe): Blue Lemons
Michael 'Wudz' Ochoki (Kenya/Sudan): I write
Mbizo Chirasha (Zimbabwe): My Painful Poetry
Marvel Chukwudi Pephel (Nigeria): Rain: A word Sonnet
Ndumi Dlamini (South Africa): Dark words

Marvel Chukwudi Pephel (Nigeria): Diagonal Acrostic: The
Juxtaposition
OjoTaiye (Nigeria): Untitled
Phumulani Chipandambiri (Zimbabwe): My Religion
Hélder Simbad (Angola): intention
Pasomi Mucha (Kenya): Sycophanta

**Part 3: Spiritual, Existential, Religious,
Inspirational, and Individual**.................................51-84

Anthony Okoto Osei. Jr (Ghana/USA): The Sun's First Born –
Opener of the Ways
Bradley Purdon (South Africa): Alive in Silver
Anthony Okoto Osei. Jr (Ghana/USA): Shango's Song is Oya's
Nocturne
Bradley Purdon (South Africa): I am connected
Ayo Oyeku (Nigeria): I Will Not Die Tonight
Mandla Mavolwane (Zimbabwe): Day Dream
Beula Kapp (South Africa): Rivers
Ayo Oyeku (Nigeria): Prayer
Harry Owen (South Africa): In the botanical gardens
Agu Raphael Gift Ihuoma (Nigeria): Have you ever wondered
Jarred Thompson (South Africa): The Epistemology of Desire
James McKeown (South Africa): Dreaming
Jarred Thompson (South Africa): For
Tola Ijalusi (Nigeria): Omi Alaafia
Ali Znaidi (Tunisia): A Google Glass Sonnet
Nelisa Khethokuhle Khwela (South Africa): Flight reflections
Ali Znaidi (Tunisia): The Sky Hides its Ash
Yeshni Sookraj (South Africa): Reality
Tafadzwa Chikowore (Zimbabwe): Death
Ali Znaidi (Tunisia): Decayed Bones and Exhaled Breaths
Michelle Hayward (South Africa): The glass cage
Michael 'Wudz' Ochoki (Kenya/Sudan): The night
Sibusiso Ernest Masilela (South Africa): Travelling Alone

Part 4: Illness, Suffering and Healing......................85-108

Nureni Ibrahim (Nigeria): Half of a human species
Marumo Moagi (South Africa): Inspired Less
Ayomide Owoyemi (Nigeria): Ode to a poison

Abigail George (South Africa): The manic depressive daughter
Ajise Vincent (Nigeria): Facets
Rana Al Hassanein (Egypt): Suicide Note
Tendai R. Mwanaka (Zimbabwe): To
Mari Ballot (South Africa): What colour is pain
Afua Wilcox (South Africa): The Day Yaa Serwaa fell down the Pit Latrine
Eliza Mabungu (Mozambique/South Africa): The glass that fell
Abigail George (South Africa): Sometimes Table Mountain and my sister
Kariuki wa Nyamu (Kenya): The Lunatic and her Brood
Vupenyu Zvoushe (Zimbabwe): I, Son of the streets
Tunu Ndanzi (Tanzania): That Talking Tree
Thandiwe Shea (Lesotho): I am dead but still alive
Myron Menon Naidoo (South Africa): A renewed life

Part 5: Memories, Nature and Environmentalism........109-124

Kelechi Ezeigwe (Nigeria): The Diary
Christine Coates (South Africa): The Summer of 69
Mimi Brako Bismarck (Ghana/USA): Nostalgia
Christine Coates (South Africa): First Weekend
Chuma Mmeka (Nigeria): Never Forget
Kelvin Mangwende (Zimbabwe): The Rainbird is dead
Bradley Purdon (South Africa): Legacies
Chenjerai Mhondera (Zimbabwe): Springs of Savanna
Ntensibe Joseph (Uganda): Homage to once a family
Nana Arhin Tsiwah (Ghana): 3rd element
Ntensibe Joseph (Uganda): To Elites

**Part 6: Colonialism, Corruption, Free Speech,
Misgovernance, War and Strife............................ 125-164**

Athol Williams (South Africa): Brentry: An African tragedy
Tembi Charles (Zimbabwe): Limitless Spirit
Ojok James Onono (Uganda): Peace in the radio
Rogers Atukunda (Uganda): The debase
Charmaine Gombera (Zimbabwe): Kwashiorkor of free Speech
Wafula p'Khisa (Kenya): neWSTODay
Hosea Tokwe (Zimbabwe): An Angry Graduate
Amitabh Mitra (South Africa): Hillbrow, Johannesburg

Christopher Kudyahakudadirwe (Zimbabwe): Stolen Dreams
Mari Ballot (South Africa): Squatter-camps
Thandiwe Shea (Lesotho): Our dyed-in-the-wool regime
Christopher Kudyahakudadirwe (Zimbabwe): A Shadow from A Dark Past
Amitabh Mitra (South Africa): Transkei
Handsen Chikowore (Zimbabwe): Payday
Gideon Chumo (Kenya): Bangui; a Poetic Coup~ I. Papa Pomp
Antonio Garcia (South Africa): To our boys who bled in Bangui
Christine Coates (South Africa): Terra Nullius – the Marikana Symphony
Gideon Chumo (Kenya): Sunset at Westgate I
Ayo Oyeku (Nigeria): Ali Goes to School
Dime Maziba (DRC): I write
Stephen Temitope David (Nigeria): Song of the lost
Eric Ngobale (South Africa): Brother (I Can't Breathe)
Dime Maziba (DRC): Child Soldiers
Gideon Chumo (Kenya): For the reign is falling

Part 7: Tribute, Dedication and Women Rights.......... 165-186

Vupenyu Zvoushe (Zimbabwe): Simon Chimbetu
Nana Arhin Tsiwah (Ghana): Yamoransa
Dime Maziba (DRC): Bye bye poet
Fayssal Chafaki (Morocco): Francesca
Athol Williams (South Africa): Walking with Bheki Mseleku
Abel Sehloho (South Africa): Mother Africa
Vupenyu Zvoushe (Zimbabwe): Silence
Mikateko E. Mbambo (South Africa): We are Conscious Women
Linda Nabasa (Uganda): Deflowered
Mikateko E. Mbambo (South Africa): The Thing Between her legs
Nana Arhin Tsiwah (Ghana): hi-life
Linda Nabasa (Uganda): Lyrical penetration
Brenda Juma (Kenya): Culture
Tralone Lindiwe Khoza (South Africa): Black eagles fly high
Brenda Juma (Kenya): Her
Ajise Vincent (Nigeria): Illumination

Part 8: Postmodernism, Family, Home and love......... 187-214

Brenda Juma (Kenya): The City Queens
Omuna Andrew Herbert (Uganda): Ode to the yellow party
Thato Tshukudu (South Africa): Grow up so fast
Kariuki wa Nyamu (Kenya): Postmodern Nairobi beggar
Ndumi Dlamini (South Africa): Be there
Refilwe Khanya Nxomani (South Africa): Homecoming
Ravi Naicker (South Africa): Strangers after a lifetime together
Rogers Atukunda (Uganda): Beyond Beauty
Lucas Zulu (South Africa): Can We
Wafula p'Khisa (Kenya): fallen in love again
Dennis brad Kunguru (Kenya): At the crack of dawn
Wafula p'Khisa (Kenya): Once Upon August (for Martha)
Ayomide Owoyemi (Nigeria): Kafanchan
Kgolagano Tshela (South Africa): Drowning in these feelings alone
Jarred Thompson (South Africa): Chemicals in the mind of "G-O-D"
Marial Awendit (South Sudan): Let a Woman
Lisa Jaison (Zimbabwe): The gift of a goodbye
Linda Nabasa (Uganda): Hard Tongue
Asiko Joan (Kenya): Dead skin
Daniel Da Purificação(Angola/Mexico): She said this is Mr. Daniel

Part 9: Translations from other African Languages.. 215-232

Ernestu Botha (South Africa): Liefde en Reen
Ernestu Botha (South Africa): Love and Rain
Jacobus G. L.Nieuwoudt (South Africa): Jy weet jou oë
Jacobus G. L.Nieuwoudt (South Africa): You know your eyes
Tendai R. Mwanaka (Zimbabwe): Maita Shava
Tendai R. Mwanaka (Zimbabwe): Thank you Shava
Monicah Masikonte (Kenya): Naahidi Kukusahau
Monicah Masikonte (Kenya): I promise to forget you
Ernestu Botha (South Africa): Die Sonblom
Ernestu Botha (South Africa): The Sunflower
Mof'Oluwawo Mojolaoluwa (Nigeria): Fitila

Part 10: Portuguese poems...................................233-324

Hélder Simbad (Angola): Dramático?!
Hélder Simbad (Angola): Conto fantástico
Britos Adriano Baptista (Moçambique):
Urgência
Confidência
O preço do meu silêncio
Augusta Jorge (Angola):
Filha das ruas
Sou este mundo
Bruno Santos (Angola):
Despreso
Materia Viva
Carmona Polá Júnior (Moçambique):
Cego Visionário
Cláudia, Minha Irmã
Odisseia dum Plebeu
Cátia Regina Correia (Angola/Brasil):
Ser um Homem-Deus
O Que Fazes da Vida
Cristina Ferreira (Angola):
Alguém Te Vê Como Mulher
A Carta
A Mulher Africana Que Sou
Edgar Ginga (Angola): Ele Nunca Disse Te Amo
Minha sedução
Albano Epalanga (Angola): Vida Aliciada
Abismo Profundo
Evaristo Fernando (Moçambique):
Meu Barco de Papel
Metamorfose Xenófóba!
Fabious Benfiquista (Angola): Negra
                              Angola
                              Seria Bom
Fernando Palaia (Angola/Cuba): Vocês me tornaram assim
Guilson Silvano Saxingo (Angola): Maus trilhos de África
                                  Cidade diamante
Ismael Farinha (Angola): Minutos Recordes
                         A Morte
Joel Fernandes (Angola): A carta das lagrimas
                         O contraste da vida

Levita Estanislau (Angola/South Africa): Um Sorriso No Rosto
Lorna Telma Zita (Moçambique): Amar é loucura
                                A prostituta
                                Porque querem que eu me cale?
Lourenço Quimbungo (Angola): Ungido de arcanjos
                                Nostálgicas pergolas
                                A Lenda
Magno Domingos (Angola): Poema 1
                                Poema 2
                                Poema 3
Marcelo Pedro (Moçambique): Criatividade
                                Erógeno
                                Televivência
Márcia Rosel Chambule (Moçambique): Desafoga-Te
                                Revolta
                                Entusiasmo
Mohamed Canhanga (Angola): Sei Que Te Escondes Por Aí
                                Quinta Feira
                                Escritos Libertários
Ngonga Salvador Luciano (Angola): Se eu parar pra pensar
                                Até Quando África
Obedes Lobadias (Moçambique): O Mundo
                                Folha Dos Ventos
                                Ininteligível
Orlando Joaquim Ussaque (Moçambique): Um ocidente em mim
                                Resolução
                                Profetizar
Rosa Ribeiro(Angola/Portugal): Paisagem
                                Filha do Tempo
Soberano Canhanga (Angola): Faixa de Gaja
                                Conte(...)Sáo
Sonia Robalo (Angola/Portugal): Carta á minha Máe Angola
                                Nós
Tony Kunsevi (Angola): Retrato Imortal
                                Artista
                                Porção Mágica da Vida
Victor de Viriato (Angola): Meu Pai, Meu País
                                Foi ontem, que teu olhar deixou de lutar
                                Tenho a patria rasgada no peito
Virgilio Chilaule (Moçambique): Renuncia
                                Sala Mana

Geraçáo Alagada
Daniel Da Purificação (Angola/Mexico): Ânsia
Poema

Part 11: French Poems... 325-334

Tchak Sami (Togo): 1°)
2°)
3°)
Armel Fernand Mbida Ebo'o (Cameroon): untitled
untitled
untitled
Samira Negrouche (Algeria) : Marine par temps calme, 1646
Cours d'eau, effet du matin, 1824
Ménerbes, 1954

Part 12: Collaborations from BNAP 2015 Poets........... 335

19 poets (English main collaboration):
Peaceful Conflict in the Land of Utopia...................... 337

3 poets (Cassoma, Guzha, and Mwanaka):
I can still see.. 343

2 poets (Mhondera, Oluwaseyifunmi):
Of love & sex in Africa... 346

**Part 13: Best New African Poets 2015
Anthology Poetics and Reviews349**

A cocktail of verse: An appreciation of
Best New African Poets 2015 Anthology by
Christopher Kudyahakudadirwe............................. 351

A Translator and Educator of Cultures, Heritages,
Traditions: An appreciation of *Best New African Poets
2015 Anthology* by Delia Watterson
.... 354

On being a pen-guine: An interview with
Fiona Mahomed Khan... 358

Thabo Mbeki's dream of an African Renaissance:
An interview with Christine Coates............................... 362

Entrevista com o Sonia Robalo.. 364
I am a simple farmer, poet, and writer:
An interview with Fayssal Chafaki.............................367

Let's begin at the grassroots: An interview
with John Attah Ojonugwa...373

Entrevista com o Soberano Canhanga 377

Impressions of the South African Launch
of BNAP 2015.. 379

Introduction

We can say *second time is a charm* as we churn out another massive literary offering in our *Best "New" African Poets Series*. This Year's anthology builds from last year's offering as we broaden it to include many other aspects. Our intention is to allow space for especially young African authors and artists to develop into professional poets and with that intention in mind we have dibbled with collaborations, "as the (slim) condition of possibility for paradise." (J Morris, Eleven Eleven Journal, 2010). We feel for us to grow as poets and professional writers and artist we have to foster close sharing of ideas, and thus, we encouraged last year's poets to enter into collaborations and pen the same poem together and we received 3 strong collaborations which we included in this anthology. Maybe it is poetic justice that the main English collaboration (written and hashed out by 19 poets) decided to title its poem, *Peaceful Conflict in the Land of Utopia*. Reminiscences of the paradise (Utopia) that through that collaboration the poets were trying to construct for Africa reminds us of Bernadette Meyer's *Utopia* or more of the total collaboration, that Jack Spicer had in mind with his first letter to Federico Lorca. "Tradition means much more than that. It means generations of different poets in different countries patiently telling the same story, writing the same poem, gaining and losing something with each transformation- but, of course, never really losing anything." (J Morris, Eleven Eleven Journal, 2010).

We also opened our doors to the many other African languages (there is no other continent that rivals Africa in terms of number of languages, even cultures etc..., yet they have remained unknown and largely ignored by the literary establishment) thus we received many other entries in Shona, Kiswahili, Afrikaans, Yoruba, which were translated into English, on top of our staple English, Portuguese and French entries. We hope to receive more in the coming years from Africa's many languages. There is also a part where we look back to 2015 anthology poetics, which includes Reviews, Literary Appreciations, Interviews with 2015 poets and a write up on one of the readings, the Cape Town February 2016 reading, and unfortunately due to life and work commitments we couldn't get, in time, a write up on the Oakland, California reading.

As can be gleaned so far this is not only an anthology publication initiative but it's a full-fledged poetry movement we are trying to build on the continent as it goes beyond the publication of the anthology through hosting of readings, performances, online engagements etc… so with that intention in mind we hope to do more after the publication of this anthology. We firmly believe the arts of Africa have not been given enough space to shape the societies we live in like say what the American arts did to its society. And it is the far-reaching impact of the American arts, intellectual and political movements that shaped American thinking, belief and society, most of which were driven by its poets like the *New American poets school (Williams, Pound, Elliot, Levertov, Zukofsky)* , *Beat poets (Ginsberg, Rexroth, Weiss, Gilbert)*, *New York school of poets (Lowell, Berrigan, Koch, Notley, Meyer)*, *San Francesco Renascence school (Spicer, Brautigan, Keilty, Duncan)*, *Language poets (Spicer, McClure, Bernstein)* and the *Black Mountain School of poets (Duncan, Creeley, Eigner)*, just to mention a few, and unfortunately the African governments, people and business has largely ignored the power of African poetry to engender these into our countries and economies. It is these artistic movements that shape the whole society's thinking and so we believe we need these for Africa to wake up from its slumber and take its rightful place in the world. We really do hope we have started this movement as a lot of anthologies have started sprouting all over the continent after our *Best "New" Africa Poets 2015 Anthology*, trying to link Africa's poets and let the poets speak together as one nation. We have worked without sponsorship in this endeavor, and we will continue in this vein, working from our pockets, but we are open to any sponsorship as long as it fosters this project. We would like sponsorship on making the anthology available in African schools, especially poor schools so that our future learners and poets gets a chance to learn and develop with the endeavor too. We are also looking for sponsorship on hosting more poetry readings and festivals all over Africa and the Diasporas after publication, and many day to day running of this foundational project, not to forget financing of copies for the anthology poets which we can't partake on our own as editors of this wonderful project. Please get in touch with us on mwanaka@yahoo.com, angopensador@gmail.com or Tel No: +263777916113, +5216624271979

Best "New" African Poets 2016 Anthology has 251 pieces from 131 poets and artists in 7 languages from 24 African countries and Diasporas, with South African and Angolan poets dominating the list. We also have a healthy number of poets from Uganda, Zimbabwe, Kenya, Moçambique, Ghana, and Nigeria, as usual. We have arranged the English poetry loosely according to topics the poets would be covering and so in this introduction we will not get into in-depth discussions of topics the poets covered, as we also felt they were the same concerns dealt with by the other language poets. Although it is true that we have a mixture of creators and artists of the letters from English-speaking, French-speaking and Portuguese-speaking African countries, the dynamics brought by Portuguese-speaking authors draws particular attention to the fact of their diversity since voices came from the Indian, to the Atlantic, to the European and American diaspora to converge on a common platform, call or understand it as the present anthology *Best "New" African Poets 2016 Anthology* expressing itself in assorted styles that go from the classic, the modern, the contemporary, the Dionysian, hybrid and, in short, this is the singularity of the "Lusophone Africanies" or the "African Lusophonies".

Essentially in this anthology the state of the art of African letters is conceived from the prism of poetry, since it allows us to find Africa in the different Africas. In the *Best "New" African Poets 2016 anthology*, what we find is the Portuguese speaking Africa reading to the French and English speaking Africa and vice versa, which is a key question within the universe of African literature.

As good sons of our mother Africa, the Portuguese-speaking African poets who participated in this compilation were touched by the call of the *Best "New" African Poets*, responding with the heart, sensitivity and the essence that characterizes lusophony, in particular when they narrate the beauty , when they vibrate through life, when they teach and share the gifts of that culture associated with the sea, when love is the issue, when they laugh and cry for nostalgia, when joy is the color of the world, in resume when "Africulture" face "lusoculture" the UBUNTU gets personified as the perfect symbiosis and the maximum expression of the human being.

In this book, when we meet with the literary poetic creation work of these magicians of words, of the feelings and the beauty of the soul, we are with the firm impression that as theme the *nationalist sense* is the one that most predominates with its pink, blue and gray tints that are expressed in parallel with *existentialist perspectives* that in turn go hand in hand with *love, desire, hankering, joy, sensuality* that transports us to *epic, lyrical, utopian* contexts without being lost in fantasy, they are artistic lines sometimes with traditional and sometimes more innovative touches. However, in contrast and to a lesser extent, almost as if there were resistant and with restraint we also find *desolation, pain, negation* that can be so sweet or so bitter that it allows the *imagination* to stop in a *lament* or end in *resignation*.

Definitely, when Africa and the Africans speak in the voice and in the pen of the creators, the scene of the words is clear, in the horizon the zenith of the mother earth that calls appears and the azimuth of differences becomes the one of convergences, thus, the compass only directs us towards a direction that is the meeting point of Africa with itself and Africa with the rest of the world and this meeting point is called BEST NEW AFRICAN POETS 2016 ANTHOLOGY. Then, guided by the hand of these young poets lets enjoy life and celebrate poetry. *Ululululu...,* we ululate!

Introdução

Podemos dizer que essa segunda vez é um luxo, enquanto nós debatemos para uma outra oferta literária massiva na série Os Melhores Novos Poetas Africanos. A Antologia desse ano tem como pilar a edição do ano passado, trazendo porém novos aspectos. A nossa intenção é criar espaços para que especialmente os jovens autores e artistas Africanos possam se tornar poetas profissionais e com essa intenção em mente temos feito importantes parcerias, "tendo em conta as escassas possibilidades para o paraíso". (J Morris, Elevem Eleven Journal, 2010). Sentimos que para crescermos como poetas, escritores profissionais e artistas precisamos fomentar estreitas parcerias de ideias. Neste sentido, encorajamos os poetas do ano passado a colaborarem entre si e recebemos 3 fortes colaborações que incluímos na presente Antologia. Talvez seja justiça poética que a principal colaboração em Inglês (escrita por 19 poetas) decidiu intitular o seu poema, *Conflito Pacífico na Terra da Utopia*, reminiscencias do paraíso (Utopia), por meio dessa colaboração os poetas tentaram construir para África aquilo que nos lembramos a *Utopia de Bernadette Meyer* ou o total das colaborações que Jack Spicer tinha em mente na sua primeira carta a Federico Lorca "tradição significa muito mais do que isso. Significa gerações de diferentes poetas em diferentes nações, pacientemente contando a mesma história, escrevendo o mesmo poema, perdendo ou ganhando algo a cada transformação, mas claro nunca realmente perdendo nada" (J Morris, Eleven Eleven Journal, 2010).

Também abrimos as nossas portas para as muitas outras línguas africanas (não existe outro continente que rivaliza África em termos de números de línguas ou mesmo culturas, embora sejam desconhecidas ou simplesmente ignoradas pelas instituições literárias). Portanto recebemos muitos textos em Shona, Kiswahili, Afrikaans, Yoruba, que foram traduzidos em Inglês, dentro do grosso de entradas das nossas línguas oficiais da antología que sao Inglês, Português e o Francês. Esperamos receber mais línguas do Continente Africano nos anos vindouros. Nesta Antologia, há também a parte que retomamos da Antologia de 2015, que inclui, recensões críticas, apreciações literárias, entrevistas com os poetas de 2015, e uma nota de apreciação da apresentação de CAPE TOWN em Fevereiro de 2016. Infelizmente, por motivos de compromissos da vida e trabalho, não conseguimos recolher em tempo útil as notas da apresentação em OAKLAND na CALIFORNIA.

Como pode ser observado, não se trata apenas de uma iniciativa que visa publicar uma Antologia. Mas se trata de um amplo movimento poético que estamos a tentar construir no continente, pelo que vai além da publicação da Antologia por meio da promoção, performances, iniciativas on-line etc. Tendo isso em mente, esperamos fazer mais, depois da publicação da Antologia. Nós acreditamos fortemente não tem se dado espaço suficiente às Artes Africanas para moldar as sociedades em que vivemos. Tal como fez a sociedade Americana. Os ganhos tiveram um impacto na intelectualidade, na arte e política da América, assim como nos movimentos que moldaram as crenças e pensamentos da sociedade americana, muitos deles dirigidos por poetas como: *the New American poets school (Williams, Pound, Elliot, Levertov, Zukofsky) , Beat poets (Ginsberg, Rexroth, Weiss, Gilbert), New York school of poets (Lowell, Berrigan, Koch, Notley, Meyer), San Francesco Renascence school (Spicer, Brautigan, Keilty, Duncan), Language poets (Spicer, McClure, Bernstein) and the Black Mountain School of poets (Duncan, Creeley, Eigner),* so para mencionar alguns. Infelizmente, os governos, o povo em geral e a elite dos negócios têm ignorado em larga escala o poder da poesia Africana como factor de fortalecimento da Nação, da política e da economia. São esses movimentos artísticos que moldam o pensamento de toda sociedade, portanto acreditamos que precisamos desses movimentos para que a África acorde na inércia, e assuma o seu lugar merecido no mundo. Esperamos sinceramente que tenhamos iniciado esse movimento, a medida que inúmeras Antologias começaram a brotar por todo o continente, depois da primeira edição de *Os Melhores Novos Poetas Africanos 2015*, como uma tentativa clara de ligar os poetas africanos e fazer com que estes mesmos poetas falem juntos como uma só Nação. Destacamos que temos trabalhado sem patrocínios nessa empreitada, e vamos continuar nessa via, investindo dos nossos bolsos, mas estamos abertos a qualquer patrocínio, desde que o mesmo fomente esse projeto. Gostaríamos que os patrocínios tornassem a Antologia disponível nas escolas africanas, especialmente aquelas escolas pobres para que os nossos futuros estudantes e poetas, tenham contacto e se desenvolvam também. Precisamos também de patrocínios para hospedagem e festivais por toda África e também na Diáspora depois das publicações e para os muitos projetos do dia a dia deste projecto em embrião. Sem esquecer o financiamento das cópias para os poetas. Pois não temos como editar e assim partilhar esse maravilhoso projeto. Por favor entrar em contacto connosco mwanaka@yahoo.com, danieljose26@yahoo.com.br, ou nos seguintes números telefónicos: +263777916113, +5216624271979

OS MELHORES NOVOS POETA AFRICANOS 2016 tem 251 poemas, de 131 poetas e artistas em 7 línguas (Inglês, Português , Francês , Afrikaans, Shona, Yoruba e Kiswahili) de 24 países Africanos e a Diáspora, com os poetas da África do Sul e Angola a liderarem a lista. Temos igualmente um número considerável de poetas do Uganda, Zimbabwe, Kenya, Moçambique, Ghana e Nigéria como de costume. Nós acomodamos a poesia Inglesa de acordo com os temas que os poetas abarcariam, portanto esta introdução não vai entrar em discussões profundadas dos temas abordados pelos poetas, porque nós também sentimos que eram as mesmas preocupações abordadas pelos outros poetas das outras líguas participantes. Se bem é verdade que temo suma miscelânia de criadores e de verdadeiros artistas das letras desde a anglofonia, a francofonia e a lusofonia, enfatizamos que a dinámica que trazem os autores de expressão portuguesa chama particularmente a nossa atenção pelo facto da sua diversidade, já que são vozes que vêm a partir do Índico, do Atlântico até a diáspora europeia e americana para convergir numa plataforma comum, - chame-se ou entenda-se como a antologia *Best New African Poets 2016* – se expresando com estilos variados que vão desde o clássico, o moderno, o contemporâneo, o dionísiaco, o híbrido e enfim, é essa a peculiaridade das "africanias losófonas" ou das "lusofonias africanas".

Em essência, nesta antologia se visualiza o estado da arte das letras africanas desde o prisma da poesia, já que nos permite encontrar África nas diversas Áfricas. Na *Best New African Poets 2016*, que em realidade é a continuação não somente da edição de um livro mas de um projecto começado em 2015, o que encontramos essecialmente é a África portuguesa lendo a África francesa e inglesa e vice-versa, o que representa uma questão bastante fundamental dentro do universo da literatura africana.

Como bons filhos da nossa terra mãe África os poetas africanos de expressao portuguesa participantes desta obra, sentiram-se tocados pelo chamado da *Best New African Poets* respondendo com o coracção, sensibilidade e a essência que caracteriza a lusofonia em particular quando narram a beleza, quando vibram pela vida, quando mostram e partilham as dádivas desta cultura associada ao mar, quando o amor é a questão, quando riem e choram pela saudade, quando a alegria é cor dos óculos do mundo, em suma, quando se encontram a "Africultura" e a "Lusocultura" se personifica o UBUNTU como a simbiose perfeita e a expressão máxima do ser humano.

Neste livro ao encontramo-nos com o trabalho de criação poetico-literário destes magos das palavras, dos sentimentos e a beleza da alma ficamos com a firme impressão que como tema o *sentido nacionalista* é o que mais predomina com as suas matizes cor-de-rosa, azul e cizento, que se expressam paralelamente com *perspectivas existencialistas* que por sua vez vao juntos com o *amor, o desejo, a saudade, a alegria, a sensualidade* que também nos transportam a contextos *épicos, líricos, utópicos* sem perder-se na fantasia, sao traços artísticos com toques as vezes tradicionais e outras vezes mais inovadores. Sendo asssim, em contraste e em menor medida, quase como se existisse *resistência* e *contenção* encontramos também *desolação, dor, negação* que pode ser tão doce ou tão amarga permitindo que a *imaginação* pare num lamento ou termine em *resignação*.

Definitivamente, quando África e os africanos falam pela voz e pela caneta dos criadores o cenário das palavras é claro, no horizonte aparece o zenite da terra mae que chama e o azimute de diferencas se transforma naquele das convergencias, desta forma, a bússola somente nos dirige para uma direccao que é o ponto de encontro de África consigo mesma e de África com o resto do mundo, e este ponto de encontro se chama BEST NEW AFRICAN POETS 2016. Portanto, guiados pela mao destes jovens poetas disfrutemos da vida e celebremos a poesia. *Ulululululu…,* nós ululate!

La presentation

Toute bonne chose a une suite. C'est pour cela que nous présentons cette nouvelle collection de notre *Série de Nouveaux Poètes Africains*. Cette anthologie s'est construite sur la précédente, tout en incluant de nouveaux aspects pour l'enrichir. Cette fois-ci, notre intention est d'offrir aux jeunes auteurs et artistes africains un espace qui leur permet de se développer en poètes professionnels. C'est dans cet esprit que nous avons doublé les efforts de collaborations pour leur donner "une condition (infime) de possibilité pour atteindre le paradis."(J Morris, Eleven Eleven Journal, 2010). Pour pouvoir se développer en tant que poète, un partage des idées est essentiel. C'est ainsi que, l'année dernière, en conjuguant nos effort nous avons pu attirer trois grandes collaborations qui seront inclus dans cette anthologie. Peut-être s'agit-il de justice poétique que la plus grande collaboration (écrite et approuvée par 19 poètes) se soit intitulée *Peaceful Conflict in the Land of Utopia*? C'est ce souvenir du paradis (utopique) que les poètes ont voulu construire pour l'Afrique à travers cette collaboration, pour nous rapprocher de *l'Utopia* de Bernadette Meyer, ou encore à travers la collaboration dans sa totalité pour mieux nous faire comprendre ce que Jack Spicer voulait dire quand il écrivit sa première lettre à Federico Lorca. " La Tradition est bien plus que ça. Ce sont des générations de différents poètes dans différents pays qui racontent patiemment la même histoire, écrivant le même poème, gagnant et perdant quelque chose avec chaque transformation - sans jamais pour autant, réellement, perdre quoi que ce soit." (J Morris, Eleven Eleven Journal, 2010)

Nous ouvrons également nos portes aux nombreuses autres langues africaines (il n'y a pas d'autre continent qui puisse rivaliser avec l'Afrique en terme de langues et de cultures, et pourtant la majorité est restée méconnue et ignorée par le milieu littéraire). Nous avons reçu grand nombre de textes en Shona, Kiswahili, Afrikaans, Yoruba, que nous avons traduits en anglais, et cela en plus de tous les textes reçus en anglais, portugais et français. Nous espérons en recevoir encore beaucoup dans les années à venir, de toutes les langues africaines existantes. Nous contemplons également ce que nous avons accompli en 2015 grâce à la première anthologie: critiques, commentaires littéraires, entretiens avec les poètes de 2015, une chronique sur une lecture au Cape Town February 2016 Reading. Malheureusement, nous ne pouvions assister à un évènement au Oakland, California lecture, dus aux maintes contraintes de la vie quotidienne et d'autres engagements.

Comme on a pu le voir, il ne s'agit pas seulement d'une initiative de publication d'anthologie. Nous avons l'audace de créer un mouvement poétique à part entière qui s'étend au-delà de la publication de cette anthologie, à travers des séances de lectures, des représentations, un engagement en ligne, parmi d' autres. Nous avons donc l'intention d'aller plus loin après la publication de cette anthologie. Nous sommes convaincus que les arts africains n'ont pas eu suffisamment d'espace pour forger les sociétés, comme l'ont pu faire les arts américains pour leur société. Ce sont d'ailleurs les profondes répercussions des arts américains, des mouvements intellectuels et politiques qui ont forgé la mentalité, la foi et la société américaine, le plus souvent mené par les associations de poètes telles que *New American poets school (Williams, Pound, Elliot, Levertov, Zukofsky)*, *Beat poets (Ginsberg, Rexroth, Weiss, Gilbert)*, *New York school of poets (Lowell, Berrigan, Koch, Notley, Meyer)*, *San Francesco Renascence school (Spicer, Brautigan, Keilty, Duncan)*, *Language poets (Spicer, McClure, Bernstein)* et the *Black Mountain School of poets (Duncan, Creeley, Eigner)*, pour n'en citer que quelques uns. Malheureusement, les gouvernements, les gens et les entreprises africaines ont amplement ignoré le pouvoir des poètes africains à inspirer nos pays et nos économies. Ce sont ces mouvements artistiques qui forment la réflexion d'une société entière, et c'est pourquoi nous estimons qu'il est temps de sortir l'Afrique de cette léthargie et de lui donner sa place légitime dans ce monde.

On espère vraiment avoir donné vie à un mouvement. Nous avons déjà vue un nombre d'anthologies bourgeonner partout sur le continent après la sortie de *Best New African Poets 2015 Anthology*, dans un effort de rassembler les poètes d'Afrique et de les laisser parler d'une seule voix, comme d'une seule nation. Nous avons travaillé sans sponsors, et nous allons continuer sur cette même lancée, en travaillant de nos poches, tout en étant ouverts à des sponsors s'ils encouragent ce projet. Nous voudrions des sponsors pour rendre l'anthologie accessible dans les écoles africaines, et plus particulièrements dans les écoles démunies pour donner une chance à nos futurs apprentis et poètes de grandir grâce à cette initiative.

Nous appelons également à des sponsors pour accueillir et animer davantage de lectures publiques et de festivals partout en Afrique et d'atteindre les diasporas après la publication de cet ouvrage. Nous avons aussi besoin de fonds pour la gestion au jour le jour de ce projet fondamental, et pour financer les copies pour les poètes participants à cette anthologie, chose que nous ne pouvons pas porter à nous seuls, en tant que seuls éditeurs de ce magnifique projet. N'hésitez pas à nous contacter sur mwanaka@yahoo.com, danieljose26@yahoo.com.br ou par téléphone aux numéros: +263777916113, +5216624271979.

L'Anthologie des Meilleurs Nouveaux Poètes Africains 2016 comporte 251 morceaux de 131 poètes et artistes en 7 langues, de 24 pays africains et diasporas, avec une dominance sud-africaine et angolaise. Nous présentons également un bon nombre de poètes d'Uganda, du Zimbabwe, du Kenya, du Mozambique, du Ghana et du Nigeria, comme précédemment. Nous avons arrangé de manière libre les poèmes en langue anglaise, selon les sujets abordés par les poètes. C'est la raison pour laquelle nous n'allons pas traiter en détails ces sujets dans cette introduction - aussi parce que des sujets similaires ont été abordés dans d'autres langues. Il est vrai que nous avons un mélange de créateurs et d'artistes de "lettres" en langue anglaise, française et portugaise. Cependant, on remarque une particularité dans la dynamique des poètes parlant le portugais. Ils sont issus de diasporas indiennes, atlantiques et européennes et convergent sur cette plateforme commune qui est *L'Anthologie des Meilleurs Poètes Africains 2016* dans un assortiment de styles allant du classique au moderne, en passant par le contemporain, le dionysiaque et l'hybride - en bref, telle est la singularité de les "africanie lusophones" ou "lusophonie africaines".

L'art des lettres africaines est essentiellement conçue par le prisme de la poésie puisqu'on découvre l'Afrique à travers les différents Afriques. Dans cette anthologie, nous observons l'Afrique lusophone lisant à l'Afrique francophone et anglophone -

et vice et versa, ce qui constitue une question clef dans l'univers de la littérature africaine.

En tant que bons enfants de notre mère Afrique, les poètes lusophones qui ont participé dans cette compilation, ont été touchés par l'appel des *Meilleurs Nouveaux Poètes Africains* et y ont répondu avec leur coeur, leur sensibilité et l'essence qui caractérise la lusophonie, en particulier lorsqu'ils parlent de beauté, lorsqu'ils vibrent à travers la vie, lorsqu'ils enseignent et partagent les talents de cette culture associée à la mer, lorsque l'amour est au centre du sujet, lorsqu'ils rient et pleurent la nostalgie, lorsque la joie est la couleur du monde - en résumé, lorsque l'"africulture" s'associe à la "lusoculture", l' UBUNTU se personnifie dans une symbiose parfaite et dans l'expression maximale de l'être humain.

Cette création poétique de ces magiciens de mots, de sentiments et de beauté de l'âme qui est exposée dans ce livre nous laisse avec cette impression inébranlable que le thème du *sentiment nationaliste* est prédominant avec ses encres rose, bleues et grises qui expriment parallèlement des *perspectives existentialistes* qui, elles, à leur tour, s'associent de force avec l'*amour, le désir, la recherche, la joie et la sensualité* qui nous transportent vers des contextes *épiques, lyriques, utopiques*, sans se perdre dans la fantaisie. Ce sont des lignes artistiques colorées tantôt de tradition tantôt d'innovation. Cependant, au contraire et en moindre proportion, on y retrouve parfois, avec un peu de résistance, de la *désolation, de la douleur et de la négation* douce et amère qui peut amener notre *imagination* à demeurer dans un *lament* ou se terminer dans la *résignation*.

Indéniablement, quand l'Afrique et les Africains parlent de vive voix et à travers la plume des créateurs, la scène des mots est claire; à l'horizon, le zenith de notre mère-terre, appelant, se dessine et l'azimut des différences amène à la convergence, alors, la boussole nous mène vers une direction qui est le point de réunion de l'Afrique avec elle-même et de l'Afrique avec le reste du monde. C'est ce point de réunion qui s'appelle *l'Anthologie des Meilleurs Nouveaux Poètes Africains 2016*. Donc, guidés par la main de ces jeunes poètes, célébrons la vie et la poésie. *Ululululu…,* nous ululate!

Part 1: Place, Heritage and Identity

I Want That Africa Go!
C. J Chenjerai Mhondera

Africa I rebuke was alive before independence and dead after
Independence;   I want
that Africa go!
The picture is no good;
Nehanda hanged a dissident, guerillas suffered revolutionaries, mass
massacred in Chimoio and Nyadzonio, Chitepo bombed in Lusaka,
civilians burnt alive to liberate Africa, dead after independence.
The picture is no good;
I want to cry souls massacred in Soweto, students demonstrating
and striking;
Hope murdered, Africa dead after Independence;
The Marikana massacre- shame, we're silent!
I want that Africa go!
Do not persecute Nkrumah like you did Lumumba in the valley of
Gaddaffi...   Nyerere
tell Samora and Seretse Khama, that Mandela was a sellout, Africa is
dead;
The picture is no good;
The pictures of a minister fat posing elsewhere in that city
Extravaganza, society thin dying miserably impoverished;
Do not rush the burial of Africa, I want to resurrect her!
Do not intimidate me, I praise no terrorist!
Do not hush me, I want to address mass!
Do not call me a dissident reporter, for I refuse to shut up!
Do not withhold writing pad, I want to redraw the picture!
Do not withhold Kodak paper; I want to print the picture!
I want that Africa dying...I want Africa resurrecting...I want Africa
living...I want Africa born... I want Africa fresh... I want Africa
growing...not the same Africa, old and dead...not the same Africa,
anemic- prescribed wrong blood from diseased blood donors of
other continents... I want Africa out of colonial womb... I want
Africa cut from colonial umbilical cord... I blast reluctance of
governments across Africa... I blast the same policies old and
rotten... I blast jacketed systems we inherited from erstwhile
colonizers... I blast old institutions, politicians and their corruption,
and systems unchanging... I praise revolutionaries... I praise
rebels... I rebuke civilians for delaying and postponing so long their
freedoms and liberty... I want Africa a mother of governments for

her children... I want Africa of talents... I want Africa progressive and dynamic!
Call me no rebel, for I lambast kings failing;
their cabinet sets of weaklings and suspects!
Give me no titles and associations I want a good picture;
Pictures of Africa living- Africa independent and interdependent,
Pictures of Africa going- Africa going forward and no backwards nor sideways!
Pictures not of dead impoverished African societies depicted in Western comedy!
Pictures not of barbaric civil wars and malnourished citizens ideal for news about Africa!

African sunrise
Roy Venketsamy

The blanket of mist engulfed the mountain peaks
Dawn was breaking, daylight infiltrating
The sun, shy as a groom
Waited patiently to enter the wedding arena.
The mist was relentless – never wanting to unveil,
But the sun patiently, and then impatiently said,
"off the beaten path, I'm here to rise."
Fear shook the mist, the battle was legendary
Mist never succeeded against the sun;
But tried desperately to stand its ground.
The African sun was strong as an elephant bull
With full might and vigour, it braved its rays
Splitting the mist apart, a memory like Moses and the Red Sea.
I stood in awe, and saw the battle won.
The sun filtered through, the mist head bowed, gave way
The sun rose!
A glorious morning
African sun shining down on Mama Africa.

Field Notes
West Africa
Chaun Ballard

1.

From our fortress high-rise we gaze out
over a city of transients, zigzagging
their way through dust, small heads
balancing loads twice their size,
pausing briefly to sniff and discuss
before going on their way.

2.

Inside our home we are overrun by ants—
climbing up walls, burrowing themselves in trash bags,
bathing in drops of unevaporated water like children
inside a dip pool.

3.

How hard they live, these cities of transients—
with nothing to buy, nothing to sell, toiling in heat,
busying themselves before nightfall, before the rush of moon
hauls them back to their makeshift world.

4.

Ants in our home exercise their right to exist
without fear of God-like feet pressing them flat to the floor
or the torrents of web that quickly overrun their streets
like an invisible hand that snatches and whirls them away.

5.

How recognizable their bodies on the street,
when just months ago they were heartbeat, sinew, and bone,
waking at dusk, clearing away sleep before racing the moon back
home.

6.

They're dead! They're dead!
The ants, they're all dead!

(Not all—but the village is gone.)

7.

How irreversible the layers
and layers of white sheets
they carry to bury beneath stone.

8.

At night I flick on the bathroom light
to find ants carrying their dead—one checks for vitals,
one runs in hysterics, one already ant-miles ahead.

9.

Don't kiss your dead! Don't kiss your dead!
But how else will they know they're gone?
How can one's customs change overnight?
How could one kiss be wrong?

10.

The ants have returned in hazmat suits.
They heave those left overhead.
They have taken Doom back
to their makeshift shacks.

Soon the rest will be dead.
Soon the rest will be dead.
Soon the rest will be—

Lagos

Nonso Charles ORJI

This is Lagos
The city draped in yellow and black ribbons
This is my birthplace
My infant sound emulating my environs

They call it the hustler's paradise
A doom to many
Succours to many more
An anomaly I still can't grasp

Where Linda gossips aimlessly
And still be celebrated
Agbero hustle endlessly
To be despised by all

Where you are welcomed
By three white men
Only to find
Blackness on every turn

Dog eats dog
Shit has lost its value
Men despise men
All for village people's praise

The city of jagaban
With each changing tide
The river source
Remains unshaken

This is Lagos
This is my city
Though not perfect
We persevere all the same.

Mdantsane, East London

Amitabh Mitra

the somali spaza shop at street corner
mdantsane
beckons
the needy
cramped within
it too waits for
a stray bullet
or a
stab

violence is Islamic
in distant african shores

death
has no color
here
in peaceful
mdantsane

only the muezzins strange strain
sets a few birds
to flight.

Victoria Falls

Handsen Chikowore

Tiny little drops draw images of untitled rains
which knocks at the throne of holy showers.
The undiscovered towers of water discos,
revive vessels of heavenly descended excitements.
Blue skies open the chorus of bliss
that uncover the mystery of virgin air

Warmth and breeze spark enlightened darkness
which bow down at the speck of mighty rainbow
Splashes of divine sheets of wonderful waters
bless sights of curiosities into stocks of relief
Where beauty and the beast collide in idle
unfathomed layers of pleasure erupt fearlessly

The vicinity is anchored by heavy gifts of trees
that dance in home of abundant branches
The oven baking sun behaves like untutored son
that invite unwelcome sweat to swim with temperature
The victorious falls never fail to rain
but continue its unending journey in dead night

Shelley Point

Niall R Hurley

Where seagulls prey on hastiness
And time itself disjoints;
Where making plans is foolishness,
That there, is Shelley Point.

Just beyond the Cederburg,
Far beyond dismay;
Deadlines hold no pow'r here
In St. Helena Bay.

A red sun rises and sets again
With not much in between,
Save the scatterings and gatherings
Of creatures rarely seen.

A fynbos sea meets the ocean blue
At a beach full of shells –
All of them: skeletons true
All with a story to tell.

Gleaming houses rise from the ground,
Each like a white church
Of Relaxation newly-found –
Their Eucharist: the earth.

A lighthouse blinks its shining eye
As deputy to The Moon,
Lest sleepy sailors go awry
And sail on to their doom.

Where Today is Tomorrow's twin,
Different but the same;
If you never get to visit,
That there, would be a shame.

Hadeda

(Bostrychia hagedash)
Harry Owen

Certainly not posh. No Knightsbridge or Bath,
no golden regency Crescent, no plum —
not la-di-dah but the bleakest raw screech,
primordial as swamp one step up
from reptile. Real.

Less pretty by far than rosellas
and fairy wrens ripe for picturing,
but heavy, squat and chucked together
with blocks of rusty parts, a spare
Concorde snout. Propped.

Like so much of here, shacks and townships,
tyres, tin and cardboard, half a forest
balanced on each woman's head
held proud, still, elegant as models.
Hadeda, This

beautiful bird. Ugly? Rough? Unfinished?
True.

wind pump
Archie Swanson

red karoo dust rises on desiccated air
wisps of bleached cloud offer no respite
barbed fences snag tumbleweeds
hadidas are mute
spinning roulette clanks endlessly
heaving pump pole shafts the barren earth

Ka"
Michael 'Wudz' Ochoki

africa: the bible came floating down the red sea

africa: the *san*(sun)/son

africa: *afar*: dust

africa: *ifran*: cave

africa: *-ica*: a land

africa: *aprica*: sunny – an ember off of hell's kitchen

africa: *ka*: the womb

africa: *africus*: rain/wind/rainy wind

africa: *lucy*: the essence; our godform/lucy: lucifer: the light

africa: broken china in the sun

africa: her literature is post-colonial, post-slavery trauma

africa: 70 coups; 13 presidential assassinations.

Identity Apples
Mbizo Chirasha

I am a fat skeleton, resurrecting
From the sad memories of dada
And dark mysteries of animism
I am Buganda
I bleed hope
I drip the honey of fortune
Makerere; think tank of Africa
I dance with you wakimbizi dance
I am Tanganyika
I smell and fester with the smoke of African genesis
I am the beginning
Kilimanjaro; the anthill of rituals
I am the smile of Africa
My glee erase the deception of sadness
My tooth bling freedom
I am myself, I am Gambia
When others sleep with bullets stuck in their stomachs
I sneeze copper spoons from my mouth every dawn
I am the Colombia of Africa
I am the Cinderella of Africa
Where mediums feast with the ghost of Kamuzu in Mulange trees
Here spirits walk naked and free
I am the land of sensations
I am the land of reactions
Coughing forex blues
Squandermania
I still smell the scent of Nehanda's breath
I am African renaissance blooming
I stink the soot of Chimurenga
I am the mute laughter of Njelele hills
I am Soweto
Swallowed by Kwaito and gong
I am a decade of wrong and gong
I am the blister of freedom vomited from the belly of apartheid
I see the dawn of the coming sun in Madiba's eyebrows
I am Abuja
Blast furnace of corruption

Nigeria, the Jerusalem of noblemen, priests, professors and
prophets
I am Guinea, i bling with African floridirization
I am blessed with many tongues
My thighs washed by river Nile
I am the mystery of pyramids
I am the graffiti of Nefertiti
I am the rich breast of Nzinga
I am Switzerland of Africa
The rhythm of Kalahari sunset
The rhyme of Sahara, yapping, yelping
I am Damara, I am Herero, I am Nama, I am lozi, I am Vambo
I am bitterness, I am sweetness
I am Liberia
I am king kongo
Mobutu roasted my diamonds into the stink of deep brown blisters
Frying daughters in corruption microwaves
Souls swallowed by the beat of Ndombolo and the wind of
Rhumba
I am the Paris of Africa
I see my wounds
I am rhythm of beauty
I am Congo
I am Bantu
I am Jola
I am Mandinga
I sing of you
I sing Thixo
I sing of Ogun
I sing of God
I sing of Tshaka
I sing of Jesus
I sing of children
of Garangaja and Banyamulenge
Whose sun is dozing in the mist of poverty
I am the ghost of Mombasa
I am the virginity of Nyanza
I am scarlet face of Mandinga
I am cherry lips of Buganda
Come Sankara, come Wagadugu
I am Msiri of Garangadze kingdom

My heart beats under rhythm of words and dance
I am the dead in the trees blowing with wind,
I cannot be deleted by civilization.
I am not Kaffir, I am not Khoisun
I am the sun breaking from the villages of the east with great
inspiration of revolutions
Its fingers caressing the bloom of hibiscus
Liberation!

The Africa I Know
Cláudia Cassoma

with glary eyes and extended lips
i see as the earth greets their feet
      as the ground brings up the sand long heated
their happiness is indescribable
                unbeatable
with the sounds of the dancer's chants
                claps from the ones who can't
it's INGOMA in the south
a deeper bass sound followed by a high-pitched one
introduce the north GOBLET DRUMS
the Africa i know is euphoria
                contagious joy from its many emporia
music is who we are
despite slavery's scar
on the old lyrics of LUCKY DUBE
the new ones from VIVALDA DULA
i see this great continent
          multitude opulent
with beauty universally represented
ANGOLA is this Africa
for all, a road opened by one
WANGARI MAATHAI is this Africa
from the oldest republic
a skirt bearing body
pink melanin in the throne
Africa is strong bone
with unstrained figure
untied from the whispers
we shout to the world
we are more than empty plates
we are your full ones
we are more than unclad flesh
we are your hairy coats
the Africa i know is profusion
it is the end of segregation
the Africa i know is Steve Biko, Oliver Tambo, Helen Suzman,
Lillian Ngoyi
this Africa is men and women, old and young

       it is the strength of a LOXODONTA
the Africa i know is singular
in a self-inflicted blindness
releasing its feral smell
Africa is peculiar
i feel as the wind tinges my peel
the Africa i know is what i feel
               is who i am
                    the scarf of a muslim woman
                    the KUFI CAP of the man
Africa is the school children go to
the seat made for all
the Africa I know is inclusive
a place where life isn't exclusive

How We Ate Fufu
Mimi Brako Bismarck

There were never chairs
When we ate fufu*
Not because we didn't own one
But because of they got in the way.
Huddled around
A centered ayowa*
Family. Friends. Neighbors.
Ashy knees from Harmattan breezes
Squat--dirty feet planted
In the warm earth
Sibling rivalry at its peak
Shoving and pushing yet
Maintaining one's poise
For to lose one's balance
Was to forfeit the meal
Pinch the velvety
Dough-with your two forefingers
And grab the mass
Of calorific glory
A quick dunk
Into the soup
Then to your mouth
The soup-peppery
Runs down your hands
Slowly streaming its way
In the dust covered elbow
And into the cut
Acquired from a good game of
Pilolo* (*You won*)
The burn.
Your lips. Your elbow
So delectable. So sensational
No time for savoring!
Quick! Get your next morsel!

Fufu- A dish commonly associated with West Africa, made from pounded yam, cassava, and/or green plantain. Usually served with a soup made with fish, meats, and/or vegetables.

*Ayowa – An earthenware dish
*Pilolo- A hide and seek game.

Lessons
Chaun Ballard

The students have become bored, unruly, seekers of new ideas. In this country where there is no Western history, no Greek mythology, or Roman classics to discuss, my students will soon ask, *Is money the only reason for math?* No, I will say, *math deals in integers, calculations, measurement of spices, cups of sugar, and how far men will go to obtain such quantities in nautical miles.* And when I return to the long division written on the board, one child will say to another, *You are a dog.* And the other will respond, *Your father is a donkey.* And I will have to report them both to the principal. Then the class will take sides and split into two groups as they head out to recess. One will return after hitting a boy, and I will ask him why he did it, and he will say, *They said I pray like a khalifah.* Later in the week, the students will ask, *Why do we need to learn math?* And I will say, *To calculate the distance between one another.* And one will say, *He means we need to give each other space.* But before I can clarify, the principal will invite us all into the multipurpose room to talk of healers and damagers. And he will stand two children up and say, *If he does this, and this one does that, are they healers or damagers?* And the children will answer all the questions correctly, and we will return having missed our period of math and most of English. And one student will ask, *Why do we need to learn rules for English?* Another will request, *Why don't you teach us history?* And the class will shout, *Yeah, history!* And I will say, *You are learning history.* And another will ask, *What do you call our history?* I will pause to think—and the class will demand to be taught history. So I will tell them of Columbus, and they will all listen intently. Then one will ask, *What happened to the people? What happened to their lands?* And I will say, *The Spanish took them.* And another will shout, *Columbus wasn't a healer—he was a damager!* And the class will all chuckle. Then one will ask, *What do you call our history?*

[First published in Sukoon]

Unsung heroes (A tribute to my dad)

Roy Venketsamy

The deafening stillness and quiet permeated the surrounding.
The sleepers lie peacefully beneath their crowned mounds;
Only the gentle breeze dares to venture across the quiet landscape
disturbing the peace of the un-weeded blades of grass;
gently swaying them rhythmically
as passionate lovers on a dance floor.
The silent sleepers made their contributions in life
Now lie peacefully with no more qualms.
Their songs have faded with time and memory.
They played their music to the fading tunes.
Only the wind is there to herald their glory
with its gentle caress over their faceless mounds.
The sleepers lie silently, peacefully
in their own glory.

The Spirit of its Searcher
Yeshni Sookraj

Dear India,
    I am finally here,

Great grandfather as my virgin feet rest upon the land of your birth,
I feel the burning pangs of the blistering sun,
that your bare backed dreams succumbed to daily on the sugar cane
fields in Stanger,
Stanger "the home of the brave" they call you,

In May 1911 you became an African, as Adinpur, India bid you
farewell,
the warrior ship Umzinto carrying your 18 year old hopes,
as you entered an era of the struggle you had suffered,
not knowing that the struggle was yet to come.

I have longed for this moment to finally meet you India,
The river Yamuna trickling away amidst its smoky atmosphere,
Loud hooting sounds like ringing temple bells thunder through my
soul,
My heart pounds faster as I search for you, where are you India?

Great grandfather, it is you that has taught me what it is to be an
African,
it is you that has taught me the spirit of Ubuntu,
        I see you amidst the comforting smiles and familiar faces
of brown skinned people,
amidst the vibrant colors and music playing in all its potency and
beauty,
where once I marched for freedom, freedom away from your dom
pass, freedom to
play in beaches, where my hair flew in the wind and my father's
hand gripped mine
tightly as we carried the strength of his India too, marching for
freedom in your honor,
"Let there be peace in our land, South Africa we love you", I
remember that sweet
song,
Blue and white badges with white doves we pinned onto ourselves,

but sacrifice and blood spilled could never make our white doves
whiter than white.

India you lay locked away within the spirit of your searcher,
Great grandfather,
I have been here before,
in my dreams,
Amidst humble souls,
lost in the treasures of your people,
I am your people,
I am you,
     I am a proud Indian from Africa.

The Naicker Patriarch

Ravi Naicker

His epitaph reads; Ponnusami Naicker
Died 31 May 1936 – Rest in Peace
The tomb conspicuous in a sea of young sugar cane.
Has weathered the elements
That battered it timeously.

Arrived on 28 July 1891
From Chengalpattu, Chennai, India
During open season for sugar barons.
His commanding voice
Stature surely earned him position of Sirdar.
Our patriarch, matriarch and infant
Transported by ox-wagon to Nil Desperandum
Indentured 'coolies' were spared
No aorta of compassion.

Their living conditions and job description
Was a crime against humanity.
Like a fish out of water
They had to find their footing hastily
Or accept flogging – as harmless and defenceless as they were.

Sundram, our matriarch reluctantly and remorsefully
Relinquished her infant for internment.

Piercing cries from often hungry
And sick children, fell on deaf ears of the White supervisors.
The mothers gritting their teeth and fiercely working.
Their motherly instincts challenged by a whip-yielding overseer.
Some neglected infants barely survived.

The various farms bear testimony
To Indians hanging themselves – escaping the Draconian style
punitive measures.

Our Patriarch won the hand from a bevy of maidens
Principally because the matriarch deteriorated in health.
Between the wives there were 22 children

Of whom only 12 survived.

1904 back in Chennai
1906 Welcomed as free farmer
Nkwifa, Glen Rosa, Glen Albyn and Glen Roy.
Parallel agenda – land was re-claimed by landowners
After virgin forests were cleared.

Hard labour produced bumper crops
Drought also swept through these lands
Forcing some free farmers into subtle slavery
At tea estates and sugar farms.
Our patriarch was resilient
The desire to succeed made his spirit indomitable.

He selflessly established a school and temple at Glen Roy Farm.
Farming on a large scale.
Drought stricken – and then our patriarch's illness.
10 May 1936 Ponnusami sat between his wives
On their journey to his beloved farm.
He passed on scarcely before reaching his destination.
Today sprouting from the grave is a stump with two branches.
The Naicker legacy – two schools and temples.

Rest in peace dear great grandfather.
Your clan has reached the 600 figure and promises to grow.
Indebted are we to you
For your adventurous spirit and determination.
Your memory shall be enshrined in our hearts.
Till we meet again.

Twelve Ways of Looking at Darkness

after Wallace Stevens
Chaun Ballard

1.

I was bred in the darkness
out of pant stank & memory
Papa held the keys to the x-y

while Momma flowered for him
like a child under the moon

2.

I slid out of her darkness
head first with bloodshot eyes
& skin that wouldn't take in the light

3.

like candlelight
we learned to count our days
in darkness

4.

the blacker the berry—Momma would say
is the dark-darker-darkness
the kind whose outer flesh does not respond
to anything less than magenta

5.

I've known the whites of too many
eyes in passion & flame
those whose souls eternalize

everything
even the darkness

6.

when Papa's roost was away
Momma hen wasn't the wiser
so (of course) the two could not be reconciled
& neither could our dark nest

7.

we admire everything brilliant
star & moon
flame & angel

never once have I heard one say
how lovely the dark is

8.

I adorn the head of Cushitic
thick-napped necks Afros
du-rags & wave caps

even Alexander turned his face
toward Egypt when he saw our multitudes
layered in the darkness

9.

God said *let there be light* & there was light
& God saw that the light was good

& they would have believed us—
if only I hadn't coveted your light & you
my darkness

10.

even if I left this section blank
(which I am considering)
the em dash would still spill dark
onto the page

11.

eleven ways to say darkness:

aphotic / obscure / ill-intended / inhumane / indistinguishable /
somber / murky / nothingness / Cimmerian / after the earth has
been cast out
or swallowed / nebulous—if anyone or anything else remains

12.

my shadow is a child

[*First published in HEArt Online*]

The Black African
Edward Dzonze

Black is my identity,
I'm found in the black of existence
black bushy hair, black the colour of my skin.
Beautified to this black at birth
I rise this black to the height of colours,
I rise this black to the height of races

I am the black African
blessed black by the mighty hand of creation,
distinctively woven into the tapestry of humanity
for the beauty of its countenance,
I rise this black to the height of colours
i rise this black to the height of races
After all,
is this blackness not to be flaunted
on a day like this?
Today, tomorrow and forever the morrow

I am the black African
strumming a tune that echoes
in the wilderness of Africa to the affirmation of our being
Found in the black of existence,
I am the black African
from my mbira player playing a rhythm
that denounces the follies of our barbarism
behold i say to a fellow black African;
the black of our skin looks best at its pristine,
the black in us feels sweet without hate
We can rise above xenophobia and civil wars
Indeed i say
in the ways of love and unity
this blackness is the greatest taste of Africa.

Black is our identity
together we can fight poverty and diseases ashore
Black bushy hair, black the colour of our skin
beautified to this black at birth
We can rise this black to the height of colours,

We can rise this black to the height of races
Behold i say
blackness was born in us to be celebrated,
It is to be flaunted on a day like this
Today, tomorrow and forever the morrow.

I too am an African

Bianca Nieuwenhuis

I too am an African:
my skin may be as white as the frozen flakes that caress the
dragon's back
my hair may be as golden as the sands that scorch the soles of my
feet
my eyes may be as cerulean and teal as the two violent oceans that
meet.

I too am an African,
for our colours were divided, but this was before my time –
I am not a product of apartheid, rather the result of reconciliation
yet we are still at odds, not yet estranged from our parents' parent's
mistakes.

I no longer want to bear the cross of the wrongful,
wicked deeds done by the descendants of the blind.
but I refuse to turn another blind eye to the deterioration of Tata's
dream –
I am not my ancestors. You are not your parents' avengers.

I am too an African.
There is no them. There are no us.
There should no longer be a dissimilarity –

We.
We are the Africans, the children of the birthplace of humankind.
We are home, here where we belong, rocking in the cradle of Mama
Africa.

Echoes
Athol Williams

Look at my face,
look
at my face, and
see my gratitude;
gratitude for the years
that have shaped this life,
this being, this face.
Look,
look at my face,
and see,
see the many faces of those
who have fought against me
and those who fought for me,
those who gave and those
who withheld their love,
their softness, their beauty.
See,
see me,
see them,
see you.

Who am I?

I am not only me, for
I am also them, and I,
I am also
you.

Untitled
Ojo Taiye

learn to use free verse
to write
depression feint in
upper case poems
use wood to tell the world
how you left a shell in the backyard
and walk into the sun
how a river became a song
in the back larynx
of a migratory bird
whose flight ends on lonely hills
how the smell of bristles
in a black robe
becomes a fish rite
in the nostrils of an elephant
how your name is clothed
with peregrine
of a possessed woman
lost in the maze
of mottled rainbows

Questions to ask in South Africa
Harry Owen

A monkey tail waves from the rear wiper
of Dumza's taxi and I ask myself:
When do things become too much? When do you
start to begrudge it, feel you've been taken
for a ride, the word 'borrow' meaning 'give',
and resent the assumptions made about you,
your character, your wealth? Why do you sense
your heart solidifying, congealing
like a crust into what you'd rather not
be: the cost of a breakfast, a chicken,
a conscience or a soul?
Named, we are owned;
spoken, we are real; lived, we become known.

Only a toy, then, but that monkey clings
to the back of the taxi, its brave tail
asking, 'What happens now? What happens now?'

Part 2: Language, Writing, Poetry and Art

Blue Lemons
Mbizo Chirasha

i am the earth pregnant with poetic skulls and skeletons of prose
dawn of my poem strip nights naked
i am the nudity of truth and the rhythm of birth
with my heart dressed in pain
bring me the poetic grapes
and the metaphoric lemons
my mind is hanging like tobacco leaves
bring me the skeleton of my passion
and rhythm of my poetic license
i see killers praying for silence and peace
i see the bleaching faith of my country
hope floating in detergents of propaganda
purple buttocks of morning sitting over fire and enduring faith
i hear the grief of slogan lashes and propaganda
sjmboks in the night of the ballot
i am you and me
my poetry is a menu of provocation
and imagination, as dove of words coo-, in the dawn
in my mental trees
i am the nudity of truth
and the rhythm of birth
i itch the syphilis of sunshine city
and the hepatitis of the city of skulls
blue lemons, black , white , brown, yellow poem.

I Write to Float

Michael 'Wudz' Ochoki

I write to right —to consecrate; to 'ohm' the flame of being into this
mortal vessel's seven spirits. I write to be, to un-become, to reach.

I channel divine epistles to the Seven Churches (Seven Chakras),
and through song, knowledge, prose and rhyme, and chaos,

I vibrate my blue lotus; by breathing, I create. I unwind syllables
on turntables. Like a serpent on the cross, knowledge is intertwined.

So I look up to the word like bread—to heal. Through meditations
of Taban,
Saul Williams, Nietszche and the magic of bleeding pens, I exhale
liberty.

Using the page as a feather, I write to float. Like a cloud with the
face of god,
I write to die, to transcend, and to escape from myself. To find
myself in ink

blotches and become one with the immortal word. I immortalize
my name in
semantics, phonetics and graphics; line breaks, syntax, stress &
sound.

I write to lie because art is a social polygraph. I scribe to transcribe
tribal
chants of my ancestors. Tears of a nation at war. I mourn. Through
the tip of the pen,

I birth new names to wrap around my tongue. I write for Africa.
For dead emcees.
For heartbroken poets. For my aborted children. For mom: I just
robbed you of

another grandchild because I loved selfishly. I write because I'm 12
years old and

this is how father buckles back his belt. And this is how mother unscreams.

My painful poetry

Mbizo Chirasha

Its rhymes are of the poverty stripped widows in Liberia.
Its symbols are of the slain cops freezing on the mortuary slabs of
Gambia
Its imagery is of freedom succumbing within bomb cry in Nigeria
Its sound is of poverty shriveled breasts of mothers in Eritrea
Its surprise is of hunger tortured children in Ethiopia
Its echo is of war caused orphans digging for fortunes and future in
rubbish dumps of
Somalia

My painful poetry
Its connotations are of the weeping of ethnic tribes in Libya
Its voice is of groaning stomachs of banks in Namibia
Its tragedy is of sewage pipes gushing out disgusting contents in the
streets of Zambia
Its metaphors are machetes slicing wombs in the valleys of Kataga
Its similes are of blood stained walls of sufferance in Tanzania
Its alliterations are of genocides and atrocities in Rwandan corridors
Its resonance is of butchers and slaughters in Burundan drives

My painful poetry
Its beat is of apartheid explosions in South Africa
Its allegory is of the crying of the Povo in Zimbabwe
Its satire is of the inking of villages in Mozambique
Its irony is barter exchange of diamond and riles in Angola
Its epitaph is the dying of the cultures in Algeria
My painful poetry is painful and never beautiful

Rain: A Word Sonnet

Marvel Chukwudi Pephel

Grey
Clouds
Lay
Hands
On
Earth
Worn
Out;
Thirst
Quenched,
Drought
Drenched;

Greasing
Season.

(First Published on Jellyfish Whispers).

dark words
Ndumi Dlamini

dark ink will illuminate
white paper
is it not ironic

vent pain, anger and hate
healing, calming and loving
medication to a disease chronic

treated with hate
abused belittled raped, writing
numbs better than gin and tonic

previously believed it was fate
she was destined to a life of misery
now flows words symphonic

a refuge for those who relate
an angel that used words
to escape experiences demonic

dark words will illuminate
white paper
is it not ironic

Diagonal Acrostic: The Juxtaposition

Marvel Chukwudi Pephel

The bomb(s)
cover (ed)
crenel (ated) …

Did the soldiers
in the merlon
escape death?
did they just sleep?

Untitled
Ojo Taiye

it is dark
there is a small star
in the bay of the sun
look!
tendrils grow in the heart
of a mad poet
caress the thighs of the moon
and see a haven of sadness
written on the backhand
of a leper teleporting
on eaves of ebon

My Religion

Phumulani Chipandambiri

Literature is my religion
of its kind,
few are believers.

Literature is my religion
with its mind,
prophets and saints.

Literature is my religion
on its truth,
many are martyred.

l believe in poetic God
of all creation,
l will worship Him till l die.

intention

Hélder Simbad

With art eyes
rip the dress
after naked

massage the body trembling and lit
with the slowness of a slug

In the port of ears
dock immorality of verbs
little vessels of bananas bunch
with silver grape
fresh from the sea honey

Inspect by kiss friendly village
and from the colossal waves of one sea
surfing with surfboard language

And after drunk with pleasure
gather in the navels well
with a symphony of licked
the enjoyment of the last drop of champagne
or take the bee language
to extract the nectar of fire rose
waving me through the dress triangle

And since then the salivate process
breaking the infinite chastity of the Siamese thigh
like camel passing through the hole of needle
one village before the lows country
Take flight towards the mystery

Sycophanta
Pasomi Mucha

Tell me how the boot tastes, O liker of, licker of big-person-boss-boots, you who sullies then raise in praise, who puts the vile in servile. Who is given to high pitched praise? Defying the flat in flattery.

Tell me how the boot tastes, O liker of, licker of big-person-boss-boots, Spewer of smoothly false extolments. That put the grating in ingratiating. Whose fawning obedience, Puts the art in artificial.

Tell me how the boot tastes, O liker of, licker of big-person-boss-boots, Who makes mortals vulnerable, Stripping their defences as you de-fence them, With sincere lies before big-persons Appending sin to sincere, A scorching sycophant, Shameful yet shameless.

Part 3: Spiritual, Existential, Religious, Inspirational, and Individual

The Sun's First Born – Opener of the Ways

Anthony Akoto Osei Jr

Somewhere, over the horizon…
Beyond the place where the Sunsets at the end of every day.
At the point where the orange ruddiness of the setting Sun begins
to merge with the Cosmic Violet of the Night Sky;
There lives a most peculiar creation.
Though a "he", most often mistaken for a "she".
Though "small", most often considered to be "large."
Though "beautiful," most often feared for "his" gaze.
He is Black and White and Gold.
He is old and young, mature and innocent.
He will bite the hand that feeds him, if given ample reason.
He will fight to the death for loved ones, if given minimal
motivation.

He lives where Day and Night are One,
And so the Sun and Moon both call him First Born.
Like a Virus, his Influence can only barely be understood.
Like a Vitamin, his presence is felt most when absent.
This peculiar creature with eyes as Brown as Mahogany.
This peculiar creature, with Teeth as White as Ivory.
This peculiar creature with Fur as Black as Obsidian and as Golden
as pure Ore.
This peculiar creature who lives beyond the place where the sun
sets at the end of every day.
An ornery creature, a mirror to those who meet him.

He smiles like a satisfied crocodile with eyes both moving and
menacing.
Eyes with an excitement that is Infectious and a Sorrow that is
Transformative.
He runs in his sleep and lays down most often when awake.
Sunlight is his Sugarcane.
The winds are his Shower and the waters are his Lotion.
But who is this peculiar creature?
What is this sentient Beast, this mythic existence that lives
somewhere, over the horizon….
Beyond the place where the Sun sets at the end of every day.

How can such a Being even exist? And why are you suddenly so curious?
What is it about this Gold and Obsidian creation that has us wondering and questioning when so much time could be spent worrying or stressing about infinite concerns?
How is he able to force us to spend time on Him more so than anything else in our lives at the moment?

His is an ornery creature, a mirror to all those who meet him.
D-O-G is what we see in the mirror of his eyes, G-O-D is what we feel within the warmth of his company.

Alive in Silver

Bradley M. Purdon

Yearning, this desire to live through the night
Burning, this fire that ascends cloaked in light
Of these wounds, I'm no longer ashamed
Wield these embers to set roses of shadow aflame
No longer does the darkness haunt me
These scars are all that remains
No more do the voices taunt me
Sylvan rivers wash away the bloodstains
My spirit soars surrounded with a sacred glow
Silver fires set alight wraiths of the shadow
The scars upon my wrists fade away
The screams upon my lips end with the dawn of the living day
Argentum emotions ardent flow through my veins
Holy auroras bloom once more ever bright
Sacred silver echoes at war with Pain
Upon my path, my Angel's Sylvan Songs are Lanterns of Light

A blessing from the Creator in every breath
I am eternally grateful to be alive
Because I clashed with Death
And with silver symphonies, I survived

Shango's Song is Oya's Nocturne
Anthony Akoto Osei Jr

Summer Rain on a Bright, shiny day,
Thunderstorms flashing on a warm Midsummer's Night.
The Imagery within the expanse of our Mind.
These symbols and archetypes describing the varying states of our
Thoughts and Feelings.
Like the Eye of a Hurricane: Peace looms with a Threat of Chaos,
A probability of Change and a possibility of Discomfort.

Summer Rain on a Hot, simmering Day.
Four Seasons, Two Seasons.
Two Seasons and Four Reasons.
North East Trades and Southwest Monsoons.
Passionate Indian Summers and Captivating Icelandic Winters.
Mother nature, unable to make up her mind;
As Metamorphic as she is Majestic.
As Calming as she is Cruel.

Thunderstorms flashing in the Heat of the Night.
Daylight brought to a Midsummer's Midnight.
Lightning Falls and the Earth Trembles.
Father sky ponders…
His thoughts, his memories raging close to the Witching hour.
The Darkness of Twilight.
The Illumination of Innovation.
Memories of battles fought and Loved Ones gone and buried
His Lightning's Brighten Heaven's Nighttime
As if furiously searching the Dark for answers to questions he
inherently knows the answer to.

The Imagery within the Expanse of our mind,
These symbols and archetypes describing the states of our thoughts
and feelings.
Like the Eye of a Hurricane.
Like the Eternal calm before the Mortal storm.
A possibility of Change.
A probability of Endurance.

I Am Connected

Bradley M. Purdon

I hear the forests speaking to me
The gardens of flowers call out my name
Groves of silver norfolks and white roses
I feel the symphonies of their evergreen songs
The snow calls me in wintry melodies
The grip of the cold holds her words in stasis
Ice intertwines like ivy in my mind
Frigid water wash over the hiemal skies
The mountains echo with my sylvan name
As valleys and canyons hum into my ears
The soil and sand runs through my fingers
As the desert overflows into my eyes
The oceans sing of tidal ballads
The seas perform an ode to their lunar mother
The rivers and springs water the forest of my soul
As lakes line the woodlands in everlasting rejuvenation
Grasslands howl in winds of the call to my spirit
Savannahs roar in unison with the arid lands
Rolling hills of the highlands raise their voices in battle cries
The plains graze the soil in herds of wandering landscape
The jungle laments of her dying kind
The pain floods my veins as rainforests turn to ash
Extinction looms over Amazon canopies
As the forests write elegies for their siblings
The wind whispers in breezes and screams in hurricanes
As rain descends and brings life to the land
The calm of the clouds breaks the silence
As storms echo with their war shouts like my electrified passion
From tundra to desert roam bird and beast
From rivers to oceans are beings of the mystical waters
Each individual sings their own song of Creation
For the Essence of Life Eternal dwells within them
As the wild sings of her freedom
She still laments of the caged beings
Each day my soul cries out in prayer
That one day the chained shall know peace
The people of the world in their joy and sorrow
Their emotions call to my mind

My heart hears that which one hides from speech
For my spirit feels the secrets they keep
The glow of the silver fires sings to my verdant name
The light that cloaks the woodlands speaks to my sylvan being
The stars in their celestial brightness shine upon the Earth
I feel the Light of Heaven within Nature
My soul is connected to Creation
I am close to the Earth and her songs
Nature speaks to the depths of my being
I feel her symphonies flowing through my spirit
In a bond of love eternal I am connected to my soulmate
My verdant crown is enveloped in the love of my Sylvan Angel
My soul sings symphonies for her as hers does for me
I feel the depths of her emotions as the passion of her mind echoes
in my spirit
Our beings joined together in loving embrace blessed by God
My soul is an evergreen forest
Nature intertwines like gentle vines in my spirit
Light shines upon my woodlands for which I am forever grateful
The Path made for my love and I is lined with divine flowers
Nature is my church to the Creator
I join with Creation in the song of worship to our Saviour
Bathed in the Light of Christ, Creation holds the Essence of Life
Life, she flows through the veins of the souls of Nature
I am connected as I experience realms physical and spiritual
As I wander worlds seen and unseen
The songs of the Earth echo within the depths of my being
As I gaze upon the symphonies of Mother Nature's legacies
I realise - I am connected

I Will Not Die Tonight

Ayo Oyeku

I will not die tonight,
my thin soul above the furnace,
stretching forth over the surface,
making a fine hue within the ether.

I cannot die tonight,
to the four corners I have knocked,
and at the crossroad I have laid my sumptuous sacrifice:
   Four goat heads
for the hovering daemons gawking into the affairs of men,
   Twelve wraps of corn pap
for the restless midgets within the innards of the earth,
   Sixteen nuts and sixteen cowries
for the eternal gatekeeper of time,
   And a pouring of red oil on my peace offering
as a libation to the surreal mothers of all ages.

I will not die tonight,
Because my soul is hidden in the lamp –
      a lamp with twenty-four candlesticks
         to illuminate,
to protect,
to rejuvenate.

Walk, I will walk,
till I imprint my feet
on the sands of time.

Talk, I will talk,
till I have my voice
embedded within the vocal chords of mortals.

Stand, I will stand,
till my once sworn enemies
accompany me to the pedestal of fortune.

And dance, I will dance,
in a rhythmic movement

to tunes played by the conquerors of the world.

So tell it to the birds of the air,
to the beasts in the wild,
to the skinks on the walls,
and even to the *anjonus* lurking behind the horizon,
that I will not die tonight!

Not even tomorrow.

*anjonu means 'an evil spirit' in Yoruba language.

Day-Dream
Mandla Ashley Mavolwane

And then the world resumes
Its deep contemplations

Pragmatism sinks to the core
How will we befriend tranquility?
Our efforts have been in vain
And our forces lead to repulsion
The aftermath has mass casualty
But humanity anticipates to be serene

An inferior voice echoes audible
Sounds of extreme anguish
Forces of nature recognise its utterance
And decide to turn a blind eye
Leaving the speech in splendid isolation
As it continues to plead for recognition

Offsprings born to Terra
Are disguised as busy bees
With a common scheme
To attain the remarkable mel
That has been hidden as knowledge
Will they discover it? They ponder

The cosmos is explicitly void
Contents are constantly conflicting
Empathy and brotherhood are extinct
Distinction hinders absolute tenderness
Oneness is a well known visitor
To the peaceful imaginary world

Difficulties carried out their vices
Inflicting agony on vulnerable societies
Numerous reforms are being implemented
To conquer the undisputed enemy
And replace the suffering with affluence
Shall we exterminate indigence completely

Humanity crumbles due to malady
Constantly hungry for more souls
A deep weep dominates tribes
Antidotes suffer clear defeats to
Extremely pitiless lethal ailments
That subdues life without hesitation

An abrupt shake interrupts
Disturbing the day-dream.

Rivers

Beula Kapp

Rivers that run
according to your
structure will flourish
excel, not to see hell.

The river that runs
according to your
layout
shall spring about
bring forth crops of plenty
the young olive trees
shall surround the spring like honeybees.

Forever your ways
shall be thought
amongst the trees.

Prayer
Ayo Oyeku

May the sun embellish the sky,
with brightness resplendent before eyes,
awakening nature in her grandeur,
with untold glories for man to pursue.

May peace prevail on Earth,
like the floods of water against the banks.
And may smiles retain dimples on our cheeks,
like twinkling eyes in the sky.

May chewed kolanut remain stuck in the corners of our
grandfathers' mouth,
And may there be chunks of meat in our grandmothers' pots.
May our neighbours bring us lamp to see at night,
And may strangers offer us blankets in the cold.

May we not sojourn when the road is famished,
And may we pluck ripe fruits from trees.
May the colours of our eyes, skins and hairs remain changeless
through weathers,
But may they not deceive us all from accepting we are same.

May the Bermuda puke her inhabitants,
That they may share with us knowledge,
On the impossibilities within our reach,
And the possibilities within our grip.

Let us pray in silence,
Let us mutter words of prayer as we walk,
Let prayers follow our thought process as we work,
And while we eat, let us also remember we feed on prayers too.

So let us pray together,
with the hush-hush sounds of kids playing pranks in the garden,
that we might hear the soulful groans of people in need,
from Syria to Sambisa,
from France to planes lost in our universe,
from the scourges of malaria, aids, cancer and poverty,

beggars on the streets,
ailing spirits jutting against their rib cages,
souls withering under sunlight,
dreams that are about to die.

Different colours,
One people,
Many prayers,
One heart.

In the Botanical Gardens

Harry Owen

I climb and sit
on the recumbent skeleton
of a gigantic tree.

One day this will be me,
an invasive alien,
bones bleached, skin-shreds tanned
to tattered strips,
DNA parched into sand.

But now the grass is a green pillow
and my bones are grateful.

Have you ever wondered?

Agu Raphael Gift Ihuoma

How the world would be without God
There would be no seas and beyond
The world would have been an empty space.
Have you ever wondered?
How life would be without Love,
How we would all sorrow on,
Just like the wars we wage on,
All of us will know no peace,
As the wars and chaos will never cease.
Have you ever wondered?
How the world would be without beauty,
There would be no roses to stare at,
As everything be in a haste to fade out
The green fields wouldn't be so beautiful,
And the gardens would seem so pitiful.
Have you ever wondered?
How the world would be without life,
There would be no doves to fly around,
And no butterflies to perch about,
The beautiful wings of butterflies would lay waste,
As a testimony of dead waste.
Have you ever wondered?
How the world would be without writers,
Nobody to appreciate the work of nature,
And nothing to do in wait for the future,
With nobody to tell everybody,
How life is a favor,
Which was granted to all creature.

The Epistemology of Desire

Jarred Thompson

i.
The curious cat
with her arched back
rubs and purrs
against the velvet wall.

ii.
Hot blood circulating in the cranium,
fluid draining and filling:
engorged upon one's self
a table set for a king
split down the middle.

Here stands the judge,
the bearer of codes and
builder of mental fortresses.

There stands the hoodless man
with pink skin:
the destroyer, the glutton,
the pin-point of the universe
where space-time collapses.

iii.
Upon what can I stand
in the shifting sands.
The real is simulated
pressed up against all sense
every hole is filled:
we eat pixels for breakfast

iv.
The curious cat
with her arched back
purrs on the master's lap.

v.
Upon the rack

twisting the screws in my back.
Tug tug till it all fades away
a gentle wave washing the message a castaway left for me.

Where is the root?
The origin with a name?
I blow out pink, blue, green bubbles
all the same.

vi.
A space craft orbits Jupiter
studying the origins of the universe,
and a homeless woman with a dog for a friend trudges
up the road.

A heart lunges in a chest
somewhere.
A heaviness settles (poisoned dew drops) on a post-apocalyptic
morning.
Our eyes are red, our skin scraped raw and our sheets smell of
taboo.

Where are those moments of pure dissolve:
I am not
You are not:
not african, not european, not black, not mixed. not white, not
cheater, not cheated on, not gay, not straight, not colonizer, not
colonized:
The negations point to the horizon
a fictitious place without history

vii.
Forces pull:
to feed, to work, to fuck, to sleep, to love, to hate, to breath.
Does it pull us away or to this incurable condition:
no life without desire, no desire without life.

viii.
The curious cat
with her arched back
purrs so sweetly in the master's lap.

Her eyes languid,
her stare, serene,
she controls all that we ever will see.

Dreaming
James McKeown

Dreamily, he slept.
Dreamily, the lion leapt.
Dreamily he wandered the barren landscape.
Dreamily, he wandered the halls of the land of the Cape.
Dreamily, he observed the multi-coloured shapes.
Dreamily, he noticed the human apes.
Dreamily, the booming voice spoke.
Dreamily, he awoke.

For?

Jarred Thompson

For the morning drizzle outside
cuddled with a lover,
or the sweat on my brow
while I lift boulders.

For the smell of spices from a cast iron orange pot,
or the lingering taste of fermented grapes
in the lull of a Thursday evening.

For the black man who waves
at a white baby
or the queer who helps the straight guy sow.

For the corrupt politicians finally serving their sentences
or the homeless woman finally getting a fresh slice of bread.

For the aborted children giving meaning to life,
or the orphans succeeding despite hardship and strife.

For music
for pain
for love
for art.
For the swing in my hips
when the strobe lights flash and the
music vibrates my ribcage.

For the conversations that last all night
and the eye contact with a stranger that lingers for weeks.

For discoveries revealing us to be insects
to Gods,
or the majestic Cathedrals
DEMANDING REVERANCE
(Its own type of gift.)

For humanity's love
(which needs explaining)

and the fault lines of the heart
causing families to slip between tectonic plates.

For tragedy
for birth
for death
for utter chaos:
reminding us that we're riders of this rock
with fists plunged deep into moist soul
we cultivate, we reap, we straddle
riding this beast till all is eventually
forgot.

Omi Alaafia
Tola Ijalusi

Stream of ages
of source unknown
and mysteries uncovered
makes a land bare.
Silence now loud in violence
answering knocks at doors,
flush of blood bears trademark
as messages of death delivered.
Do you hear
the water rumbling,
rising fast above temperature?
Do you hear
the living mourning,
singing to the dead?
Today, I ask
if you hear
that the water
has been troubled.
Tomorrow, I will call
through your broken windows
your throbbing heart
revisit your fading pasts.

*Omi Alaafia is a Yoruba word in Yoruba Language from South Western
Nigeria meaning Water of Peace.*

A Google Glass Sonnet
Ali Znaidi

I just want to respond
to the rainbow's request{temptation, indeed.}!
I just want
those flimsy colours
to last. Just want
those sparkles to last.
Just want
those tropes to last,{although
I don't like ropes}.
There must have been a time
when gazing at the rainbow
wearing a Google Glass is amazingly experiential
because you can discover and capture the true potential
of virtual colours{your inner self, indeed.}!

Flight Reflections

Nelisa Khethokuhle Khwela

Giant masses of water
Shining like golden coins
Steep hilly mountainous regions
Stretch across the land for hours
Metal wing slicing through the air
The created bird charting across the sky

I look down at the earth.

How are we so small yet feel so consumed by life?
As I looked down at the creased duvet of land, I realized:
If, as small as we are, own the mountain tops
Can't we own everything else?

The Sky Hides its Ash

Ali Znaidi

Ash is in itself death.
Ash is cooked on the oven
of shadowless breaths.
Rife with poesy,
words of exodus are carried by the wind.
—Alleys, meadows,
and scattered dandelion seeds.
It rains. It keeps raining.
Blueness oozes out from the wounded clouds.
—Blue marrow staining the bones.
Although time is fleeting,
the sky is always there hiding ash
between the layers of the isthmus:
the distance between breath
and the reverberating blues
of a broken harmonica.

Reality
Yeshni Sookraj

Starlight twinkle from afar,
into the distance we gaze,
a body,
a mind,
fueled with the energy of the African earth,
that resonates the tales of our slave forefathers,
where we lay of our heads to rest on the fortunes of their great
suffering,

the sands of time,
I yearn to grasp within the palms of my hands
and find those stones that keep us,
for if we could give joy and feel joy,
then why not yearn for that which drives us,

it is the very ounce of reality,
our knees are bruised,
we bite the dust,
we conquer with faith in grim reality,
we reach for the light,
we reach for the starlight twinkle.

Death
Tafadzwa Chikowore

I came and went as I did please,
Amid the flowers, in the light of the spring,
Roving through the fields with a careless ease,
To a courtyard fair, where I did sing.
In the summer's heat or in the winter's face,
I came and went as one might grace
A regal wedding, or a gilded ball.
I danced in the haze of a waterfall.
Yet now the wind is my only brother.
Its egregious chill is the one thing I know,
As a throng of rice is thrown for another,
Into the somnolent grave I go.
Death, why do you seek me,
When I have never thought of you?

Decayed Bones and Exhaled Breaths
Ali Znaidi

The fig leaf is a cover.
The sky is a cover.
The river is a cover.

The desert is nudity.
Sand is a cover.
Granules are full-stops
stopping moving bodies.

The sea is nudity.
Foam is a cover.
Waves are questions
without answers.

A cloud is a cover.
Rain is nudity.
Raindrops are exclamation marks
falling on imprisoned bodies.

Breaths are nudity.
Bones are covers.
Days are not but underclothes
covering our limitless limitations.
Days are not but decayed bones
and exhaled breaths.

The glass cage
Michelle Hayward

Come with me to the place where few feet dare to tread
But where many forgotten souls pace up and down in dread
Tip-toe beside me through the halls as old as age
The place I call the glass cage

Enter into the place; stop to listen to the white flamingo's song
As he taps his beak at an uneasy pace on the glass entrapment all
day long
His is a stubborn song that will stop you in your tracks
He will not relent until the glass cracks

Do not fear to feed the creature that cannot make a sound
Rage races through his thoughts, though he bound
His gaze is forever chained to the sky like Orion
No longer a hunter, yet still a lion

Sit with me and watch the old mischievous fox
Trouble follows shortly behind her dishevelled locks
In a reddened rush, she taunts the delicate fawn
Before retreating to safety, for she too is a mere pawn

Before you leave, peer up at the brightly lit skies
Dare not look away, dare not narrow your eyes
And once you have wandered off this page
Do not forget those in the glass cage

the night is a sea
Michael 'Wudz' Ochoki

١

the night is a sea
and stars are memories of merry, sly, black pearl, and our child: the
brightest star in a cloud

the night is an apology:

sly: i'm sorry for becoming a knife and a coward
pearl: i'm sorry for becoming an eye for an 'i'
mom: hello, it's me. i bear your father's name like a birthmark. he
was a rock, had bigger feet and longer fingers. i'm told, artists have
longer fingers so as to mould anything out of clay, like god.

٢

nights like this, Arabic songs scissor the night into shreds of
abstract syllables

٣

the wind smells of mirrors. it's the fragrance of heaven seething
through the windows of stars.

the wind is jazz, a duvet — a smoke of high grade weed from god's
lungs.

٤

save for the lull of crickets, a boy and a girl giggling, a loud snore,
the neigh of a horse...it's a calm night; i almost stretch out my arms
to swim in the serendipity.

٥

instead

،
i brew

myself
black
coffee
because
i'm told
that's
what
writers
do
.

11.57 pm

٦

...and tomorrow, your shoes must shine.
'cause your feet are made of star dust.

Travelling Alone
Sibusiso Ernest Masilela

I passed across the face of Timbuktu
In search of shrines or hieroglyphics
Welcomed by the hot and dry shingles
I saw a Muslim woman facing north
Kneeling and reciting over the Quran
Asking death to feel the loss of folk,
She must have been the only voice left
Her brothers and husband lost in carnage
Her children forced to do child labour
Just to serve the interest of the guerrilla,
I then looked for directions to the West
Perhaps fill a better attitude in my pockets
And felt dust plunging a free-fall on the air
I guess we are all not so free after all
We suffer a conflict of power and territory,
Vestiges and corpses formed our wastelands
Si-moom exhuming desiccated bones
All hindered by broken conversations
Craniums placed on spears as zone flags
Car metals burned or galvanized with blood
Vultures are watchmen camping on dead trees
Hiding lunar moon behind a monochrome,
No sheep survives a den of hungry wolves
Footprints erased by whirlwinds chasing tourists
Only the mephitic scorpions print ellipses
Sahara boiled by heat wave itching on the skin
Our lips cranked but our souls will be purified
If all our remains are buried down South,
Niger showing marks of what were once torrents
The all Seeing Eye has started execrating on our rivers
Drought will fulfill its mission by creating thirst
We are not sure if the Robben Island is full
And the only sign left on our map is poverty,
Somebody please! Call for daughters of Modjadji
To cry proverbs on the sky and conjure for rain
We pray for the velvet clouds to bring us wet salvation
Grow green leaves and shelter us under Marula trees

Part 4: Illness, Suffering and Healing

Half Of A Human Species

To all sickle cell victims

Nureni Ibrahim

I diagnosed the genetic cactus on his bedridden gene
Bones contorting like a rotten flowering shrub
By the ancient hills of sickle syndrome
The trend of mystical ailments
Pounce the veins, tissues and bloodstreams
Zest with no spiritual vaccine
The flowing clog of blood vessels
In seconds, minutes and hours
I diagnosed
He deceived the seeds of his ailment
With his hale and hearty face
Like the pretentious death of a tortoise's hibernate
Look at the Corridor!
See apron, stethoscope and the theatre sets
Prepared for the patron of loosen cells
Oh! Poor miserable teen
Where are the anemic genes that drag thee forth;
Unknowingly unto this planet?

Inspired Less
Marumo Moagi

I sit and ponder on the thoughts of my heart,
It speaks in words I only hear in part.
I so desperately wish to hear what it says,
To understand and know its ways.
It seems somehow it has stopped beating,
It needs CPR because it's not breathing.
Numbed by the tear and wear of days,
Pains that pierced through as sharp as the suns' rays.
Dull to the sweet song of love or the melody of laughter,
And to the heartbreaks that follow after.
It no longer speaks to me but it speaks in foreign tongue,
Sings dirges I've never sung.
O' speak to me again in words I remember,
And to your command I shall surrender.
No more will I drown you in thoughts uninspired and words half said,
No more will I depress you with whispers said upon my bed.
Live again and I'll let you be.
Treacherous as you are I'll give you freedom of speech.
I'll forsake my mind and give you my loyalty.
Inspire me once more and I will treat you like royalty.

Ode To A Poison

Ayomide Owoyemi

She froths at the top,
ebullient of the poison within.
From jars to mouths ajar,
in bars and personal lairs,
the solvent transmutes,
intrudes and precludes egocentricity.
By it the mind goes
flip flop and fits and stops,
in hops, skips and jumps,
but at times
it turns to a dour slop.
It rouses unwilling muscles
and unfetters neurons.
The surreptitious bubbles
to the surface,
in babbles, jabbers
and repeatedly pressured
Sphincters,
till the haze swoons
and catalepsy moults
into the rueful
hangover.

The manic depressive daughter
Abigail George

The furniture is there but it also isn't there.
What I am seeing is not real. It's
Like the memory of water's hiding
Place inside a lake. Fire for eyes. Moth
Wings for limbs. Milk flowing
Through bones. All rage and sadness
Standing at attention finding them
Instead of the fluid emptiness in a vessel. You are
My sun. All feelings shatter the sunset,
The dawn in ravishing intervals. You
Have to see it the way that I see it. That
I am damaged. That the people I have
Loved have damaged me. My face, the
Reflection in the bathroom mirror, is a
Museum. It speaks volumes. Grief is
Like silence. It has its own soul. I only
Had to learn how to love myself and

Then all this sadness would end. Rage
Would find the exit out. Some escape.
This voice within me has no ending, only
A beginning. You're asleep so you don't
Remember. The stillness that came
After the hunger. The forest. The earth. Gravity.
Most of all the red path of the volcano.
Haunted, so the night swimming began
In earnest. I used water to trace vertebrae.
I praised asylum. I exalted the keys that came
With freedom. I was a fossil but knew
Nothing of choice. I knew what touch
Was and in the end longing for it almost
Destroyed me. I tried to live up to your
Expectations.

facets
Vincent Ajise

at an infirmary
sponsored by men who speak
through their lungs.

a woman tears
flood the hallway with
   rust & riddles of grief.

a child's mouth
is cupped in awe
as his ass is being
diagnosed as an harbinger
 of worms & gore.

 .

a monk stares
at the bubbling-rear
of a nurse, wishing
he could barter his celibacy
   for the tsunami brewing.

while a bohemian whose head looks
like the shape of an avocado
sits with his legs scissors-shaped,
 humming the language of machines
to a god who understands only
the accent of the Swahilis.

Suicide Note
Rana Al Hassanein

Fading away from this world
I sense the beauty of what's beyond
My eyes see spirits
Mourning to join death
Skin shines no more
As beauty lost with sins
 Fears devours within
And heart's cries to vent
I tried to sail away
But I reached no shore
Your universe is extrinsic
Your voices murdered instinct
Ashes to ashes
Lust to lust
My veins to be hewed
And face to be dimmed

To

Tendai R Mwanaka

To let this poem trot blindly the way youth and stupidity runs back
down the never ending source of remorse and genetics
To have glass shattering anger at this poem but
To still manage it until I finish writing it, you reading it
To let me skip to the past where grief gives way to a recurring
dream of finding whole other houses behind my mirror
And the bricks of my whole other houses were tears

To know that we will never know whether it is luck, strength,
blessing, curse or weakness to have survived where others could not
To know that suffering is like that too- five horizontal lines drawn
in pencil grounding the canvass of our life
To traverse that canvass, leaving black leaking spaces for air
To be untitled like everything else that takes too long to arrive
To be ill without falling ill

To think in a low voice so no one can see us
But no thought comes but only the wind
To be incapable of following our thoughts from one sentence to
the next one because the sentences breaks down and the gaps
between words become too long, too big for the words to connect,
to hold together

To feel guilty whilst escaping our own shadows
To feel guilty for walking away from our shadows and all the while
remaining behind
To be like a bazooka that hasn't lived up to its boom blast potential
To realize everything that I had declared buried, done with, is lying
open to a second viewing

To know that she is going out with other boyfriends, she is on the
prowl, whilst I am at home waiting, wilting, curving the darkness of
my home with the chisel of my loneness
To storm abuse at my own reflection in the mirror
So that I might not feel this alone, so alone
To know of this loneliness so barren, is like my dried and shrunken
testicles
I am dog eared in many places it looks like I have a body

93

To feel the cold pain eating me from the centre of this body

To feel our suffering weighing more than what it weighed before
we ever got here and what happens here weighs what it weighs
To live by burrowing in for we are people buried alive, and our
tunnels seem strangely aimless, uprooted, gutted, fallen in….
To be a lorry tipper that vomits the sands and stones on our mind's
tunnels
To know that children with deep eyes will be silent at the world just
like old man with funny coughs
To be but a soul, formless, loitering around until emancipation
To burn each day, with more knowing, with more estrangement

To abandon misery until it becomes a mere concept, a poem
To leap with hungry aim
To be as ambitious as an argument
To run against the river
To question yourself about how to make it from one margin to
another
To knit my heart back together every time I get up and it forgives
me again and again
To move desperately towards meaning, where travelling becomes
the basement of everything
To have an imagination fatefully embracing the birth of the world
of appeal
To know that learning is life, that learning is the colour as life

What colour is pain
Mari Ballot

Light clouds drift by   soundless   white
a black bird soars free
I hear my own coloured sobbing   (as if it is not mine)
see the secret sound of pain
am I one child too many?
am I too much not like her?
unwanted   like the cold bare blue walls
bruised   but brave   as the grey roof
broken   withstanding loud storms
silently   I too cover up   pretend maybe   if I had a dog......(it
would defend)
maybe   if my father did not leave maybe   if gran did not die
maybe   if I looked like her
maybe   if I wash the windows more ...sweep the entire floor...
that frightening familiar smell my home   my hell
it is not a place where people laugh or play (a silver spider too
crawls away)
her thin mad lilac lips shout
the yellow sun shines suffering
lights her unkempt brown hair
red blood trickles on the door (I curl up more)
love aching   glass breaking cries creeping through the room
wind whimpers softly soaking up sadness trashing thumps
the passage funnels fear a mess of blurred colours
I know   nothing that I'll do   will ever please her
and that tonight she will cover herself with guilt
and I lying on the undone stitches of the sheets (she once
mended)
I will hug her mother's torn patchwork quilt....

The Day Yaa Serwaa fell down the Pit Latrine

Afua Wilcox

Serwaa, sweet Serwaa, with your lips: watermelon pink,
Your smile: coconut white,
Your spirit brought light from the coast to Togo.
Your tiny frame,
Was too small to abstain,
From being swallowed to the heavens below.

Yaa Serwaa is missing,
It has been 3 days now and we haven't seen her,
The whole village looked for her, and she couldn't be found.
She was not in the playground; she was not under Mrs Anno's
banana trees,
She was not playing ampe* on the high street, nor was she down by
the reeds.
Serwaa had just disappeared.

Serwaa, sweet Serwaa, with your lips: watermelon pink,
Your smile: coconut white,
Your spirit brought light from the coast to Togo.
Your tiny frame,
Was too small to abstain,
From being swallowed to the heavens below.

That overcast morning,
The clouds wounded the sun,
The dust was exceptionally mischievous,
It was caked between my toes and chalewote*,
The children gathered with a rattle of whispers,
They said they found Serwaa in the pit latrine.

Serwaa, sweet Serwaa, with your lips: watermelon pink,
Your smile: coconut white,
Your spirit brought light from the coast to Togo.
Your tiny frame,
Was too small to abstain,
From being swallowed to the heavens below.

I have always associated the grave scent of the pit latrine with hell,
But in all honesty, I've never fallen in myself,
I have never seen the universe that is beneath the earth surface,
If Yaa Serwaa fell in there, then surely it cannot be hell!

Serwaa, sweet Serwaa, with your lips: watermelon pink,
Your smile: coconut white,
Your spirit brought light from the coast to Togo.
Your tiny frame,
Was too small to abstain,
From being swallowed to the heavens below.

Yaa Serwaa was the sweetest girl I knew.
Her hair was always thick with pomade, not a strand out of place,
her cocoa skin always buttered to match. She had a bright smile,
sweet watermelon lips and a gap between her two porcelain incisors
so God could mimic the tongue that uttered the soft spoken words
she said with sunshine.
Yaa Serwaa always helped me with my books,
She played with me when Maame cut my hair and everyone else
wouldn't play with me,
They said I looked like a boy.
Yaa Serwaa didn't mind,
 She told me I looked like a girl.

Serwaa, sweet Serwaa, with your lips: watermelon pink,
Your smile: coconut white,
Your spirit brought light from the coast to Togo.
Your tiny frame,
Was too small to abstain,
From being swallowed to the heavens below.

If Yaa Serwaa fell down the pit latrine, then that space down low
must be heaven.
God knows how wonderful Yaa Serwaa was.
When Nene was buried they put him in the ground and Maame said
he was going to heaven.
The pit latrine heaven must be a very special heaven,
If Yaa Serwaa fell in it, it is surely a wonderful place.

It must have walls lined with kelewele* and cassava cakes, kube* and bofrot*.
Its floors glazed with Fan Ice and pineapple juice. Banku* and okro soup falls from the sky!
I think God made it smell the way it does to put off non-residents, and protect this heaven,
If everyone knew what was down there, we would all be diving in and stealing these great treasures from all the legitimate citizens of this holy paradise!

Rest in Peace Yaa Serwaa
Sweet Serwaa, with your lips: watermelon pink,
Your smile: coconut white,
Your spirit brought light from the coast to Togo.
Your tiny frame,
Was too small to refrain,
From being swallowed to the heavens below.

*Ampe is a simple game played by school age children in Ghana.
*Chalewote is a flip flop.
*Kelewele is a Ghanaian snack made from plantains.
*Kube is a type of Ghanaian toffee
*Bofrot is Ghanaian donut
*Banku is a Ghanaian staple food made of maize meal

The Glass That Fell

To my younger sister Sindile Mhlanga, may your loving soul rest in peace.
Eliza Mabungu

I woke up to the loud noise of a breaking glass,
I woke up to the breaking sound of the thing I held on dearly to,
I rose from the bed,
Paced around my kitchen in search for it!
I looked and couldn't find it.

It must be the window,
Windows are also made of glass,
So fragile but yet so endangering!
Every window I checked was fine,
The bathroom one was even closed for a change!

Something screamed at me,
"Check the compartments where you keep your fine china!"
I rushed, I was worried and I had to look!
I opened them, to only find everything in order.
What is it that must have fallen?
What is it that fell and hurt my ear?
The sound too deafening to bear.
The glass fell; I heard it even in my heart!

It was then, then when I felt the cut,
The cut so deep that I couldn't bear.
It was then when I realised you were the glass that fell!
You were broken in pieces,
In my heart you were the glass that cut so deep.
In the compartments of my heart there are glasses,
These glasses I hold with care,
They are those kind of glasses you boast about to special guests!
These fine glasses are always handled with care!

Maybe I shouldn't have treated you like glass!
Maybe I was right, it is just in your nature!
You fall and you cut!
I should have known but you fell on your own,
You broke and now your cut is so deep!

I am now brokenhearted because of the cuts,
Because of your broken pieces, my heart is broken
Your cut so deep, you are the glass that fell!
You are the glass that broke!

In the compartments of my heart,
There's a glass that fell!
The cut so deep, it hurt!

Sometimes Table Mountain and my sister
Abigail George

She's like the ocean. Her perfume is carried
To me in waves. Vibrations. She is a bird.
She is my enemy. Sometimes she is my friend.
We have everything and nothing in common
At the same time. Her eyes are made of
A strange language. My life to other people
Seems to be filled with courage but to tell
You the truth it's not. Most days it's glass ceilings,
The memory of the 'mother city' Cape Town's
Table Mountain, and my sister. I'm
Running away from her again in this poem. In this
Version of my life I am truth. I believe in
Fear. My sister believes in summer dresses.
Lip gloss, peacock-blue eye-shadow. Kohl-
Rimmed eyes. Accessories. Accessories.
Magazine hair. She's Brazil. She's Rio de Janeiro.
I'm the Sahara. She's Hollywood. I'm a
Starless sky giving slowly birth to salt and light. The
Colour blue. Her mouth is like a wedding guest.
I write my poems and everything is fine. I
Put my sister in a time machine but she keeps
On coming back as herself. She doesn't
Change. Inside of her there's a code I must
Crack. A system. I know the fingers of cities.
I must find the marrow in my bones. Keep the muscle
For myself. All this love is surely not meant
For me alone. She's a diva. I'm just playing a minor role
In her major life matters. She's art history.

The Lunatic And Her Brood
Kariuki wa Nyamu

Christmas dawn
found the rain-sodden lunatic _{mou}nti^{ng} ^{Gi}ko_{mba} market's garbage
_he^{ap}s, whilst repressing an obstinate cou_{gh!} With intent of nourishing
her ravenous brood, whose sires will without end be   a
n   o   n   y   m   o   u   s!

Christmas noontide
the towering s ☼ n blazes her bare back
          as city centre believers on microphones, yet again sing love,
          accord and charity, in celebration of Kristu's birth, while the
          famished woman parrots mellow carols, awaiting the
          cheerful hands of *Imanueri's* envoys to
s t r e t c h   out to them!
But, ugh! They blatantly RE^{BUKE!} and *haul her* _o U ^T *of feast!*

Boxing Day dusk
finds the weather-beaten mother and her malnourished daughter,
fighting over stale Christmas steak, next to garbage on Grogan
road, until the latter gives in! Thus the mother of children _{thr}o^{ws} it to
the twins, as her daughter hurriedly scavenges a blueberry muffin
          infested by myriad worms…
     Then, Ma _{mi}ⁿe_s a sachet of milk from the smelly decaying
          stuff, and ^{gu}z_{zles} to her fill, this time, unmoved by the twins'
hunger pangs! She then ^dri_{ps} what's left on their foreheads
pronouncing, 'My lovely puppies will take this, for milk is gold!'
     Hmm, utterly ecstatic, they lick it as it ^{sp}il_{ls} do_{wn} their little
noses!

New Year's Eve
I sp**O**t the *frail* and forsaken one intently   s o r t i n g   o u t musty
*chapatti*s from the _{hi}ll^{-high garbage hea}p_s in Muthurwa, as her often sick
twin lads pitilessly consumed by malnutrition (glare at a marabou
          ingesting something filthy in its goiter-like bag, then dangles
          it do_{wn} the throat) as the hostile-friendly Ma rummages
          through _{bi}n^s, the frayed brood wait on, with demanding
          hollow ëyës, yearning
to s_uc_kle the shrunken breasts, only for Ma to gi^{ve} them a l**OO**k that
seems to say,

'*Mbaga**, whom do you think I'm fighting for?'

New Year's daybreak
the ill-fated ones ₉et ᵘᴾ and return to the flooded gutters, singing
merry, merry Christmas
Though branded outcasts of social order, and the grubby
seeds going through hell… they must fight to ₉ᵣoᵂ and blossom into
urbanites who're within tolerable limits!
Oh loving God of small things, we meekly beseech you to
SMᴬₛₕ their
horrific bug of lack, ill-health and misery!

But hey, come on people!

Won't you ever bud an iota of compassion
and fight maltreatment from the wild world
and suffocate the ache that the shabby
and odorous ones SUFFER?

*A Gikuyunized word for 'bugger'

103

I, son of the streets
Vupenyu Zvoushe

To what oracle shall I moan and kneel?
To what temple shall I plead my case in a shrill?
To what religious podium shall I cough up my misery?
I know no life.

Being born on the other side of the bed is a crime I committed
It saddens me when I lead a pared life
It is not by choice that I was born out of wedlock
I wish I could find the womb that brought me forth
For since I was me, it's me and myself

I labour on day's end to eat to my full
As I urge my hunger into a stupid lull
I only exist as a human silhouette
Foraging for nothing but untouchable illusions
I fill like nothing but a pack of dust

To whom shall I unload my pain?
I am tired of this life am conferred with
Insomnia and hunger
Hate and nakedness

People see me as a disgraceful black number
Too insignificant to remember
From the tomes of statistical data
So I plead to be remembered

I desire harmony with the rest of the world
It is my daily plight to fight this fight
I dream of a life that is, never is
So help me make my dream come true

That Talking Tree
Tunu Ndanzi

Bound to one ground,
No left nor right,
To just be stuck and wait
Waiting for that push,
Wind blows to be thankful.

That tree that talks with many invites,
Invites to unknown meetings,
Meetings with meaningless agendas,
Meaningless I insist
Yes meaningless
Because all it does is just talks
Screaming success with no actions.
Can't avoid that dry laugh,
Being weathered to feel that coldness
Unreality thought to be reality.

That hunger that eats my worthless life,
That sacrifice to that tree,
That tree that grows strong
Eating up even the left bones
Selfishness.
Ignorant that's our spoken memory,
That's how glorified our memorial is, to that
tree that talks.

I Am Dead But Still Alive
Thandiwe Shea

Chagrined, brooding, crestfallen, bleak
All these emotions, I am agonized
Coerced to X-out my unborn baby
I fell to my knees, clutching my head in despair
Excruciating, ineffable, hoarse, staid
Pain became unbearable
Tears welled up in my eyes and began rolling down
my cheeks like rivulets
I tried to stop them, but they were refractory

20 weeks
"Her body has grown bigger,
Her head and body are more in proportion,
She weighs about 10 ½ ounces now
She is also 6 ½ inches long from head to bottom
And about 10 inches from head to heel..."
The nurse had explained in elation
The thought of holding her made my eyes glitter with tears of joy
Little did I know it was just Evanescent, Ephemeral
Sighs!!!

I chided feebly, deplorably
But illegitimacy is untenable in my culture
I had to acquiesce
Now the pain was cumulative
It developed into angst, malaise and lassitude
Overcame with all senses of weakness, decrepit
I lost balance and fell down in swoon

I woke up the following morning
The nurse delivered the news
My baby is stillborn
Mother Nature has taken its cause
I broke down in tears
Until my voice was no longer audible
Something in me died
I died alive
I am dead but still alive

A Renewed Life

Myron Menon Naidoo

Into the deep
                          Blue sea
I see.

As free as the fragrant
Of the fresh crushed salt.
With its healing power.
My wounds are
Healed.

The bright yellow orange
                                        Shimmy rays.
Too bright to see.
But its beauty
Too full to see.
Another glance…

As the breezy waves shrives off
Gold and silver glaze
                          As the silver fish ride again.

Part 5: Memories, Nature and Environmentalism

The Diary (1963)
Kelechi Ezeigwe

You and I, your mind and mine *is* entangled in a circle of nostalgia
at how far we have gone away from time back. 1963, we were
young, the air sifting through our thick hair. We sat before a round
table, you on flare pants handling a camera, another on floral print
and me on sunshade, while we watched the family in a get together,
it seemed life had just started. We clustered together on the wet
grass, a corona of love binding us. There comes sounds of vibrant
laughter and giggles, a flash of light and there on our faces are still
smiles, coyness, and longings that lasts just as long as photographs
of us placed on the wall. Today some faces are beginning to blur
out- *where is she, something like oil has spilled over some faces here!-* we
recognize her but tomorrow we find vanished faces, and we recall
their memories from pictured outfits- *look! you remember he wore this,
the floral print-* or if you look to throw a stone away, white marbles
with engraved names we knew and called and cackled until it
dissolved into echoes and gloomy bouquets we place in memoriam.
Each, we are sure are gone to places, but what kind of place is so
far for a return, 1963 till ..., what they left behind, only
photographs on the wall- *Chika on cornrow (black and white), a
saddening laughter on her face;* Faded Christmas, love cards littered on
the dinning- *with love from Uche.* Another, *I will wait by the seashore till
this feeling come alive.* A well packed wardrobe of clothes we go to
inhale the scent, something nostalgic. The nostalgia life brings to us
and take away cruelly, so that we remember memories that come
and go off like wisp of smokes, we cannot hold it, for all we have
lost and loved are those memories that come and go and do not
stay in the palm of our hands, else we remake them. *LIFE- sluggish
saw that splits in a twinkle of a second- you move with unimaginable craft that
throw us apart into unreachable realms.* Realms as wide as two nostrils,
we outstretch minds to reach each other but it becomes wider as
1963 till now, the gone times when grasses were green and laughter
were vibrant and we gathered in a family re-union, holding hands
and taking snaps. We now relish those moments in this garden of
wilted grasses, the memories made with the people we knew, who
left a broken door behind when they walked away for good. We
have no idea where life flung them to.

The Summer of '69

Christine Coates

That summer we didn't die,
we cycled out of town into the country,
by a stream we barbecued sausages,
walked across the narrow culvert.
The river dropped away, it seemed a hundred foot below
but I know how memory shrinks.

That summer we didn't die,
although if my mother knew what we were up to –
we went to the beach all day, our bodies tingling from sea and sun.
A blue-bottle stung me and you took me
to the dunes and peed on my leg –
it was the most natural thing to do.

Later you made us all dinner, and when
the others were sleeping and my mother passed out
from too much wine,
we sat on the bed, your hand up my shortie pyjama top
a whisper of a touch, then an eager puppy pulling at my nipple.
Is this very bad, I asked, that summer we didn't die.

It was the summer my father died,
my sisters ran feral like baboons when the leader is killed,
but we didn't die that summer –
we danced to Dickie Loader and the Blue Jeans,
we French kissed and
your hand progressed to inside my panties.

That winter we listened to the moon landing;
getting out of Klerksdorp was a greater challenge.
The sixties were ending – you left for a job in Joburg,
called to say you'd bought a red Alpha Spider.
I never saw it – you'd written it off – no scars to show.
I met a boy with a blue Capri and another with an old green Morris;
the next summer I was riding with boys in cars,
but that summer we didn't die.

Nostalgia
Mimi Brako Bismarck

There was a time
When we were children
Right before a thunderstorm
When the wind whirled.
We took our mothers' ntoma*
Tied one end around our waist
Held the other ends over our backs
And parachuted into childhood innocence
As we raced down the dusty, red streets
Your face--black and shinny
Revealed crooked teeth and jaundiced eyes
I would've married you
Even then.

*ntoma- *Traditional African printed cloth*

First Weekend

Christine Coates

That night by the lake
remember how we talked in your old green Morris
how the stars watched us fall.
Sitting in the back I wanted to know cars and rain.

That first night in Elgin
under eaves and red quilts,
in the morning opening the window
to mist and apple orchards.

That drive to Hermanus,
how we stood on the sea wall, me in fake fur and boots,
you taking photographs.
Were whales watching us then?

The tea and sandwiches at the Princess Cafe,
the jukebox playing 'Die Tantes van Nantes',
you selecting Simon and Garfunkel's
'Bridge over Troubled Waters'.

Now I see how you were
the bridge I crossed,
the pier that shored,
that harboured me.

Never Forget

Chuma Mmeka

I could never forget the days of folly
From the old youthfulness of yore.
Those long and busy days
When sweat creased the brow
And the reward was sweet.

How we welcomed all the evenings
With hearty calls and happy timing,
With proud relief and anticipation.
How the evenings stretched to night
The nostalgia and the feeling of woe.

How my Parish rode out every night
Honking horns and missing hisses
Prowling like hawk for cheap prey
The height of our extreme foolery
And silly courtship with destruction.

I can't forget the wild merry making:
The groovy hangouts at Fleeks joint
That culminated in Baby's place;
How we' all step into the Next Level
To play some more and look around.

Why forget the club and drunken nights
The rascality and the convincing lies
The sweet nothings and careless lays
And the mornings always full of regrets
For a wasted time and loss of money.

Do you really want me to forget all?
The fair game that did come to me:
The rich and the very wretched
The just comes and the old schools
The pretty, the simple, even one-eyed.

Even if I try, I cannot really forget
All the fun and pleasures of the night
The threesomes and the orgies
The exposure to risk and illnesses
And the marrying of diverse demons.

How can I possibly succeed to forget?
When the memory is ever before me
The guilt and wastes confronting me
When I fear for the future that comes
Not knowing how I may be judged.

The Rainbird Is Dead

Kelvin Mangwende

The rainbird is dead, its black people wings
covered the unperfumed sordid people
unbawn they walk with a forlorn hope gnarled
ramble flimsy shadowed horizon, bayuon
cops held guns and truncheons, stood on the
balwork to protect the pillage covered the
rubicund face with glass shields and the mass
shall bear the brunt. Frenzy seemed
barefaced the masters, hunger impregnated
their bellies. Empty promise in their naked
minds, the sole-hearts painful, the bumper
hunger harvest on their barren heath, sooth-
people their bones rattle, but each shadow
being a forlorn in the midst

Legacies
Bradley M. Purdon

The verdant winds sing of the ever-glowing winter
The evergreen flowers lament of their fallen brethren
The frigid season is both beautiful yet deadly
Fires flicker in embers of ephemeral warmth
Footprints of man and beast line the frore snow
With the next day do they fade from present and memory
Claw scars and fingerprints embedded in the trees
For marks left upon the snow will disappear
But legacies left on forests remain eternal
Evanescent melodies of hiemal lyrics douse the fires of pain
Seconds later do the smoulders burn once more
But silver sylvan flames bring starlight to the darkened woods
And the blazing pain fades with the coming of the light
Floral branches listen to whispers in brightened woodlands
As they speak of ancient days archaic
Days the snow does not recall
For only the forest knows of her beginnings
With each winter season is the snow made anew
But the evergreen woodlands remain cloaked in holy light for
eternity
Beneath supernal stars of Heavenly blessings
For the verdant forest, enveloped in love, travels through lifetimes
and realms
Yet always remains with her beauty and her legacies

Springs Of Savanna
C. J Chenjerai Mhondera

Springs of Savanna, have you dried yet?
Or you're waiting summer to revive your energies?
Look Sahara is dry, and Sahel is withering cursed by Lord of never-
coming-summer!   Springs of
Savanna, have you dried yet?
Or gods of Savanna have a case, blood of Mubvamaropa to dry
without flowing?   Are
mighty rivers of Savanna to flow?
Or until another downpour, winters have no traits nor trace of
giving summer a try?
Are we lone in this forsaken desert?
Or to loan a desert is to bring hunger and thirsty?
I want to hide no more! I might die.
There's hunger, widespread. There's poverty and pestilence.
Has Hermes phoned to skies above, if there shall be rains?
If ever to come, where shall they come from when trees big, fall by
Smith's chain-saw?   Did I say the
forests have all disappeared?
Oh no, I said off-shoots have seen no age to transpire!

Homage To Once A Family

Tales of a bird

Joseph Ntensibe

The last time I visited
Mahogany and all the make wailed
For a family perishing.
Brother monkey, wobbled for a place to live
Me, I flew and I nestle now in a hot
Rock (your niece and nephew has no playground)

-Cousin, wind blows furiously for she's
Housed no more
I know uncle rain is gone forever
-His brother sun is too merciless now
-I hear our once neighbor snake vigorously taunts
Our enemy (congratulations)

-Our choir orchestrates no more
-the auditorium was cut down
My melodious soprano is fading away
The symphony is tainted with tears.
-Our conductor Sparrow
No longer can waive the baton
'cause he has flapped featherless for rest
In vain

-How I long to be home again!
 Perhaps my creator will say
-Goodbye sister.

But before I bid you farewell
I think I have heard a rumour:
Of these our tormentors (some)
They miss the choir
The eye of the sky torments them the same...
And
A new blanket is being woven
It is slow but steady
Their young souls seek to see us fly
And

I see them resurrecting out home
I have heard some of my cousins whisper songs of hope
The laughter of some of my cousins whisper songs of hope
The laughter of some hyenas echoes in our new homes.
The central wind blows to calm northern winds as the east and
western winds join
the spectacle…..

Perhaps not yet….its not yet.
We can and we are soon gliding to new winds of glory
For a new blanket has been planted.
The streams are clean now…
For a new blanket has been planted.
I will glide in harmony.
We are living again
Going back home
Our home…

3rd element
Nana Arhin Tsiwah

dear goddess . . .

the law was a spirit —
& man
cosmos

when we die
leaving behind
rotten smiles:

roots sing —
herbs become saturated
with tears

every flowered child
when it has withered
lives in two circuses:

spermatozoa
&
spirit

To Elites
With pain and regret
Joseph Ntensibe

Whoever taught sharks to swim?
Eagles to fly
The storms to ravage
The seas to protest
Who teaches babies to
Cry-when in need?
Lions to roar when in
Pain
Snakes to strike when attacked

Mr. Elite, how many books are you to open to know this!
How many chapters are you to read to see this!
How many verses to peruse to see your pain

How many words are to
Write your pain
How many letters are to
Reveal your sorrow?

Mr. Elite do you need Einstein's hair to
Know your downfall?

How many ears do you need to hear
the drums of revolution
What symphony can be played to wake your
rotting educated spirit
What voice of change
can touch your stinking
enlightened heart.

Should we summon Che'
To touch your
Porridge brains?

-oh- mercy me
You are too bright to
Know your problem

Too smart to see pain
Too clever to reason with wise fools
Too wise to know the truth!

But —damn you who think
Its brains and brains
-damn you all
Rubbish brains
-huggers of the rotten system

Part 6: Colonialism, Corruption, Free Speech, Misgovernance, War and Strife

Brentry: An African tragedy

Athol Williams

It was 1820, the year of Brentry,
that we got new tongues and learned
how to bow and curtsy. Visitors came.
They came to save us
from our memories. They came to save us
from the diamond demon that pierced our
sheets like satanic fingers, and the golden
ogre that lay beneath our beds waiting
to suck out our souls. We got new gods
new kings, new sorrow. Everything was new
at Brentry. But all we wanted was our old –
our old sorrow, old tongues, old memories
now buried beneath pomp and progress
that looked a lot like mine dumps to us.
They said their gods answered prayers
so we prayed to their gods for Brexit,
but they must've lied or we did it wrong,
because the visitors would never leave.

Limitless Spirit

Tembi Charles

Braving tumultuous oceans they anchor on Land.
Then gallop at great speed; stop, measure and claim.
Amidst bloodshed and tears,
Cries of anguish, beggings and pleadings,
They proclaim: This is our Land!

They march over mountains armed with pick and shovel.
Inspect, test and dig despite my groans.
Deep within my bowels they wring golden yellow and brilliant
white.
Celebrating: We can have what we want!
For Land is ours!

These hawks ride high on clouds and their hungry eyes hover,
Machines hum - chop - pile - chop and pile.
They plant rows and rows of frothy white.
Notwithstanding bitter-sweet sweat, breaking backs, and displaced
voices!
These scavengers rejoice: This is our Land!

I whisper: Pay heed! I am Land!
A limitless Spirit: Leave me be! Leave me free!

But they have no ears.
Brilliant white loses its dazzle and golden yellow becomes black.
Green rows an ashen brown.
And engulfed in my bowels, breathless and dying,
Bent, black bodies dressed in soot,
Lungs painted black, the dying-dead,
Also cry out loud:
Land was ours; now lost to us forever!

My laugh bellows: I never belonged to anyone!
I can never be measured, restricted, contained and owned.
Land is I: Leave me be, Leave me free!
I am Limitless Spirit!

Peace in the Radio

Ojok James Onono

We hear it on the Radios
We hear on televisions
That Northern Uganda is now peaceful
Northern Uganda is free of war
But NGOs fled the peace
People left the IDPs without counseling
A mistake the government never did
Trauma at its peak
Camp Resettlements for us, meant land wrangles
Alcoholism sings a louder song than war now
Gender based violence is another master
Drug abuse is almost the king
Poverty is sky rocketing in the peaceful north-
With the guns going silent
Hundreds of children born in LRA captivity
Have their own version of the peace on radios
But the peaceful North is now field for researcher
Pasture for gamblers, Ground for gamblers
Just because of the peace in the Radio.

The debase
Rogers Atukunda

Remind me, grandson, what was the day?
A Friday, grandpa, January 15, 2016
And you say it was a tea story?
No grandpa, I said it was on TV
Ooh, but did you say it was a primary debase?
Grandpa, a presidential debate
I see. And the old man who spoke big words, was who?
The judge, Justice James Ogoola, grandpa
Eeh, that one, did he really say the *debase* was the *sin*?
No, he said the debate was the thing
Did I also hear Mbirizi?
No, not Mbirizi grandpa, the name is Joseph Mabirizi
Ooh that one, okay, but did he really say he was *adapted*?
Mnh! That is what I heard, grandpa!
You are sure he didn't say abducted?
For sure grandpa, he said *adapted* two times
And what did the lady Kyanwa say about women leaders?
Kyalya grandpa, Maureen Kyalya
Aah, never mind, but did she call them dummies?
[Our hardworking mothers are like the display dummies!]
Hnh! That is what I heard grandpa
And that Amani (Amani?), what did he say about his stomach and
God?
Grandpa! It is For God and My country! And the name is Amama
Mbabazi,
But wait…grandpa, are you trying to mock him?
Ooh, him? Tell me, what was that he said about *erections*?
That he has never witnessed a stolen election since independence!
Hahaha, hihihi, hehehe, my ribs, my ribs
What grandpa?
Never mind…but tell me, what did he say about serve houses?
Not serve, grandpa, he was talking about safe houses
And he wants to serve our goats, macron and chips?
Microchips, grandpa, that was Abed Bwanika
And he also wants to empower them down there?
No, now that was Mabirizi. He was talking about women
And all the debasers don't know oil papers?

Indeed grandpa, they don't! But one wants to take the oil to
Kenya…
I see, but, why was one chair empty?
You mean the one for Museveni, grandpa?
Yes, he was my hero president when I was a young man
He is still the president, grandpa
No wonder he missed the debase!
The debate grandpa, DE-BA-TE.
But why miss the debase?
He said it was childish grandpa,
Did he mean childish or challenging?
I don't know grandpa but he said it was for kids
Kids? You mean a young one of a goat?
Children grandpa
Did I also hear him mention peace or pieces?
He was talking about peaceful elections, grandpa
Waw! I love fairy tales
What grandpa?
Ignore me…and what is this man of eyes bringing
Ooh, you mean Kizza Besigye, grandpa?
Mmh, he means to bring us new walking sticks?
No grandpa, he talked about walking with swagger
Hmh!
What is it grandpa?
My friend, these eyes have seen, these ears have heard,
these hands have touched…enough, enough!
Are you okay grandpa?
My grandson, you are yet to see!

Kwashiorkor of free Speech
Charmaine Gombera

My tongue is glued between the walls of silence
Where the oven baking sun is overwhelmingly bitter
I am saturated with winds of news, still sinked in silence
Where my uncaptured feathers vomit suffocated pressure
My mind is boiling with unearthed information
Yet I am forced to bow to the throne of silence
Where dictators behave like deep tanks of poison
Waiting to block the passages of my writings
I am totally thirsty of speech like deer longing for water
I am awkwardly dying from absent free speech
As I cannot breathe without rhythm of freedom of speech

neWS TODay
Wafula p'Khisa

That my senator was clobbered by his wife
because of a mere bedroom dispute
until he sought refuge in a cell
That the president cheated on his wife
before putting a ring on her finger
with the other woman in the ministry
That my sister went to China
to acquire new curves & skin, reshape her bottoms to look
bootyfull
and have sponsors salivating to savour her
Isn't tasty enough to assuage our longing conscience

they are mere hearsays, smuggled for free
at funeral wakes and beer parties

we want hot, disturbing news
whispered only in bed or darkness;
news that burn tongues like hot pepper
news that'll have tongues cut, for they make & break!

Tell us about war and victory
that our sons, pulled from the family breast, went to harvest death
in El Adde
Or the sweet bitterness of hell, our sisters are lured into, in Middle
East
Tell us, who sold the soul & will of people
for a mere political token
and watered dry earth with innocent blood
to appease evil gods of greed, power & selfishness
but wanders around, free!

Tell us who will disappear or die next, in this quagmire of injustice
so we may dig their graves & start mourning early
why aren't governors behind bars
after gobbling chunks of the taxpayer's money
yet their laughters & lavish lifestyles are the soul of existence of
media?

Let's know why little Sudan burns
and no diplomatic magic, has soothed Kiir and Machar
to believe the state is bigger than their wild desires
Why did the world watch Burundi butcher her people
and ignore the habit of some African chiefs who've clung to power
like a man to his shadow?

Let's know why uniting African is a dream impossible
and our resources, history & progress are claimed by the West
why is Boko Haram, Al Shabaab & LRA growing strong every day?
Why can't we recover from colonial hangover
and chat our own path into future as free men
without blindfolds of alien gods, songs, tongues and philosophies?

An Angry Graduate

Hosea Tokwe.

Every day he enters the industrial sites
Searching employment without success
Finding little hope for any job
Tears wailing in his tired looking eyes

All day long he wears his worn faded green shirt
Now he gazes in the seemingly lifeless blue sky
Cupping his rough arms for a better view
Waiting for a tomorrow, the same today as yesterday
Hoping for a better day, as fear lingers that his life
will get worse

Out he fishes his dirty notebook to write
Dreaming about life in the capital city
Which has failed to provide him a descent living
For back at home a wife and child wait pitifully
The burden of supporting them weighing on him

Now he stares at his soiled khaki envelop
Full of certificates that has given him sleepless nights
Now he wonders, asks himself why he has spent all these years
Toiling for this Engineering certificate
He remains angry, blaming the limited horizons
of the fading city life.

Hillbrow, Johannesburg
Amitabh Mitra

At Hillbrow, a Zimbabwean girl curls in darkness before a growing night. She is one of three million Zimbabweans who have to flee to South Africa. Only her eyes glow in perpetual hunger, her neurones numbed by daily beatings from her Nigerian master. She is a tree now, other girls from Kwekwe seem to see her in borderless sunsets beckoning them to come. In the eyes of another sun she longs to die but not before her earnings slay in dreamless sleep the drought of lives succumbing slowly. Her mind, body and tonight her smile is encrusted on this debt. There is dearth in dryness, she says in impeccable English, Can I be your master for tonight, Sir, I will show you what even the cranial saw wouldn't show after you have sawed my skull in a bid to understand the cause of my death. I live through many a death; each one seems to ridicule the other in its severity. Each death lives through many others like many birds perched at an infinite corner of a shadeless sky. And as I idly die I laugh at the vulnerability of your godless seasons and even at a person like you who have thoughtlessly caught up on writing about me. You wouldn't believe, I have an honors degree in English. I tore it to bits after humans tore my humanitarian time. She left me finally in neon bright on other strata, swinging her hips towards a darkness dressed as a car purring in the far corner.

Stolen Dreams
Christopher 'Voice' Kudyahakudadirwe

In the moulded past we believed in the freshening future
The inviting future was just a dream away from the past
It was so vivid we could caress it with our calloused fingers
We could hold it and cradle it like a baby in our hands
That dream was real - our lives were destined for change!
You and I looked at each other through the settling dust
The dust we had raised during the creation of this dream
We smiled and invited each into this waiting dream.

Time strode down our lives in slow motion like a giant
Our very own bodies registered it with wrinkles and grey hair
We peeped through its days, weeks, months and years
Trying to get a glimpse of the promised dream there
We shaded our eyes from its brilliance with our open hands
We wanted to enjoy dreaming it; it was ours to dream it
We wanted to enjoy living it and hand it down to our children
But as time strode on waving its hands at us, saying goodbye
Little did we know our dream had been stolen from us
Thus we knew the dream had never been ours but a carrot
That turned us into donkeys yoked to the cart of poverty.

Now is the time to re-dream the dream that has fizzled out
We are living in the yesterday of tomorrow's dream
Come, fellow citizens and reclaim our stolen dream
Come, fellow citizens, quick before the dream is lost again
Let's hurry into the future of our lives and pick up the pieces
This is the time to put together the shards of our pilfered lives.

Squatter-camps
Mari Ballot

Senseless-shelters   shapeless-shacks   insanitary-ineptness
incurable-cruelness unspoken-fears   twisted-times of torn-tongues
of traded-souls of raw-tears   nicotine-numbed-nostrils fettered-
fingers   hungry-haunted faces withered-wilted-eyes rows upon
rows …rows upon rows upon rows   of patched-together-pieces
warped-walls of discarded-cardboard-boxes   corroded-corrugated-
tin-roofs metal-odds asbestos   stolen-splintered-planks
scattered-sods of unnoticed-weeds   destitute-dunes of uncured-
unmet-needs   among the mixed-monochrome-minimals   alleyways
of agonies of lies of rampant-rats   smashed-glass   trampled-tins
scrawny-scum-dogs sniffing fruitless   pissing on littered-plastic-
packets a polluted grey smoke-and-fever-filled puking-place where
sound is a scream a cry a stiff-death-rattle where breathing is a
battle   language is xenophobia mixed F-formed
words…famine…fear here where voice is a curse a whimpering in
a wrenched-worn-out vagrant-wreckage-world where comfort is   a
door a mud-floor a torn-old-oversized-coat a sip of murky-water
luxury… a swig shanty-sex a wasted-windowless-frame a chunk
of coir or foam bed a pain-killer   a purple-paraffin-primus-flame…
the violent air shivers… who's-to-blame?

Crawling insects   the million flies   the why's ghetto-ghosts
tangled-wires squalid-sores soul-suffering destroying-fires   the
quivers-cries   this disease devours   digs deep …a child convulses
cringes like a crushed-worm a slaughtered-chicken squirm in
delayed-despite a bulged-belly-baby upon a battered-breast dies
with open-sunken-empty-eyes saliva-spatted-spaces   a flowerless
bleak-beaten-stench-struck-sky sated-septic-sewers reek   desolate-
despair bashed-buckets leek   distorted-destiny unwashed-sweat
jobless- worthless-idleness   lethargic-loitering festering-fading-
figures skeletal-limbs they pain in prejudices choke in intolerances
suffocate in terrifying-torment   do they hate?   can they love? …
they are ironic-chronic third-degree-victims in a culture-conundrum
cast-asides ignored by a first-class corrupted-economic-parasitic-
politically-wounded-world…on this huge contagious-communal-
burial-ground not a stone engraved for the enslaved…in Africa they
cannot keep a book of the dead …their unlit unfed uneducated eyes
cannot read …their starving ears do not hear… their outstretched-

hopeless-hands their infected-hearts ...are begging for more than bread!

Our Dyed-In-The-Wool Regime
Thandiwe Shea

"Catch him up! Catch him up!"
She screamed helplessly

Jeering or sneering!!
A demagogue yet a despot
Dilettante yet glib
Suave but yet malinger
Idyllic in appearance but yet full of faux pas
He stole from her

He is of biblical proportions
Covered with loose folds of skin, swarthy
Blackguard
His eyes are glossy
His forehead creased
His nostrils flared
His mouth twitched
His jaw clenched from embezzlement

Wry! Ironic
Fresh out of a bandbox, that's more like it
Smartly dressed in glittery, flamboyant suits
Still quaint, humorous
Attending black tie events
Deep inside deceitful, out-and-out, outward,
Overweening, wayward
Far cry from his slogan

Impecunious!!!
Her face is contorted with rage and fury
Her voice crackles with anger
Sadness clouds her features
She approaches him menacingly
She wants answers

She wants what is rightfully hers
Her home becomes a bandit territory
She comes to blow with him
Gloves are off...

She doesn't want to get down to brass tracks
Her situation is cut and tried
Our people need an elbow grease
She needs a rescue
Our regime needs to get a foot in the door
He needs to cater for the people

A Shadow from A Dark Past

Christopher 'Voice' Kudyahakudadirwe

Thirty-six years ago, on a Friday evening,
My young past walked into a crowded bar.
It took a casual seat on a rickety bar stool,
Ordered a stiff cocktail to quench its thirst, and
Then it lit a weed cigarette and relaxed, and
Sipping and puffing, it waited for my future.

Almost two decades later, my future arrived late,
All bruised and bandaged all over and limping.
Its bloodshot eyes were streaming teargas tears, and
Bulging baton bumps were all over its head, and
It was jobless and its pockets were yawning.

My future stared at my nauseating past and scowled.
It spat at its broken unpolished boots and walked out.
I stood there watching this unfortunate fallout
Of two strangers meeting for the first time.

I wanted to bridge the gulf between with hope;
To tell the two that crises were resolved always
Not by hanging them out on a line like clothes.

The weed smoke lingered in the already fetid air
I looked at my past; it had cleared out of the bar.

So here I am - a shadow from an empty dark past.

Transkei
Amitabh Mitra

in transkei
we drove on roads beyond roads

the sun and sky set themselves apart
and people there talked about new south africa
i wanted to get braids done on the
roadside
and dance to hip-hop
with others
being played by a blind musician
his head moving
his eyes behind dark glasses
negating all......

nothing has really changed
only a dog among hitchhikers
just wanted to cross the street

Payday

Handsen Chikowore

At the blink of midnight link,
Money dive into unbalanced river bank
restoring the sanity of the wallet
Loan sharks swallow it instantly disallowing
strangling interest from being entertained

The indecent jaws of direct debits
draw the residue without pursuing permission
At the doors of Mr B (Bills) and Lady D (Demands)
the standing odour is stuck at axis of exceeded limit
creating CCJs drama more entertaining than ITV

The cheque is bounced like baseball
and the debit card is terminally ill
Cash is slashed from broken cave of credit
to the limitless pit of unfit debit wells
The shockwaves invite third parties
hungry in legal intercourse and dirt collectors
who ascend into the mountains of insolvency

Bangui; a Poetic Coup~ I. Papa Pomp

Gideon Chumo

I

Papa Pomp proudly paraded himself
In the coronation, decking out his decorations
The fabric of his commander's cotton coat,
Exaggerated in explicit embroidery, propped up
From beret to boots with dazzling golden medals
Ever awarded and rewarded in every array
Each, a bone bounty from his military *mutineering*
The symbolic spoils of his slain enemies
Being a petite tiny-stout orphan from nowhere
The colossal coat spigot outward from waving,
A miniature Statue of Liberty is the result—
The Torch his flywhisk—basking for the cameras
Obsessed with press attention, played PR acrobatics
Stage-managing theatrics, like declaring his country
Bankrupt and greeting guests at his costly castle
By kerosene lamp—but its glow turned upon himself

II

Mama Pomp, who wore Roman royal robes
Was upset to see her style so upstaged
Quickly skipped the rest of the procession
Immediately summoned her expat stylists
To design her a fashion of matchless spectacle
But the local tailors who had printed her clothes
Mismatching her half-grinning face—republic's face
Showing an inch of an inkling like she were in labour—
Were arrested and fed to her personal piranhas
And ligers at the aquarium of her lavish villa.
Parisian *fashionistas* flew in to fine-tune her tunic
That could accommodate her jewels and bracelets,
Even if importing the magnificence of Eiffel Tower
Adorned in empress frock coats and pearl slippers
She'd spare no costs—to cosset a coquette
To parade a performance; to crown an extravagance
She then amassed all degrees from Fruitcake Campus
More numerous than thermometers could count
In honorary coronations with Napoleonic connotations,

Craving covetously the scents of French basilicas
Bonaparte himself, her hero and guru from the grave
To her like God Embodied; an ideal model to follow
Then wearing her crowns on her illiterate head
She assigned herself assorted masculine titles:
Genius of the Carpathians, Supreme Sheba,
The Unique Miracle of Fruitcake Republic
Tigress Who Knows No Defeat Because
Of Her *Tigritude* And Supple Pounce, MBS,
The *Cockeress* Who Goes From Cock To Cock,
Grand Dark Knight of African Admiral II, etc
Never mind the real Dark Knight threatened to sue.
And renamed all the months, weekdays, streets and
Villages, after herself, her mother and her titles

III

But Papa Pomp the peerless champion
—never minding one more inflated feat—
Enacted in his tiny little dramatis persona
A life-sized scene. A slapstick production
But in a blood-splattered performance
He made Mama Pomp open a hypermarket,
A clothing line selling only designer uniforms,
And exercised his pervasive imperial powers
To ratify a new law that all republican children
Like the national team; like all doctors in lab coats
Must wear the national uniform bearing his badge
And available only in Pomp Hyper Chain Stores
With a special label—buy-two-get-one-free—
Of course, the price was in sky-rocketing ratio
A smart maneuver, a limited family monopoly
Killing a bird with two stones to ensure its demise

As expected, the poor children threw tantrums,
The scam of earth couldn't afford new uniforms
Even if subsidized to sustain the bleeding GDP
That had hemorrhaged the rotting Fruitcake
Protests, unrests and school closures followed.
The uprising punctured Papa Pomp's Beast
A state of siege is declared; all kids rounded up
His famous temper exploded on state radio:

145

'Napoleon faced similar insolence. But taught
The madding mob a lesson with 40 canons.'
Nothing is ever learnt from blackboard ghouls
—conjugating verbs really pissed off Papa Pomp—
And under the wrath of his gold-plated walking cane
Sharper than ebony pencils in slicing small skeletons
Slaughtered on colossal scales his African fruitcake
Using a Marxist model that solved problems quickly
'One man, one problem. No man, no problem.'

To our boys who bled in Bangui

Antonio Garcia

Our multi-coloured Flag flies high
It mirrors our rainbow nation
Red stains the nation's flag
A reminder of our Struggle

'94 was the reward
Never, never and never again
From the heavens, seas and mountains
Were the words echoed

What was the struggle in CAR?
How could this be?
That we allow your sacrifice to fade
Why did you bleed the ground red?

What was the reward?
Teddy warned
That soldiers die and old men talk
Now our history cries

A Nation new, A People old
For them you served
And so you paid the ultimate price
For us it is forbidden to reason why

Our blood is paint,
The canvas is the battlefield
Commanders plan as artists paint
What was the price of your masterpiece?

A gun salute for the fallen
Our ancestors launched spears in the sky
A folded flag and anguished tears
Your blood and our memory thins

Your story remains untold
Your sacrifice unrewarded
How shall we remember?

Our boys who bled in Bangui

The life we choose is sacrifice
There is no greater honour
Soldiers, I salute you
Your blood paints our pride.

Terra Nullius – the Marikana Symphony

Christine Coates

Do you hear the shouts of men, the creaking clanking mines?
Do you see the empty land, this land that belongs to no one?
It's just a landscape, a landscope, a parcel, a portion;
the knobkerries beat the rhythm, the pangas, the sticks.
Do you hear the spinning wheels, the sounds at the edges,
the beat of fists and feet?
This is the Marikana Symphony, the Marikana March.

Do you smell the dust of that hill, the sickle-shaped leaves,
bare land, crown land, rock rocking away?
Do you remember that April when we would be free,
when life was changing?
Since Sharpeville 52 years – ways of closing our eyes.
This is the Marikana March, the Marikana Symphony.

Do you see the colour of men telling stories
of treasures below the land, finders keepers?
where people are invisible, ways of forgetting.
It's the man of trees, he walks, he talks.
They're just paper words, they won't save you.
It's the beauty of terra nullius, it's the Marikana March.

Night is coming, papers blowing.
It comes on the wind, the rusted bushes, miners on random hills.
Can you hear their marching feet, the sound of sticks?
It's the Marikana Symphony.
Go wash your faces seven times, let the long knives fall,
these bullets won't harm you.

Do you see the colour of that day, the dust, the rock, the dried-out
trees.
do you watch until it becomes a kind of blindness, report, retort?
It's dreamtime, time for rude awakenings.
It's a small koppie framing the story, marking,
lettering each murder site;
it's yellow stars painted on rock, dirt, dust, thorns.

It's the beauty of terra nullius, it's the Marikana March;

we've become what we most despised.
It's just a landscape, a landscope, a parcel, a portion.
Look in the dust, it's the empty land, land belongs to no one.
Night is coming. It's the night of terra nullius, it's the Marikana
Symphony.

terra nullius: In International Law **'terra nullius'** *describes territory that nobody owns so that the first nation to discover it is entitled to take it over, as in "finders keepers"*

Sunset At Westgate I
Gideon Chumo

White Widow Web
(www@death.die)
Sun set one sad September 21st morning
On lonely basements of The Westgate Mall
To a restive Gold-Coast intellectual octopus
Who like a cheeky child in our Candy Land
Grabbed many a goody; pocketing poems
Into his regal and striped *abatakari* tunic
A Charlie chewing with a chock-full cheek.

Prowling as well were Winkies of Wonker
In red *Arafats* along heartbeats of karma
Sudden as his hideous faces of madness
Facing bonkers, not Makkah al-Mukarrama
Crawling, as unseen as the devil at prayer.
None noticed an ill-fitting bidding requiem
Lurking in depths of torments, of shadows
So sad a farewell in the Sabbath of sorrows.

An inconstant open sore of our continent
That preached a Synoptic Hadith of horror
Filled the mall with bloodstains of despair
In a symphony with a distorted harmony
Spreading terror-ism rehearsing 'La ilaha, ...'
With dry husky voices at its forced recital,
Mouthed in metred threats invoking Amina
And coughed up as al-Kafiroun Suratul-Error

Kofi's a Kaffir in Qur'anic question marks
As AK 47s cock; Kofi's like 'La il...' comma,
Couldn't recite 786 Sword Verses of Qur'an
Nor knew the length of the Prophet's beard
Rat-a-tat! White Widow shot him a full stop
'Burn in hell with sulphuric smell. Period!'
Missed periods put into point-blank ranges
Painful period for un-periodic mocking poets
'A Prof? Who knows not Grand UmmibintWahb!'
Priestess-queen spat to her drones of *Shabaab*

151

Who as scared baby jihads had hung on her hijaab
Hid under jihadi skirts, breastfed on time bombs
Licking wounds, from bullets fired by fathers' lips

Now Jihadist Johns harbour erotized hatred
Fixated in infantile form of infamous honour
Silently, had witnessed their mothers' abuse
Her scars, now living in them as an extension
Regressing to revenge her dishonour, and yet
After battering our maids into earthly widows
Carnally crave for 72 fecund eternal virgins
So as to re-live immortal dramas, even when
The satanic stage is their final *halaal* hellhole

Woe unto our Annan of tolerant hope
Radical but in rational borough of belief
While random users of terror gospels—
Nay, abusers, miscreant mis-users—
Against innocence, stinging as bees
Hurriedly read the religion of peace
From upside down, and left to right,
Use it as weapon, as full stop to reason.

"What desires did you wish to posses?
That you already did not have?"
Was it black coffee? Was it a book?
Perhaps researching another novel?
A dramatic episode in life's chapter
Riddled with 4-Seven *fatwa* bullets
Immortalized as a latter day Hamlet
With cosmic ironies beyond us all
Wordplay won't cheapen this puzzle
Adieu master wordsmith. All is well
Past pastures over the still stream
Is Parnasius, a sweet beau-la land
In that centre, a centre that hold
Is poetry of how well you lived.

'Twas a very meticulous vetting process
To separate the sheep from the goats
Taking orders barked on mobile phones

Bowing down in prayer between attacks
To cite Thuaiba and her blessed nipples
Motherly domes off your phallic minaret
Searching hope in barren face of lunacy
To seek force of the sickle and scythe
To export a violence into our sunrises
To have your evil ways in our sunsets

The Closing Chords of *Jibriil* you crow
As phony muezzin who doesn't know
That poet Kofi rides *Firdowsa* Chariot
On wings of his poetry as every griot
Via labyrinths of sunset, Westgate
Flies he, into sunrise, Heaven gate
And woven into the Almighty's Cloth
An Immortal Bard, not born for death

Holy Hitlers of dehumanised factories
Fuhrers and poisoned misanthropists
May maim unarmed men, butcher boys
Assault pregnant women and kidnap girls
Explode (in) buildings, burn piles of books
Issue edicts, erase history, strip streets
Pave it with dead dreams, littered bodies
Raze civilizations, spit on to our cultures…

But can they decapitate and put to death
The memory of Professor Kofi Awoonor?

Notes:
1. 'La ilaha, ill-Allahu' is a Shahada, i.e. a confession, 'There's no god except Allah.'
2. Amina bintWahb, the mother of the Prophet. Invoking her name, to extremists, carries a similar connotation as what some Christians deem Mariolatry, invoking Mary, the mother of Christ.
3. 'Grand…queen…drones…bees', a (counter)extremist psychoanalytic theory of maternal infatuation with the ummi (mother), the matriarch in the hive, who birth the umma (the Muslim populace) with workers and soldiers, guarding her colony.

4. '786 Sword Verses,' terrorists highlight these verses, yet in the Holy Qur'an, the word 'peace' is mentioned twice as many as the word 'war,' and unequivocally condemns war.

5. White Widow, aka Samantha Lewthwaite, the widow of the London 7/7 bomber, and suspected as the Westgate Mall mastermind. Irony for a 'White Woman' to bark orders (and from a cell phone) to the caliphates who have reservations with the female gender.

6. Annan i.e. Kofi Annan, a peace mediator, former UN Sec. Gen. and Nobel of Peace laureate, it's interesting to note that the Westgate siege took place while the world was celebrating International Day of Peace. Further, Prof. Kofi served successful terms, like his namesake compatriot, as an envoy to many countries including as Ghana's ambassador to the UN, where he chaired the UN Committee Against Apartheid in the critical years of 1990 to 1994 during South Africa's transition to democracy, and 'one of the few people on earth who knew firsthand how utter desperation sometimes made people into terrorists.'

7.Parnasius .i.e. the mythical mountain home of the muse

8. Thuaiba, the Prophet's first wet nurse, after his mother died. A nourishing symbol i.e. a nursing figure, her significance is radicalized by extremist paternal clan culture.

9. Jibriil i.e. Angel Gabriel, said to make the final call before the Last Trumpet.

10. Firdowsa i.e. paradise

Ali Goes To School

for the BuniYadi boys
Ayo Oyeku

Ali goes to school,
wearing a brown sandal,
with a backpack slashed across his back,
and a pen stuck at the back of his ear.

Ali goes to school,
to open his mind to global knowledge,
burying his head in books
and experiments too.

But Ali never forgets in school,
to tell Binta how much
education would take their tryst far away,
and open a world of possibilities to them.

Boko!
Haram!

Western education!
Forbidden!

Ali
jitters
under
his
bunk
When
a swift hurricane
teleports vicious men
with guns,
swords,
and amulets,
into the walls of his hostel
leaving litters of papers
beneath a miasma of sorrow, tears and...

Ali will not return from school,

155

because he is lying on the floor,
with caked carmine
on his face,
arms,
and body,
bringing back memories
of the massacre
at Kigali.

*Two years ago, 59 students of Federal Government College BuniYadi were gruesomely murdered by Boko Haram terrorists at night in their hostels when some of the boys were fast asleep.

I Write....

Dime Maziba

For the love of words,
I write.

Not to change the world,
But to enhance human rights.

I write to express my feelings
Because they still oppress my healing.
Slavery was once in the chains,
Neocolonialism is twice in the brains.

Oh blow! Blow dear hurricane!
Wash away all the warplanes.
My pen bleeds red ink,
Not like a soft drink,
But the blood of the East of Congo

I write to open up a case
Before money come to erase

I write not to be a journalist
Main medias don't see my birthplace
Destroyed by the same capitalist
Those who claim superiority of their race.

My blank pages is spotted of red
cruor of innocents cries
The sunshine can make it dry
But 8 millions of my people are dead,
And my history remains unread

I dunk my feather in ink of gore
to express my bitterness,
Politicians sing a lullaby of deliverance,
The sluggish river of despairs floods.

Song of the Lost
Stephen Temitope David

Come to me like the pungent wind of forgotten feasts
Cackling jackals tearing at repugnant carcasses of lost hopes
Oil doom!
Oil boom, and boom sticks in fecund violent hands.

Sing to me, the lies of hiding species
In creeks of lonely shacks
lost sharks!
From many lands,
Fecal matters in the eyes of the deep.

Tales of vanquished pipes,
Oily blood on sale,
Costly airs of fire!
Who can buy?

Come to me like a shield in the face of poisoned arrows,
Poisoned waters and bloated fishes,
Pregnant tales of blood told by lazy mosquitoes.
Why does my blood fill the barrels?
My drained veins fed on empty pots!
While his flowing regalia divides the rivers of shame.

Brother (I Can't Breathe)
Eric Ngobale

I have sat stagnant on the matter
Hoping my silence would speak volumes
Preventing nouns and verbs from taking form
In the hopes that mankind would correct themselves
That we would do what we do and a hashtag would be the usual fix
Weeks in and we got the tag line, *#NoToXenophobia*
A bit long, but straight to the point and direct
If only we could engage in less violence and more dialect
Give voices a chance instead of fists
You see, brother I can't breathe
I'm being smothered by shame
I am an African and my people have disappointed me
They sight abject poverty, unemployment and famine as excuses
Preaching about rights to enjoy their mother land
Forgetting their responsibility to respect life
Are they wrong to believe they are entitled to a heritage
But then again are they allowed to use another as leverage
My sister, I'm struggling to breathe
I'm having fits of short breath
Due to the thoughts of our potentially soon to be struggling
economy
We used to get along but things have become complicated
Maybe instead of democratic, they feel things should be dictated
We used to be neighbors but now they've developed a God
Complex
I miss life when it was at its simplest...
My friend, I think I've forgotten how to breathe
If memory serves it involves cooperation and unity
Unfortunately there is none of that in my life anymore
Friends have turned to enemies
While sticks, stones and fire have become the language of the land
Blood flows, creating rivers on the land
My ninja, I'm not sure if I want to breathe
I've seen too much pain and grief
Hate words and terms suddenly surround me
Social media has become my enemy
I see videos and I'm afraid
I see videos, all I see is dead people

South Africa,
I can't breathe
I'm out of breath from shouting bring back my Africa
I'm losing hope in humanity
I feel like I'm chasing impossible dreams
Hoping for the Ubuntu of yesteryear
South Africa, help me please
I am seeking peace
Asseblief, mayibuye iAfrika

Child Soldiers

Dime Maziba

I'm young
But I've chosen the battlefield
Instead of school seat.
For rhetoric has failed to protect us,
Machine gun will whisper deafening words.

I used to stare at
Hungry flies flutter over inert bodies
The nose on top
Beseeching God's pity.

The mirror of life has carved up
The solstice of my exquisite joy.
Don't I fear a bloody death?
Do they fear the fetal one?

I shall not come back.
The cistern of my tragedy
Sprinkle burning flames
Of a spoiled child's dream.
I missed the fetal death
but they won't miss the ignominious decease.

For the Reign IS Falling

Gideon Chumo

Grand mufti of Tehran's terror
Hajj Errorist Al-Goatee Imam
Imagineers an opium podium
Of guile less mass sloganeers
To rehearse his Mahdi reign
And pray for latter-day rain

He counts golden beads
From a majestic minaret
But obscure his azure skies
With the colossal contempt
Of Ilyaas to the rainmakers
Until an entombed Isis
Stirs up in cold coitus
For virgin fertility figures

Lo! A messiah he behold
In the shape of a crescent
Of a salaam-saluting cloud
Floating into a dry terrain
'O this nimbus so pregnant
Seeds a peace sovereign!'
His racing spirit thirst

Alas! It's not.
Nastaghfirullah!
Rain brewed in hell
Dropped as Hades hail
Drone in as a dead Godot!
Doom-ka-boom
Rat-a-tat as fleets
Of Alladeen bandits
In Arabian night-time

He prayed for the rain
And saw a dark cloud
Flying above a black flag
And his tongue did wag

Behold a heavy heaven
That'd lull a boiling sun
Greeting his arid terrain
As heralds of wet news
His Zamzam in Firdows

His empty watering hole
He hoped would be full
His crops a green jungle
His infertile farm fruitful

But hell no!
What on earth..?
When he thought
It's peace and safety
A sudden destruction!

Roaring rain torrents
Wearing suicide wings
And blood-stained blasts
Explode in dust and sand
Descend on the dappled land
Ten Plagues to Egyptian kings!

His yields; his losses
Fields filled by sand hill
And in abundant oases
The fool is thirsty still.

The lonely dawn open
On landscape so barren
And where are the men
Who recited masha Allah?
Calling a Caliphate mullah?

There are only debris
And domes downcast
Under ashes of history
To witness to the past
Unmasking the sheikhs
Who sired shabaabs of Isis

To hide behind bushy beards

Part 7: Tribute, Dedication and Women Rights

Simon "Chopper" Chimbetu

Eulogy dedicated to the late king of Zimbabwe's Sungura music, Simon Chopper Chimbetu.

Vupenyu Zvoushe

Smuggled from us is this maestro – Guru
I see no reason why I should not take my hat off
Many will agree with me that he was a true civil patriot
Over the years he waxed and churned life with music
Nurturing it to great greater heights

Chronicles will concede his dynamic trait
He breathed from his heart social fireworks
Onward he crooned palatable vibes
Propagating in his fans the joys of life
Painstakingly without coercive manipulation
Every soul ate his fine-tuned tempo and the
Reason to mourn his departure is overwhelming

Chapters of his mortal life maybe closed
His critical approach to life will linger forever
Indeed he was a man in his own class
Morale seemed to preserve his wellbeing
But life couldn't spare him any more life
Eventually his life subsided and came to a halt
Today as we reflect the passage of his time
Upon this day we say "Rest In Eternal Peace"

Yamoransa

A tribute to 'FANTE-DOKONMAN'
Nana Arhin Tsiwah

i—
i've not told you of how we came here
aligned along this uncircumcised road

like the peaceful Tano
undisturbed
by quarrelsome pebbles

ii—
there is witchcraft
in every wrapped kenkey
seated on bewitching tables

that numbers vehicular —
movement . . .

Bye Bye Poet

Tribute to the late AIME CESAIRE
Dime Maziba

The gloomfull intruder
Lumbered in the forecourts of fears.
Unfading footsteps of blood
Has left sorrow in our longing heart.

Aime Cesaire's poetry rain
was spluttering over the roof of life,
Beseeching the deaf ears of death.
"We beg you! We beg you!"
Oh!
Rhetoric doesn't persuade
The curtains of death
nor pay the bill of breath

tomorrow,
I will jot poetry in creole language
with hieroglyphics signs
and Cesaire writing style
to hush machine-gun fire
of my torn soul.

I write this poem in a dim night
Of a winter cold because poetry is
Like a roaring lion calling his lioness from
The den of his words
But Misunderstood by flying birds
Who report to ears of the wind,
The anger of carnivores.

Francesca

A Poem Devoted to Her Highness Princess of Armenia
Fayssal Chafaki: The Poet of the Kingdom of Morocco

Francesca! What shinest ov'r 'tis rainy cloud,
Recumbent, alone, 'nd mo' gazin' into the sky,
Actin' fool, the moon, or the stars tha' feel proud,
Now t' be seen sparklin' frea my place to Italy?

Cheerful Lady! I knew the charm o' old Rome
Exceeded thy fair lands, crossed the sea, 'nd came
Soft, gently blown, sailin', drawn wi' rhumb,
Castin' the distance a line fo' the perfect dame.

After thy pretty Italian wards caught my ears
Fast was the trip, loud was the noise, few I heard
Reading thy moves, I did feel yonder my fears,
As thou stepped the first, the second, 'nd the third.

Nay my lady! Thou mayst go far yet shalst return
Cure me! I who'd keep lookin' at thy eyes ev'ryday,
Endeavourin' t' mak 'em my best tales to learn,
So long thy eyes do shed an everlastin' fervid ray.

Cast my darkness! Thou art my dear sun so bright
And thou who shine fo' me now, not the light,
Free thyself! Thou who but love me aright,
Reavin' my sole heart wi' tender 'nd delight
Ask my warm tears how they've droppeth downright
Not odd they defied the most darkened night
Candid men do whatever they can to win the fight
Enthusin' me are the battles I took 'gainst the knight
Steady, omniscient, valiant, kind, vested in white,
Compared to my Arabian Fame, lost in sight,
An ocean o' love I am when I compose 'nd write.

Fascinatin', solemn, far too pretty, thy Highness!
Rich, humble, poetic, frea Rome, na Babylonia,
Ay! Let the Poet bespeak thy noble kindness,
Namin' the Queen o' Hearts the Princess o' Armenia!

Cherishin', acute, friendly, wise 'nd famous,
Elegant, active, attractive, distinguished 'nd loyal,
Such beauty before whom beauty is anonymous,
Call to mind her pure blood is royal.
Able, prominent, precise, nice 'nd neat,
Fabulous her Hame, dear her name t' us!
Revivin' the early spark o' cold 'nd heat
As if love first dwelt in her splendid palace.

Na nymphs, na faeries, na ev'n the Old Bards,
Claimed craved clutchin' cadent composition
Eve, said they, proffer 'tis angel, O Lard o' lards!
Seekin' t' show respect t' thy rank 'nd position.

Chants, if be devoted to thee, Highness, must excite
Alterin' the best choice, na ane mere foresight
Falterin', fake, flatterin', faint verses na t' cite,
Reasonable enough O lovin' soul t' ignite
Ane whole obscure path t'ward peace wi' might,
N'ver claim the Coarse Bard be impolite!
Chivalry, courage, adventure, wisdom, 'nd wright
Excessive poems fo' my Princess wi' rhymes infinite,
Sheen she is, I would only the strong ones invite,
Canst thou perceive tha' splendiferous twilight?
Ane Bard who greets thy Highness day 'nd night.

Walking With Bheki Mseleku
Athol Williams

He was not taught to walk.
He received no lessons
in the mechanics of motion,
or the intricacies of balance
and its complex feedback algorithms
to correct, self-correct, or auto-correct
the way our spinning planet does
in our tumbling universe.
Yet he walks.
He walks with the rhythm of the oceans,
he walks to the melody of the wind,
he walks with the beat
of his mother's heart in his chest,
and the song of his father's tongue
in his fingers. He walks.
And as he walks,
music comes.

Mother Africa
Abel Sehloho

The impeccable creation of your landscape
Haunts with creatures that sing
the saddest songs from your hollow core.
The sun elopes with the stars
Over the highest mountains.

The soil has footprints of your soldiers.
The water is dense with their bravery,
Stronger and powerful with each struggle.
Fear weakening with each battle
Oh! Mother, such beauty you are.

Your stories awakens the uninspired,
With rich history of nemesis and artillery
You still stood the test of time.
The predecessors paved a path of hope
For successors to horn and pursue,
Oh! Africa, such spirit you have.

The clouds gather to soften your pain,
Rivers run to erase it to oblivion.
Your shape speaks harmony
Your heart beats gracefully.
Peace shall reign for our grandchildren.

Silence
Vupenyu Zvoushe

Silence may mean fear
Silence may mean brutal
Silence may be venomous
Silence may be vocal
Silence may be golden
Silence can be a fight against a fight
Silence can be a voice of a voiceless

Silence speaks of that irrational mind
Silence speaks of that mouth that laughs
Silence speaks of that cynical eye that mocks
Silence speaks of that insensitive ear that eavesdrops
Silence speaks of its hallowed silence
Silence speaks to be silent.

A proud young decent woman
Full of energy, robustly focused and graceful
Is silently torn apart
She is silently molested and raped
Abused by avid readers of the center pages
She silently stares at her dwindling life
Ravaged by the ripples of silent life
As she is incriminated by society of indecency

This is a silent horrid stigma
Many are victim of circumstances
They silently battle to justify their innocence
Yet subtle silence is all they have
Their silence is totally ignored
They have a fight to fight
Can Silence be sanctified?

We are Conscious Women

Mikateko E. Mbambo

We have emptied ourselves
And hung on the windows of our Souls
The curtains of Aloneness

Our breath wasted
In the many races we ran
Blood flowing from the soles of our feet, shaping their path
We have sacrificed
Dreams we have carried from our very existence
To nurture those who give us up
Our Being misused
Till She herself embraced forlornness
Placed in fading backgrounds
We made our wombs their homes
They fed from our burning nipples
To contextualise us as the weaker sex
Our essence bottled
Shipped across the shores of wailing seas
Stored away and never to be freed
We were at the forefront in those racial wars
Wounded and swallowed by the earth
And in their history books we occupy just a subsection
We are conscious women
Mindful of our aptitudes
We are Power!
Remember us...

Deflowered
Linda Nabasa

I want you to hit me again
with your slave like hands, this time I won't bargain
I want you to take me on that bloody train
Swing me then throw me out in the rain.
Not once, not twice
You got so busy
Thinking you'd get rid of me that easy
You fist punched me in my mother's womb,
I shouted mummy is your husband crazy
And even though your punches made me dizzy
You anxiously waited for the bloody thighs
So you could go to the bar and give your drunkard victory speech
As my mother lies in excruciating pain
And I on the southern gate of heaven, in the queue for babies who
never got to be birthed.
Shame on you, for I curved my tiny body in pain.
I was fierce
I was never going to give you that victory speech
So when you saw no blood, you slapped hard on her tummy
I shouted help me mummy
Please fight mummy
Speak man; if you don't love me then why did you make me
Speak man, why did you penetrate my mother's flower
Then choose to deflower me at eleven
Speak man: I counted to seventy seven
It was seventy seven times you humped on me.
You held tight my tiny waist
Speak man, why did you use your power?
To penetrate my little flower
You, leader of the tribe of cowards
First man on the line of drunkards
Known in the books of the unemployed,
Speak you mother, father
See am a good girl, I called you father
Men that beat women can never be forgiven
Men that defile, rape young girls will forever have their own line on
judgment day
And we your victims will sit and watch you, watch you, watch you,

burn!
Skin dripping from bones
Burn!
Tongues, running dry
Burn!
Bones to ashes
Burn!
Ashes to nothing
Burn!
We will watch you
BURN!!!!

The Thing between her legs
Mikateko E. Mbambo

Misogyny with his hands around her neck
Then his fists against her head
Excruciating kicks to her belly, her spine
For
The Thing between her legs

Sexism in his egoistic acme
Looks down on her with insolence
Restricted in all extraordinary spheres
Because of
The Thing between her legs

Male Superiority though tanned with atrocity
In her Feminism armour
She will justly conquer him
Regardless of
The Thing between her legs

hi-life
Nana Arhin Tsiwah

there is live music in womanhood
like riddles of a tranced bard,
a foot tapped is a reading note
on a deep-pressed phonograph

there is *'welcome home'*
- a reawakening from Osibisa . . .

there is *'me yantaban'*
- a soothing midnight pat of Kojo Antwi . . .

there is *'edukuro mu nsuo'*
- our Amakye Dede revolts the heart . . .

when mfantse court drums beat in triple wake
- an Ambolley is felt – *'hey baa, ono ye dokon, dokon'*

shoes tap
lips squat
brains ejaculate
. . . mechanical larynx arrives

Lyrical Penetration

Linda Nabasa

Your love in my life showed me a new dimension.
Your soul giving me this heartfelt sensation
As I stand in front of this mic
I can only hope my spoken word can bring some sort of lyrical
penetration
Now don't get me wrong,
Am not here to compete
I just want to defeat my feminine competition
As they use their bodies
I will use my words to show you
that
I love you
I need you
I get what I want,
So I will get you
Because you keep asking
how will I know she's the one?
How will I know the one?
And I just have one question for you brother
Are you blind?
Cause am the one
I have always been the one
You can go ahead and ask me why
Am a stress relieve pill
That tender succulent meat on the grill
Am hotter than heat
I dance to the beat
Am sweeter than meat
I make a very good feast
So don't be deceived my brother
By those thighs in micro miniskirts
Those boobs that just want to pop out
Those lips that are willing to give head
To any collar
That has some dollars
I got all that my brother
I just choose to not show it
To every tom, dick and harry

I choose to only show it to you
So when you see me dressed in those long skirts and jeans
It doesn't mean that am old fashioned
It simply means am keeping my self-warm for you
When you see me in those tight jeans
It doesn't mean that I want to impress these losers, suckers
These young boys that call themselves men
I just want to show you a little
And tease you
Keep the rest for the bedroom penetration
But as I said
Am not here to compete
so ladies, don't be scared
am only here to defeat my feminine
Competition
as they use their bodies
I will use my words to show you
that
I love you

Culture
Brenda Juma

The river waits,
The farm waits,
The children waits,
The cooking waits,
The clothes waits,
The dishes waits,
Conjugal rights waits,
Culture stipulates.

Bruised face,
Broken arm,
Red eye,
Tearful face,
Painful heart,
The reverse action,
Culture supports.
Behind the mirror,
Lies bitterness and helplessness,
Psychological trauma,
Emotional torture,
With strength,
Holding on,
For better for worse,
Culture stipulates.

Black Eagles fly high
Tralone Lindiwe Khoza

She flips her wings, though her heart is broken
Stirs within, and hopes for better days
Her pride is the wall that keeps others away.
Her wisdom echoes to the ends of the earth.
The black eagle flies high.

Those that pursue her, move between dawn and sunset to catch her
twig.
She is the ultimate catch, but you must sweep her off her feet
And him? He must catch me first, she says.
Some suitors' rhythms are pure; some are filled with greed,
feathered hidden agendas.
She smiles wide with her beak of strength, and stands out in her
circles.
The black eagle flies high.

She wears her blackness with pride & elegance
And hums bitter-sweet sounds of hidden scars, blood stained sins.
But love covered a multitude of sins.
She feeds hope to her young, in a decaying society, morally
questionable- know-it-all
And she flocks together with those who mirror her depth.

Hides from the world for his betrayal,
For trying to stone her the ground, but she has risen from the ashes
and
Her beauty she wears with pride and elegance, and hums bitter-
sweet songs of Africa.
She lies in her bed waiting for clouds to open,
For she knows her help comes from the heavens.

The queen black eagle flips her wings, though her heart is in pieces.
Stirs within, and hopes for better days.
Her pride is the wall that keeps others away.
Her wisdom echoes to the ends of the earth.
The black eagle flies high.

Her

Brenda Juma

The stone will open her eyes,
Eventually.
The stone will open her ears,
Eventually.
But the stone will not breath,
Eventually.
The stone will be dumb and deaf.

illumination
Vincent Ajise

"she was free in her wildness.
she was a wanderess, a drop of free water.
she belonged to no man & to no city"

~ roman payne

the day our aunt who lives in the city where men
are gods & all other organisms subordinate
came visiting, we sat underneath the effulgence of dusk,
discussing about the wreckage on her skin,
each one of them bulging like origami-statues
 tending towards the hopeless refuge of restriction.

it was then we knew of men who buy somatic moons
  & seas—the tender arcs & bubbling rears of dames,
just to oil & illume the totem between their thighs.
it was then we knew about the reign of misogyny:
the utility derived from the hatred of all things bright & beautiful.
it was then we knew about the heresies
of self-imposed gods, the barbaric dogmas that annihilate
time & wit, were just creations of certain naysayers
to stifle the girl-child, to make her name dissipate into atoms of
rust.

Part 8: Postmodernism, Family, Home and love

The City 'Queens'

Brenda Juma

The city has its definition,
The rural has its definition,
I bet you have yours too.

In the city,
It is defined by,
Fake beauty,
Fake boobs,
Fake butt,
Fake hips,
Fake skin tone,
Fake hair,
Fake lashes,
Fake teeth,
Fake eyes,
Fake nails,
Fake,
It's a competition.

Expensive makeup,
Expensive hair,
Expensive fancy clothes,
Expensive heels,
Expensive bags,
It's a competition.

Expensive hotels,
Expensive night outs,
Expensive drinking sprees,
Expensive hired cars
Expensive gadgets,
It's a competition.

Fake rich boyfriends,
Fake social media posts,
Fake over edited photos,
Dirty secrets,
The reality shows we emulate

It's a competition.

It only lasts for a while,
It ends painfully,
Engulfed in guilt,
Dirty secrets leaked and shared,
Insults on social media,
Organized gangs,
Threats of guns and knives,
Depression,
Is it a competition anymore?

Ode To The Yellow Party
Omuna Andrew Herbert

On my death bed
I would like to share
A toss to the yellow historicals
Who braved with 27 guns
And rid us of that governance.

I would like to tell the nurse,
"Yellow blood please,
I am a post '86 youth.
A UPE and USE graduate
In *bodaboda* riding.

I would like, for civility,
Be wrapped in *bisanja*
Like the night dancer on a third round dance
And lead brethrens to that bus
Of steady ….

"Nurse, please make a sack cloth for me
To harvest that money.
My ancestors too need foreign exchange
For their bank
To pay off the ghosts there."

"Where are my hands nurse?
My social media accounts are dormant.
The guardian of the leopard's balls,
King of the kingdom of U…
Has granted me the VPN codes."

Before I bid thee farewell,
Send my greetings to Kaihorror
And Chigundi.
I aspired to work with you, but –
My name, nose …

Lay me peacefully at Kololo
In a yellow mahogany casket,
Secure from the noisy rats.
It will be a worthy grave-arrest
From non-patriotic citizens.

I leave some simple requests –
A stately funeral,
A total recall of all my debts,
An assured government post for my family,
And, …

Grow up so fast
Thato Tshukudu

All I see is wrinkles on my peer's cheeks due to an overdue use of anti-aging crème.
Leaked secrets through screenshot pics but less synchronised outbursts of laughter in concaved cliques.
Click clock time is a tick so we flick intimate moments together and form brick walls.
Plant seeds of lies that manifest into a fatherless kid, mothers that have to maintain a nine to six and teens that rinse their parent's efforts for a quick fix.
Minor's voices stuck between the larynx unheard and unsung like miner screams trapped between the claustrophobic concaves of death pit.
Shifting tectonic plates of relationships terra firma to form earth-bound bodies of hate-hoarders roaming around with words as fists.
Confidential tales grow tails of metamorphic proportion and let out deadly hisses of snakes.
Suppression of depressants with antidepressants that sent us into psychiatric wards with cut wrists.
Condolences texts that were accompanied by emotionless emoticons but I was just yearning for your brief visit.

We have lost valuable minutes searching for fame as social gimmicks, losing self-confidence to socialites we aim to mimic.
We are too timid to realise that we are the only generation that was not oppressed with limits.
We are the only generation that is still too timid to realise that we have so much Change embedded within us but we are afraid to emit it.
So we shut our mouths with duct tape and voice our faux thoughts through typed texts of quoted lines plagiarised from a poet's rhymes on Facebook pages for a hundred likes.

It is our greatest plight how Instagram posts boast four images of better quality whilst we are striving for a society of serene duality.
Admit it. We are the only generation that is too timid to realise that we have so much Change embedded within us yet we are too afraid to emit it.

Postmodern Nairobi Beggar

Kariuki wa Nyamu

Chilly Nairobi s☼nrise
as I'm pacing towards Ngara market
stern and all ears, I hear, *'Kijanaa[1]'*
from a grimy guy gawking madly
'S^{to}p I tell you something…'

I perplexedly turn; l👀k intently at him
as he wildly pronounces, *'Aisee[2]*… some coins…'
thrusting his filthy palm of hand to my side
Good grief!
I disregard his frantic gesticulations and
HO^p the stinking **black** wastewater past the narrow bri_dge
only for him to beLLOW
'Oooo, so you won't even s^{to}p!
All right, stay, me I myself will come,
Niga wewe[3]!'
'Ah! You call me what?'

Rudely SHO^{CKED}
I ignore his haughty diction the more
'What might have ^{en}tered his mind?'
I ponder as he stubbornly follows me,

I, awfully taken aback,
Walk qui_cker
        'GHASIA[4]!' he   re^{bukes} again
'Can you be of help to anyone?
and the way you guys YELL prayers
and attend day-long sermons…
What charity are you taught?
Hmm, is that what you call wisdom?'

Ugh! I'm lost between

S^{to}ppi_{ng} by to fli^{ng} him a coin

and overlooking his nuisance the more
as the city's attention now turns to me!

But, can't any one of you here help me
tell this *mburaribuu*[5]
to bugger [off]
and   le   a   v   e   me   ALONE?

[1] *Kiswahili name for a young or youthful person*
[2] *Kiswahili manner of calling attention of someone, usually that of a young person*
[3] *Africanized words for 'You nigger!' usually offensive*
[4] *Kiswahili word for 'useless,' usually derogatory*
[5] *A Gikuyunized phrase for 'bloody fool'*

Be there
Ndumi Dlamini

When the stars of the night sky sway to the howls and hoots of the
forest, be there.
When the moon is shy and crescent, crept up behind the nimbus
clouds, be there.
When the palm trees along the beach roads stand tall against the
rays of the sun, be there.
Just be there.

You don't have to speak. Just let me feel your presence and your
warmth through the gentle touches that grace my skin.
We don't have to be heard nor seen. Just let me witness the joy
reflected through your eyes and I'll open my heart to your secrets in
silence.
We don't have to rush or be compelled by time. Just lay with me in
this transient forever, until the waves depart from the shores with
no return.
Just be there.

When your jovial spirit is dampened with sorrow, I'll be there.
Like a phoenix, I'll fly over to burn away the sadness and bring
warmth and light to your wake.
When your soul is lonely, stranded on a dance floor, I'll be there.
Like a hibernated bear awakened in spring, your soul will find new
life in my presence.
Just be there.

When the birds stop singing and the butterflies don't flutter. Be
there.
When your mind is overthrown with emotional clutter. I'll be there.
When the sun melts away the rocks, and sand dunes run like butter.
Will you be there?
Our souls simply long to be together.
So when they meet under the willow tree, where the river hums
gently, let's be there.
We just need to be there.

Homecoming
Refilwe Khanya Nxomani

Slowly, petals peel from each other
Likewise, fingers from one another,
Separate.

Stems grow high.
Directioned.
Likewise, arms from shoulders,
Trunk into the atmosphere.

Jovial fibres, flutter in the wind
and likewise, appendages convulse in joy
Bending and flapping like petals in a hurricane.
In a gale of elation.

Strangers after a lifetime together
Ravi Naicker

My Alzeimers must have come to you as a shock,
a tsunami that swept through your life,
erasing a life in compliance with order;
my once elephantine memory fading into oblivion
before your benevolent eyes.

When I became a global village of my own
you unstintingly lent me a hand,
shadowed my altered life.
I had become a stranger to you
but you still embraced me.

Sometimes I catch a glimpse of your smile.
You wait upon me with the patience of a saint,
the door of your heart open, without reserve.
Those happy moments we shared together
when our children played in the garden
or – the clock had advanced -
when we sat near the hearth during winter nights
stealing glimpses of the fire consuming the log,
whilst we read our favourite books
exotic fish swimming the length of the tank,
you and I aging with grace, our home emptying.

Therefore, cherish the gift of memory, savour it,
as you hug a snowman before the sun rises.

Sometimes you look at me hoping for a response
but I stare at you like a piece of old furniture.
Your tears cascade down your cheeks.
I weep too and you wipe away mine.
We look into each other's eyes
and memories of a lifetime go by.
Sometimes I smile and it's like manna to you.
I raise your hopes only to see your hope defeated
even as our tears catch the light from the candle.

I would cross the world to have back my memory,

reciprocate your love.

Beyond Beauty
Rogers Atukunda

I still recall-
That rare creature
A Mutooro girl
With a thick mass of falling black curls
Onto her tender face kissing and tossing
Like a lily in a cool after-drizzle-breeze

Abooki*, how can I describe her face?
Those brown watery eyes,
Pleading, oo, pleading-almost dosing…
Like two moons lighting up the sky
That honey-dripping mouth
And lips, so succulent-mmnh!
Glowing cheeks and a pointed nose
A neck, graceful as a crane's
In the breeze, gently swaying
So slender, so youthful

The daughter of Bachwezi*, how can I put it?
Rounded shoulders
The mango-like breast pulsating with life
The slimmest, most fashionable waist
A pale peachy skin
So smooth, so soft

Oo, how shall I say it?
Firm, well-curved hips
On legs of bamboo
Upon which I gazed, gazed
and gazed-more wildly…
Then, I saw, a perfect beauty!

*Abooki is one of pet names Batooro of western Uganda use. Batooro are also said to have originated from Chwezi empire aka Bunyoro-Kitara which ruled the Nile Valley

Can We...

Lucas Zulu

Can we close the vast distance
between me and you?
And begin to
mend the broken bridge
as we begin to cement our ties again
can we stitch a jarred hole

that had been torn apart by our brittle words
with a passion for a dove and olive branch
as we restore the
harmony between   can
we rind off our hurt feelings
while they are like lime, the first buds of
spring   and cease to stow the fresh lemons
for another day   as we engage in
casual conversation, lets share their tang.

fallen in love again
Wafula p'Khisa

... mine is a heart seasoned by fiery fires of grey
the moment mother expelled me after troubling her womb before
time
I didn't shed a tear when the knife ate my manhood till noon
I didn't smile after winning a thousand hearts with a simple lie;
until I was dumped after warming their cold thighs one winter
I swore by the graves of my departed emotions
never to touch broken breasts of a maiden & be a priest;
But I found the metal guard of the Seminary locked at dawn!

Then you descended from the silvery cloud yonder
with a smile that could turn the wrath of gods into sensuous
laughters
Was it a song of redemption I heard you sing whilst still on wing?
Oh, *mwana wamai*, my heart melted in your watery presence
Expelling dark memories of the past via the tiny window of the
present
I wore a smile, and wound my fragile hand round your waist
and like expectant sailors ashore, readied to sail across the serene
island of future; stretching hands for us
I knew I had fallen in love again!

We are now trapped in the angry waves of the present
and the yester-dreams and beauty have long vanished into stores of
memory;
thus leaving the bitter sweetness of the future a mystery, wrapped in
giant mists of grey
I pray that we stop not rowing, even in the eyes of storms
We didn't come all the way from home to throw a feast for sharks!

Endure the smell of every bullshit my tongue vomits
Because a moth ate my morals whilst still an infant
Pick me up when I fall, and I swear, Arreba
I'll never kiss you at night, unless the moon & stars cheer us
lest the witches spoil our bliss with awkward dances!
I'll never let you step on delicate earth, lest it break open and
swallow you
I'll walk with you, in full glare of the sun, in the middle of the road

and everyone will move to the periphery to give way:
acknowledging that indeed, I chose best!

At the crack of Dawn
Dennis Brad Kunguru

At the crack of dawn
I wake to the beckoning of a new day
And with my mind astray
I raise my heavy head to peep through my window
All is misty and biting cold.
I fix my sorrowful eyes to the cloudy sky,
All is biting cold and lonely.
I feel my crackled lips trembling
Trying to hold onto the memories of that last kiss
From that one person I truly miss.
The cold is biting so deep
Yet there's not much I can do
But seek solace from the birds in yonder
Welcoming a new day
Unaware of my burrowing tribulations and confusions!
I raise my shaky fingers to reach my window pane
It's burning cold!
From a distance, I see the blurred smile of the sun
Trying to pierce through the thickened clouds
Then I turn to look around-
"Welcome to emptiness'
-those are the sounds I seem to hear.
There's not much to hold
No much to yearn for
And not much to live for!
All is empty.
Then feebly like a chameleon dancing on a twig
I turn to seek the cold embrace of my empty bed.
A sob or two escape my insides
I'm sad, life is sad; all around me is cold and sad.
I lose the courage to carry on
Afraid of my distant tomorrow
Afraid of my burning insides,
Oh God!
Why is life so absurd?

Once Upon August (for Martha)
Wafula p'Khisa

I was bitten by a snake once
whilst combing the wild, searching for treasure
And the poison is still fresh in my blood;
it rises when echoes of the past knock at the window of memory

I don't want to suffer another heartbreak;
the classroom is yet to churn out trained doctors to fix broken
hearts
I don't want to chase frogs in all rivers
for fear of untold miseries each could spit into my vulnerable
system
So I sneaked across the forbidden line
and elected you, to hold my heart
to melt not in times of extreme heat;
to freeze not in times of terrifying cold
but dance appropriately to the rhythm of the love song
whispered silently by blood in our veins...
 I stopped singing elegies for my shattered dreams
I stopped idling on village footpaths, ogling at young maidens from
the river
when, like an angel sent from yonder lands, into my life you toured;
nursed my wounded heart & gathered its multiple pieces--
longing for healing
And breathed your finest breath into my starving lungs
Whilst we licked each other's dry lips
amidst the wild August cold
I cherish our laughters, echoed beyond these moonlit footpaths
when you baptize ugly situations into mild jokes
by the magic of your deadly tongue
and strive to outdo me
in solving this great puzzle holding us in debt, birth to death.

Why aren't our people dying of hunger anymore?
Because the soil surprised us, and every granary is sagging with
good harvest?
Why aren't politicians hiding from voters anymore,
and fighting for space at funerals and churches?
Because the season of sowing is nigh?

With my equation balanced, it doesn't matter, dearest
If there is a time I ever felt alive,
It is when I am trapped in the web of your embrace
For there is no warmer place on earth
than the paradise between thighs of a woman!

Kafanchan
Ayomide Owoyemi

At the platform I waited,
by the milling crowd orbited,
as time stood still,
on the dead clock.
You will come they said,
you will come.

The rails stretch
like strings on a guitar,
cold metals frozen in form and time,
I awaited their strumming,
At kafanchan, she said,
there, wait for her.

Repeated hoots rekindled my hope,
chugchugchug,
the crowd is percussed to silence
and stillness, I move,
I thought, from here,
we will pick our odyssey.

Hope faded with the receding coaches,
I am the dead clock,
left at the platform,
orbited by the milling crowd,
Bauchi, she said,
I have moved on.

Kafanchan used to be an important railway terminal in Northern Nigeria. Bauchi is a town in Northern Nigeria, it lies beyond Kafanchan on a train route

Drowning in these feelings alone
Kgolagano Tshela

She could not call to mind how they became close but I guess it is true when they said: those whom we do not remember how we met are the ones that become part of us. Before she met him, she was living in a dark world. She was hurting, she was in pain, and she was drained.

And he came along, he handed words to her like crushed blackberries in the palms of his hands, firm. His smile was like a wheelchair because even at times she was at her worst he was able to carry her heartbreak and transform it into a heart. They started sharing moments and I guess that is when she gradually fell for him. She kept everything to herself as it was not her intention to fall for him. She tried to ignore her feelings but even a blind man could see that she does care. She cared to a point whereby even in his absence his presence was felt. She cared too much and I guess that is why she was hurting. She got so much to say, she wants him to know how everything is fine when he's around, how she's a slave to his touch. Deep down she's scared of what would happen if the ice would break in an unpleasant manner, so she smiles and sits around in hopes that he will notice...

Chemicals in the mind of "G-O-D"

Jarred Thompson

If we're all chemicals in the mind of "G-O-D"
then me and you were chemicals on either end of a synapse:
secreted into a void,
we met
we fucked
we changed each other
things were communicated
to the larger body
electro-chemical firings
produced sparks of incandescent light.
then the thought died,
another connection was introduced
another skill was learned: disconnection.
Oh the wonders of neuroplasticity.
The ability to take the pain
consume
love it
and let blood pump into smooth, blank regions
But the neurons remember
("G-O-D" remembers)
the chemicals burned and left an imprint.
Now every impulse flows through your corridors
every chemical fills holes hollowed out by you.

You are recycled
I am recycled
and when "G-O-D" thinks of us
we are billions of neurons apart

Let a Woman
Marial Awendit

Let a woman not be stolen
From a sleeping rib
That we may not find
Our path into half-bitten
Do-dare-not-eat apples.

Let a woman
Come weaving life
Like the moment
Before a kiss
Or a bud
Brewing dreams
Of trees not living.

If a woman must pass
Like one intruding harmattan
And from her veil a man reaps chills
Then *Black Pearl*,
Had we not walked under glaring lights,
One small quiet night, along a freed street?
Where our words not pregnant buds spelling the night's fog?
Silent witness?
I was blown by her wind
Before time undressed
Her cunning

And I knew we had met
To part.
Who traps the wind?

If a woman must come singing
Like a breeze
But leaves a hurricane,
Shattering life out of windows
And china,
Then that *Weech of Wandy*
Came sowing
Wings of blooms but left

With knives hungry to intercourse
Bellies
        And I knew she had come to go
To jail.

Again, let a woman not lay herself
A Red Sea to cross
  Where breaking a sea
For one man to cross
  Is strangling an elephant
To catch a maggot.

Let a woman lay herself
A river where a one deep diver
May not drown
But let a woman
Not be one licentious
Nile; getting dirty cleaning crevices.

The gift of goodbye

Lisa Jaison

You are broken and irreparable, and I am leaving.
Swore if our paths should ever meet again
I forget you, forget every memory and every experience
I have dug deep into the core and under-belly of my conscience and
buried you under the massive rubble of everything you did not do
right.
Farewell, adieu, it is done.

You deserve my enraged silence to forget you
To not exist in my world, and be deleted to nothing
A non-entity, echoing the non-event that was you and I
Move on, we never happened!
I am neither bitter nor mad, just pleased for tomorrow has the
certainty of no you
Relieved to say you are a bygone

A black blot of nothing, like the darkness -that's you
Harboring all ogres of the dusk living within you
Empty and desolate with no glimmer of light
Blocking the sunshine and swallowing up the light around you.
A huge black shiny blood sucking leach
To be discarded and escaped

I am glad it's over; I will never see you again
Glad I survived you and those two horns you couldn't hide
Glad I have today and tomorrow without you
Glad you are a dead part of it all
Glad I conceive to feel nothing now that that switch has been
flipped
I bury and bid you so long

Return the favor, and erase me from your sick memory
We will never be friends, acquaintances or ex`s
Bury me like I have buried you, as you crawl back to the dingy
shadowy hole you came from
I will be damned if I mourn a living being
I rue that you ever crossed my path but walk away with bravado

When all is said and done I stand tall, and embrace tightly the gift
and the power of goodbye within me.

Hard Tongue
Linda Nabasa

I have leant my lesson
Never to hold out my heart
Leave my chest hollow and open
With hands drenching in thick red lover's blood.
He doesn't crave for such mess
And me causing a fuss
Is only a waste of his busy time.
and even when I shout 'FINE'
He don't even have the energy for a verbal fight
Am like that luggage he lost , however much the airlines calls ,
he won't pick it up.
My heart is now back in my chest.
It's a badly sown job
But hey...... at least am alive
and well covered for the next guy
who won't even see the stitches.
I still have my pretty face
the body is in constant trial and error.
in and out of the gym motion
as I fight the turn ' to junk after breakup emotions'
But it'll do for now
the body, I mean
With my new self-that's cold.
I will smile
Laugh at his jokes
I will sit with him but I will be absent
Cold
Wet and folded in a towel even a microwave cannot dry.
My soul hidden down a tunnel
covered by my plastic self.

Dead skin

Asiko Joan

Tis midnight,
He tip toes in,
I lie
Wide awake,
My senses dead.

His breath almost awakens my bile,
He spreads his hand,
And presses my breast,
It collapses cold in his hand,
It is smaller now,
Older and wrinkled?

His hands are rougher now,
Grazing my still stomach,
As he moves them lower,
The hairs underneath recoil,
As if running away from a crawling monster.

Underneath, seems dead than I,
His persistent hands rough it up and down,
He curses and pushes me on my back,
My bum is colder,
His hands roam all over,
To hold on,
But they won't.
He stops and grunts,
His body facing the wall,
He snores.
I guess, he now knows,
I am dead skin.

She Said This Is Mr. Daniel

To María del Carmen Fonseca López, in your bed in Texcoco
Daniel Da Purificação

I
Wrote my feelings
In
My first English poem
From
My weak-lazy-poor vocabulary
When
She was in her bed
When
She looked at me
And
My blood changed
And
My skin run away
When
She said
Hey you PLAYBOY
Come here
Show me what you can do
With a woman like me without feelings

Part 9: Translations from other African Languages

Liefde en Reen

Ernestu Botha

Verdrink in liefde en reen
Sonder dit is daar droogte

Geen beheer oor liefde en reen
Wanneer dit daar is beteken dit niks
Wanneer dit iets beteken is dit daarmee heen

Ons bid vir n druppel reen, vir n sopnat soen
Ons sit emmers uit,
En wag vir die vrugbare seisoen
En kom sy nou, en gaan sy weer
Gebreek dat sy wil gaan,
maar te Trots om te keer

Die reen is weg,
maar darem was ek Reg
Alweer

Love and Rain
Ernestu Botha

Drown in love and rain
Without it there is a drought

No control over love and rain
When it is present it means nothing
When it means something it is gone

We pray for a drop of rain, for a wet kiss
We set out buckets
And wait for the fruitful season
And now she comes and gone again
Broken that she wants to leave
but too Proud to stop her

The rain is gone
but at least I was Right
Again

Jy weet jou oë

Jacobus G. L. Nieuwoudt

Jy weet jou oë
hoort nie op myne nie
jy weet gedagtes proe
nie soos medisyne nie
denke soek nie
blyplek nie
vingers soek nie
lêplek nie
arms vou toe
rank om my tempels
hande klam op my nek
sweet soek 'n lekplek
Sondag sit ek in die kerk
Sondag soek 'n lêplek
drome vra nie hoekom nie
ogies soek dinge
wat fluister
wat wegkruip
in die duister
lang gras liedjies
Engels bly weg
Hier's dit donker.
Ligte lankal weg.
Toe oë
nat broek.
Oop mond
tong soek.
Hemel koek
proe so naak
hare grys
koppie wys.
Vee roep na die oggend reën
ietsie om te drink
dis so droog in my
byt vas
arms vry.
Jy weet jou oë
hoort wit

omgedop
sodat die spieëls van die lewe jou nie kan
kry.

You know your eyes

Jacobus G. L. Nieuwoudt

You know your eyes
doesn't belong on mine
you know thoughts don't taste
like wine
ideas aren't seeking
a place to stay
fingers aren't seeking a place
to lay
arms fold shut
creeps over my temples
clammy hands on my neck
sweat seeks to leak
Sunday seeks the week
dreams don't ask why
tiny eyes seek things
that whisper
that hides
in the dark
Anglii stay away
it's dark here
lights left
now there's only fear
Closed eyes
wet trousers
Open mouth
tongue seeks
Heaven cake
tastes so naked
hair grey
head wise
To prod calls the morning rain
Something to drink
it's so dry on the inside
hold on
arms free
You know your eyes
belongs white
tipped

that the mirrors of life can't
have you
flipped.

Maita Shava
Tendai R. Mwanaka

Mhofu yomukono, Ziwewera
Hekani mutekedza
Vakatekedzana pa Janga
Wakapiwa mukadzi munyika yevaNjanja
Hekani mutekedza, vari muhera mukonde
Zwaitwa mhukahuru vemiswe inochenga muviri

Ah, ko mazwi angu angapinda sei muninga yepfungwa dzenyu?
Ndingataure here kubudikidza nemi, muromo wangu
urikukwakukakwakuka, mwoyo wenyu wanyorovera
Munogona kundiudza zvose, Shava
Nhasi, ndichaedza kutaura nomunemi
Iyi inyaya yenyu iyi, Shava
Ndononamata kusarasa rwungano rwenyu irwu

Ndakakusarudza iwe nokuda kwako chete
Uri munamato wangu wakahwandiswa
Uri ngirozi iri munzira iri pakati pepasi nedenga
Tirikuenda kunyika itsva pamwechete

Paivapo pataisangana, tichinwa, kuseka, kutsvodana
Zvisiisii zvichitikurudzira nezvidimbu zvemimhanzi yenziyo
dzatairangaridzwa
Tsvodo? Nganiko? ah, handingakuudzei
Ndakakugumbatira nguva refu zvangu pawaiva wati raremangwana
Muromo wangu unenzara yokuda kukuswada mandiri.
Zvishomanana tsvoda dzichinanga pamurumo pako
Mune ramangwana ngwanani, ndokunyorera *wamukasei* tichisasana
zvechihwandehwande hedu
Dimwe nguva, ndaisatomboziva zvandaitaura zvangu

Zvikwawu zvandakatsetsa kubva mumakodo kuitira rudo rwako
Mwoyo wakapetunura mwoyo wangu
Kuitira tsanga yembeu yomwoyo wangu
Irikumerera muvhu rako, muti wangu munyoronyoro
Ivhu remaruva angu anoyevedza kudairira nziyo yorudo rwako
Uri furafura rangu rinonwa kubva muhana nhete yemaruva angu

Uri patya rangu romuninga dzepfungwa dzangu, diziro remapapiro angu atyoka
Kunge shiri mbiri dzehurekure, tamhara pabango regore rokudenga
Tichanyora nomwoyo yedu yasunganiswa paganda regore iri
Mumvuramvura nohuhwandi hwemvura yemakore tichakura pamwechete
Nhasi ndonokupai mwoyo wangu nekiyi yeninga dzepfungwa dzangu
Semubikiro wezvinonaka, Shava
Rudo rwako rwunondizadza nemufaro nemanyemwe sehari dzezvinotapira
dziri muninga yenyikadzimu chisionekwi.
Ndawuwudza halleluiah, Ndawuwudza halleluiah, Ndawuwudza halleluiah.
Ndinokudai Shava, Ndinokudai Mhofu, Ndinokudai Ziwewera.

Thank you Shava

Tendai R. Mwanaka

The Great Eland bull. The Runaway
Thank you very much. The one who carries heavy loads
Those who challenged each other at Janga
Those who were given wives in the country of the Njanja people
Thank you my dear mutekedza, those in uHera Mukonde
It has been done Great Animal, those with tails that are intimate with body

Oh, how can one person's words enter the soul of another?
Can I speak through you, my mouth keeps moving, your heart is
still
You can tell me anything, Shava
Now, I try to speak through you
This is your story, Shava
I pray never to lose your story

I chose you for you
You are my hidden prayer
A saint as a point of moving from earth to heaven
Herding for a new country together

There was a rendezvous, a drink, a laugh, a kiss
Hummingbirds motivating us to sound snatches of remembered
songs
A kiss? How many? Oh, I couldn't say
Holding you longer each time we say goodnight
My mouth hungering to take you in
Slowly moving each kiss closer to your mouth
In the morning I would text you *goodmorning* and flirt in codes
Sometimes, I didn't know what I was saying

The oars I carved out of my bones for the love of you
The heart that opened my heart
For the wheat of my heart
Sprouting in your soil, the plant of my tenderness
The soil where my roses blooms to the tune of your love
You are my butterfly drinking from the soft heart of my roses

You are the twin of my soul, a sanctuary of my broken wings
Like two swallow birds, we have landed on an arm of a heavenly cloud
And engraved our joined souls on the cloud's skins
In the balmy and bounty of the cloud's rains we will grow old together
Today, I present my heart and the keys of my soul to you
As a dish of delight, Shava
Your love overwhelms me with ecstasy like clay pots of sweetened drinks
In the cave of the mystery of myth
I chant halleluiah, I chant halleluiah, I chant halleluiah
I love you Shava, I love you Great Bull, I love you The Runaway

Naahidi Kukusahau
Monicah Masikonte

Wewe ndiwe ndoto pekee iliyowahi kutimia kwangu
Wewe ndio Wimbo pekee niliowahi kuupenda
Uliondoka na kipande kikubwa cha moyo wangu
Uliniachia pengo lenye uchungu moyoni mwangu lisiloweza
kujazwa na yeyote mwingine
Uliniachia makovu yatokayo damu kila moyo wangu uukumbukapo
moyo wako
Lakini naahidi kuwa nitakusahau
Bado mimi hukuota wewe
Bado mimi huliita juna lako ninapohisi woga
Bado nina ladha yako mdomoni mwangu
Ningali nina kipande kile cha moyowako ulichoniachia
Lakini naahidi kukusahau

I Promise To Forget You

Monicah Masikonte

You are the only dream that ever came true to me
You are the only song that I ever loved
You went with a big piece of my heart
You left a painful gap in my heart that no one else can fill
You left me deep scars that bleed every time my heart remembers
your heart
But I promise to forget you
I still dream of you
I still call out your name whenever scared
I still have your taste in my mouth
I still have that part of your heart that was left with me
But I promise to forget you

Die Sonblom

Ernestu Botha

Die sonneblom blom wanneer die son op kom
Die son kom op vir die sonneblom
om te sien hoe sy glimlag as haar oë oopgaan
en sien haar af soos hy oorgee aan die maan

Sy slaap vredevol, hy slaap vol vrede
hy is hare en sy is sy rede

Saam sal hulle slaap en saam ontwaak
Tot die gras blou en die lug groen raak

The Sunflower
Ernestu Botha

The sunflowers blooms when the sun rises
The sun rises for the sunflower
To see her smile as her eyes open
and send her off as he hands over to the moon

She sleeps peacefully, he sleeps full of peace
he is hers and she is his reason

Together they shall sleep and awake together
Until the grass turns blue and the sky green

Fitila

For Ayobami
Mof'Oluwawo Mojolaoluwa

Eniyan lo n sore eniyan
Only humans befriend humans
Ore eni lore eni
One's friend is one's friend
Ayobami lore temi
Ayobami is my friend
Baba ore mi ku
My friend's father passed away
Baba ore mi ku
My friend's father remains
Digi ore mi fo
My friend's mirror is broken
Digi ore mi ku
My friend's mirror is intact
Fitila ku
The lamp has gone out
Fitila ku
The lamp shines still
Oba oke ni digi ti kii fo
God is the everlasting mirror
Oba oke ni fitila tii kii ku
God is the lamp that never goes out
The everlasting mirror is with you
May you look into Him and find your dreams
The eternal lamp is your guide
May you look by His light and find your way
A dara
All shall be well.

Fitila means lamp in Yoruba.

Part 10: Portuguese Poems

Dramático?!
Hélder Simbad

Acto I
Cena I
O poeta com a retina nos tempos
rabisca versos com dentes de aços
versos pedras nos sapatos de deus

Cena II
A vida do poeta no telefone
atravessa os segundos da fibra óptica
Os olhos fotografam a coreografia dos perigos
(Esquizofrenia na frenética alma)

Cena III
O velho
qual camaleão mestre
apoiandando-se à bengala
o porco de óculos a ler o passado
o engraxador da cor da graxa
a criança que dispara brincandando
tudo assusta

Acto II
Cena I
Uma prostituta latino-americana
ou uma deusa grega e angolana
a mando do general Kahoyo

Cena II
Uma boca salta do jornal e dispara:
- Há beijos que induzem comas
O poeta é o prato na mesa do gazeteiro
qual Jesus chicoteado por afiados verbos

Acto III
Cena I
Uma carta sem lirismo
o pescoço na corda da morte
uma ausência gritante

versos queimados
ou escondidos
no bolso da verdade

Conto fantástico
Hélder Simbad

Eu digo:
Pelos intermináveis esgotos do sonho
canalizo o energético poema
ligando-o aos fios eléctricos
por onde se escoa o sangue

Eu digo: passa o poema
(sonhando) passa o poema que me sonha
bombeado pelo frenético palpitar
do coração marimba

Não!
O espírito do poema
ou a baba de deus
escorregadia e pegajosa
desce
pelas velozes cordas da luz
ou pelo triangular ciclone
e me golpeia pelas laterais

Poema com dentes de morder
Poema que me sonha

Invocar um instante apocalíptico
como um cristão
rico
de pobreza
e morrer neste instante
sonhando um inacabado poema?

Sim!
Seria perfeição
o sonho de um deus realizado
no limite do infinito

Eu digo: esqueci-me
Porras

Como direi?!
Um poema viajante
com cintilantes rosas
polvos e rosapolvos
a voar por mares
(sonhando)
a flutuar por céus
(sonhando)

Um poema
com origem em si
percorre
o frágil corpo
em transe
seu impulso
giranda pelo cadáver
fora
impedido
pela tampa da caneta
explode-se-me

Seu ímpeto atravessa
a carne dos dedos
os transparentes abismos da caneta
a tenacidade da tampa
a terra que não sonha
o sonho da terra
e vai além sonho

Do alto regressa
sonhando se sonha
e seu nome será
alguma coisa
sem género

Urgência
Britos Adriano Baptista

Eu preciso partir
Para qualquer lugar
Partir daqui
Partir de mim
Partir somente

Eu preciso partir
Para horizonte qualquer
Para ser eu e nada mais
Pois aqui nada fui
E nada sou

Eu preciso partir
Sem demora
E levar comigo
O nada que fui e sou
E nada mais

Eu preciso partir
Para gente alheia
Lá serei um qualquer
Menos o nada
Que aqui fui e sou

Eu preciso partir
Com os meus eus
Para voltar para mim
Cheio de eus que não fui
E não sou

Confidência
Britos Adriano Baptista

Estávamos a sós entre o teto e as paredes,
Eu e ela a sós.
Embrulhamo-nos num olhar,
E num beijo novelesco beijamo-nos novelescamente.
Incorpóreos, abraçamo-nos como se fosse a última vez.
O suor floria-nos a pela como flor espreitando a terra
Na queda da madrugada fria de Junho.
Despimo-nos por completo e atiramo-nos numa cama de papel
Coberta de virgem neve, estávamos num céu terrestre.
Já que não se faz amor, inventamos amor,
Num tempo em que o tempo nos aplaudia encantado…
Despidos da aprisionada lucidez, vivemos a nossa maior liberdade.
E num demorado êxtase, um orgasmo mútuo fecundando na palavra
Deu origem a este poema.

O preço do meu silêncio
Britos Adriano Baptista

Queres comprar-me o silêncio?
Eis a minha condição:
Leve contigo a fome e miséria
Que me inventas.
Desligue os brinquedos de pólvora
Que matam meus manos e manas
De crianças ao idosos,
Lá nas matas do medo.
Lá onde não parece Beira
Que seduzia-me os olhos.
Lá onde há sangue correndo como os rios
Prestes a vomitar águas em cheias.
Leve para longe de mim
Esse teu falso sorriso,
As promessas não cumpridas,
A utópica ideia de desenvolvimento.
Leve contigo o peso da ira
Que me amarrota o semblante.
Leve contigo esse sofrimento e humilhação
Que em mim plantas com injustiça.
Devolva a felicidade que me roubas.
Dê-me os teus palácios de Belo Horizonte.
E leva esse horizonte vazio
Esvaziando o meu olhar.
Em troca dou-te a minha humilde palhotinha
Em xipamanine,
Lá onde ladrões são ladrões...
Venha viver aqui!
Venha viver no gueto.
Venha viver no avesso da cidade.
Em troca deixa-me viver no teu luxo,
Assim talvez seja bom para nós os dois.
Leve contigo esse teu falso capitalismo
Que merda-me tudo e descapitaliza meus bolsos,
Minhas contas bancárias e faz-me dever-te...
Dê-me toda a tua riqueza
Oh príncipe da luxúria!
Dê-me o teu sorriso

E leve-me as lágrimas que me habitam os olhos
Nublados de tristezas.
Dê-me o amor que não tens,
A sensibilidade que não sentes.
Dê-me tudo de bom
Que não tens e seja o que não és comigo.
Devolva tudo que me tiraste injustamente...
Prenda-te nas tuas injustiças
E desprenda-me das tuas mãos insanas.
Mãos que me submetem a ti e ao teu regime ditatorial.
Dê-me liberdade
Oh bom diabo!
Por fim deixa-me urinar no corpo da falsa democracia
Sepultada na tua mente, e chorar de alegria
No túmulo da tua ignorante inteligência.
Só assim terás o meu silêncio.

Filha das ruas

Augusta Jorge

Porque tiraste-me da rua
Para que eu seja sua

Cobria-me do frio dela
Acompanhada de suas estrelas
Do seu luar
Das noites escuras e chuvosas

De dia vivo o sol
Que faz-me sentir tão quente
Que nem uma cama ardente
Eu vivo nessas ruas

Onde o pão é só em pensamentos
A dor aperta no meu peito
Eu vivo nas ruas

Não sei o que é um abrigo
Porque nunca me foi dado
Eu sou da rua
Onde a solidão é o meu colchão
O silêncio o meu rumor

O coração não sabe o que é a paixão
Eu represento a minha própria ruína
Por tornar-me heroina
De tanto sofrer, nem sei mais o que é ser feliz
Ainda assim vivo a rua

Sou este mundo
Augusta Jorge

Um lugar onde todos vivem
Mas ninguém encontra-se

Esconde-se num semblante
Que apresenta ser salutar
E nada é surreal
Quase tudo parece brutal

Não me abandone nesse ciclo vicioso
De dor sem fim
Onde alguns comem capim
Onde sem mais esforço
Deito-me onde haja algum enconsto

Lugar onde vivo frio e calor
As cores e o incolor
Mas tudo com muito amor.

Despreso

Bruno Santos

Veneno, em forma de cianeto

Respirar o ar do epicentro,
Catalogamos falsos,
E os colocamos selos
Made In China...

Circuncisão mental,
Aonde prepúcios
São o proprio
Hipotálamo...

Conforto debaixo das árvores

Folhas caiem neste outono
Virtual,

Sapos e rãs coacham no lago
Do meu pensamento...

Não me despreses,
Sou um homem de valor,

Sou exclusivo aos teus olhos,
Não me despreses,

Observa a minha mudança,

Sou feio sim,

Mas mudo,

Porque hoje sou uma lagarta,
Mas quando sair do Casulo,
Serei uma linda borboleta,

Que estará em cima a voar
Sobre as vossas cabeças!

Materia Viva
Bruno Santos

Correr atrás dos sonhos,
Materializamos ideias,

Organizamos momentos
E escrevemos poesia,

Renovamos os momentos e
Planeámos palavras,

Articulamos a gramatica,
Depositando frases,
Amamos e romantizamos,

Forjamos e lapidamos,
Transcendemos, nos
Movimentamos parados,
Mas somos o que somos,
Liricistas, ativistas, verdadeiros,
Viajamos com a caneta,
Para mostrar que somos artistas!

Cego Visionário
Carmona Polá Júnior

Sou eu o cego e visionário,
Vou seguir cegamente a minha visão nesta senda
Até onde as cores não mais existirem e
A diferença entre preto e branco não mais ser diferente...

Até onde a força de gravidade perder a sua capacidade de atracção,
Tornar-se fraqueza, o sol perder o brilho e
A terra se separar de seus movimentos de repente...

Até onde todo o sempre se tornar nunca e
O tempo perder a sua existência...
Até onde a minha voz deixar de ser eco, me livrar de todos os
alteres sociais e
Descansar pesos na minha consciência...

Até onde todos os sabores da vida e da ciência perderem o gosto e
Não importar mais o desempenho,
Tudo que faço converter-se em legado, eu não mais existir e
Morrer a única vida que tenho!

Cláudia, Minha Irmã

Carmona Polá Júnior

Cada vez que eu penso em ti,
Rochas de sentimentos Caiem sobre mim
Apedrejam a minha alma,
E abrem feridas com fundidade sem fim!

Cada vez que eu penso em ti,
Se desata o nó do silêncio das minhas cordas vocais…
O barulhento silêncio da sua partida,
É violentamente esquartejado pelo pacato grito sem som!

Cada vez que eu penso em ti,
O rio que há em mim, Lentamente transborda…
As suas fracas correntezas tiram-me a resistência!
Sinto muitas saudades suas, Minha irmã, minha gorda…
Tu perdeste a vida mas tu não perdeste a existência!

Odisseia dum Plebeu
Carmona Polá Júnior

Sou plebeu de nascença,
Desgraçado na minha opulenta pobreza;
Fui Nascido e educado como gente sem poder nem influência!
Desde sempre fui Ignorante sobre coisas básicas.

Sou Combatente veterano de guerras pacíficas…
Tornei-me general de toda incompetência militar!
Guerrilheiro das mais inseguras trincheiras...
Fui um pobre desertor do seio familiar!

Fui, sim, roubado por Velhos Soldados…
Treinado para resistir contra a resistência!
Fui Ensinado a não ensinar o que sabia,
E aprendi a não aprender o que aprendia!

Eu, assim como os outros Plebeus,
Cresci, reconhecendo a minha pequenez
Nunca tive sede de poder,
Mas sempre tive fome de comer!

Ser um Homem-Deus
Cátia Regina Correia

viverás obras completas
No enredo dos seus próprios Passos
Realizará com o ímpeto
De tuas Mãos
no intelecto ,na força
Do teu próprio espírito
Eu & Eu
Realizará os presságios
De caminhos nunca
Antes trilhados
Através de uma intuição mágica, aptidão nata
Fruto da Genética
De africana Realiza
Presságios cantados
Pela voz do seu ancestral
Conduzirão a tua dança e a dos teus irmãos
Coreografado por zambi
Em dias de festa
Onde a paz e a união
Do teu povo
Te farão recostar a cabeça
Tranquilo em teu leito.
Segredos da noite
Toda madrugada
Levado por suspiros
Meu calor
Atravessa estradas
Entra na maresia
perpassa intransponível
Pelo vento
E corre mais rápido
Que a luz do sol
Que inda logo chega
Pra pousar em teu corpo
Antes do nascer do dia
Amanheces com um sorriso
Da visita que te fiz
Em espírito

Nos nossos encontros
De sonhos

O que fazes da vida?

Cátia Regina Correia

No sono leve ou profundo
pálpebras tremulam
saem involuntários
sussurros segredados
balbucios
Meu espírito dança
languido em sonhos
e meu eu me conta segredos
viaja, conhece mundos
aprende idiomas
nunca dantes ouvidos
metafísico
O sol daqui brilha forte
e não queima minha pele
eu sou o sol de meu
uni-intra-multi-verso
Alma translúcida
fonte inesgotável de energia
Sou a arte, penso e sou ouvida
crio teorias e as desfaço
analiso, julgo e absolvo
grito quando me dá vontade
Aqui o som não tem volume
e todos sentem seu vibrar
o pranto nunca é contido
o riso desagua em rios
gargalho lágrimas em harmonia
Viajo, sobrevoando os mortais
já não sou de carne
em meu culto
sou divindade
Recito versos sem som
e há mãos estendidas
catando minhas energias
como quando corríamos
atrás de vaga-lumes ao crepúsculo
Vivo amores, caso, descaso,
enamoro de outros e de mim

253

já tive filhos e netos
vivi séculos
lembro de dimensões
que já estive e as que ainda
comprarei passagem
Encontrei Deus esses dias
ele sorriu pra mim
e disse que meu cabelo estava bonito
se despediu dizendo
"a gente se vê... Se olhe mais no espelho!"
Acordei!
De dentro pra fora
sou o viajante
de fora pra dentro
passageiro.

Alguém Te Vê Como Mulher

Cristina Ferreira

Ó mulher! Como farsas sua dor!
Turbulento é seu mundo adentro
Por fora só lindos jardins de flor
Nos lábios teu sorriso é um espectro

Nas calçadas do quarto fremente mendigas
Um membro quente que te dê desejos
Que te ame com amor como nas noites antigas
E com ternura te adorne de carícias e beijos

De rastos rastejas e imploras que te entre
Que pela última vez mate sua fogosidade
O fogo cresce uns centímetros abaixo do ventre
Em troca recebes desprezo e insensibilidade.

Quem te tem, não te sabe ter, beber ou comer
Deixa-te com fome de formas a humilhar-te
Enquanto houver comida haverá quem comer
Ó mulher! Tão linda que és, quem irá negar-te?

Um dia um amor qualquer flagrou-te na rua
Ouviu teu desabafo e decidiu te compreender
Com suas palavras despiu sua alma e deixou-a nua
O que aconteceu depois disso ninguém precisa saber

O estranho te deu o amor que teu amor te negou
Nunca te deixou implorar, pois seu amor te pertencia
Jurou pelos deuses te amar como mais ninguém te amou
E disse que um homem de verdade é o que você merecia

Agora vives dividida. De um lado o amor do outro a traição
Chorando dizes: Não importa o quanto eu esteja dividida
E nem importa a opinião social sobre a minha traição
A viver esta paixão proibida hoje mesmo estou decidida

Como quem vive num lar feliz esta traição tu nunca quis
Mas a muito cansaste de existir para quem se recusa a te ver
Sabes que a sociedade repudia, mas antes disso tu queres ser feliz.

255

Por isso te entregaste todinha ao primeiro que te viu como mulher

A Carta
Cristina Ferreira

Confesso ser um erro autêntico ter te conhecido
Depois daquele beijo eu já deveria ter partido
Mas a rubra paixão caminhou forte em sua direção
Dos teus carinhos me fez refém com tamanha morbidez
A escuridão nutriu um cósmico segredo de embriaguez
Fez nascer nos dedos, o amor e acendeu o fogo da paixão

Simbiose de dois corpos despidos tacteiam aquele quarto
Espelho, retrato. Ouve-se o nosso fremir no guarda-fato
Baloiçando num ir e vir, as cortinas fingiam não nos ver
Quatro paredes. Lá estava eu a sois com minha nudez
Simultâneas indagações do tipo: Como me irias ter
frSeria bom, seria a primeira ou esta seria a última vez?

Longe das túnicas és um egípcio com um deus pequeno
Quando embravecido atormentaste todo o meu inferno
No amarelecimento dos meus papiros fizeste história
Com sua Intrepidez faraónica mostraste-me seu poder
No clímax abcidei e de olhos fechados contemplei sua glória
Sublimada, em êxtase perdi a noção de ganhar ou perder.

Hoje compreendo melhor, como os tempos são rotatórios
E como os juramentos dos amores eternos são ilusórios
Numa única noite foste capaz de me amar duas décadas
Senti-me incólume, Despida daquela mulher quotidiana
Por um efémero instante fui o símbolo das mulheres amadas
Em dia de plenilúnio senti o prazer da natureza humana.

Como quem a pele arranca amarguradamente preciso esquecer
Não nutrir-te mais em mim lentamente fazer-te em mim morrer
Como quem a si próprio se diz não, sepulto hoje a nossa paixão
Nosso amor jogar nos desertos do esquecimento. Comida de besta
E não chore se eu não suportar sua ausência e morrer de solidão
Quando terminares rasgue a carta porque terminou nossa festa

A Mulher Africana Que Sou

Cristina Ferreira

Nasço, junto às nascentes do Nilo
Sangue quente, pele escura.
Faço jus à lei de Gloger.
Esculturais seios nus ornam-me os peitos.
Pífaros, nos lábios dos ventos que dançam
Nas quentes áreas dos desertos de África
Numa orquestral polifonia entoam Cânticos,
sons de Rebita e meus seios
Dançam ao compasso dos meus passos.
E os pássaros dão louvor a sensualidade
E a raridade da Mulher africana que sou
De Cabelos crespos e curtos. Pernas lapidadas.
Pés despidos de um calçar
Escrevem sobre as áreas de um deserto num
Dos cantos qualquer de África uma
História que Historia Não contou.
Corpo despido… a pele bronzeada de suor.
Fazem realçar esta cor do asfalto num olhar
atento do sol. Missangas são correntes
nas mãos e nos pés. Sou Negra!!!
Lágrimas caem em cascatas
Quando penso que dos musseques do Mundo
já fui escrava… ufa! Nos musseques do Mundo!!!
Com pincel, minhas lágrimas apago, pois fui Rainha
Nas Metrópoles do Mali entre um povo como eu…
Um povo como eu honrou-me.
Um povo como eu Chamou-me Rainha.
Conheci o corpo por trás das Vestes de Sundiata Keita
em taças dei-lhe de beber Os vinhos do meu amor.
Flutuei na exaltação dos Bendré tocados por mãos nuas…
harpa-cítara, harpa-alaúde Inarticulação
de palavras fazem a voz do artista… Cantando
a beleza da mulher Africana que sou
Quem dera o mundo visse… com os olhos de Africa
E não com os olhos da errata historia
A supremacia da mulher Africana.
Lamentavelmente o mundo é Bartimeu
por opção Só vê o que quer ver.

Ele nunca me disse te amo
Edgar Ginga Sombra

Cada dia vivo uma curiosidade dele
> Sempre me tem de um jeito diferente
> A noite bate a porta e voamos no ritmo dela
> E voltamos às madrugadas
> E nas despedidas, ele não diz: te amo...
>
> Ele é gentil, simpático e atencioso
> Sabe seleccionar minhas cores
> E trepar minhas paredes...
> Consegue quase mudar o meu mundo
> Mas ele não o completa dizendo: te amo...
>
> É cavalheiro, especial e perfumado
> Sabe ler em mim quando lhe necessito
> E não me deixa piscar em outras direcções
> Seria perfeito para o meu mundo
> Se tivesse me dito:
> te amo...
>
> Será que ele conhece o sentido da minha vida?
> Porque beija meus pés todo amanhecer
> Frases bonitas sabe desenhar para a sua garota
> Me faz bonita ou caminhando sobre as nuvens
> Mas nunca compôs para mim a frase:
> te amo...
>
> Ele já me presenteou estrelas e céus
> Manda-me bilhetes de ouro
> Palavras sem tumultos
> No dicionário cuidado ele vive
> Só não sei se tem a palavra te amo
> Pois, nunca me disse:
> te amo
>
> Tento derramar rios de lágrimas
> Obrigá-lo a dizer que me ama
> Ou mesmo a acabar com tudo
> Mas receio sempre estragar a festa

> E ver o seu lado leão
> E mesmo por pena, ele não diz:
> te amo...
>
> Já me deu até metade de si
> Tudo com ele é como se fosse um sonho meu
> Como se tivesse nas mãos as chaves da minha felicidade
> Só que, mesmo por saudades
> Ele nunca me disse:
> te amo...

Minha sedução
Edgar Ginga Sombra

> Não pergunte
> Não há tempo
> Não quero ouvir
> Os seus discursos
>
> Me devore
> No silêncio
> Mostre no teu olhar
> Todos os desejos
>
> Hoje é jogo livre
> Se é na rua ou na praia
> Não quero abrir os olhos
> Só quero contigo cavalgar
>
> Se há um erro
> Vê se desliga
> Deixa-me respirar
> O sol da tua boca
>
> Se não há razão
> Se é invasão
> Não é hora, não
> Para donas regradas
>
> Nesta voltagem alta
> Se és cadeia
> Me serre com a mais forte
> Corrente da tua paixão
>
> Os toques da minha canção
> Levantam a emoção
> E nesta parede em que te prego
> Está o calor da minha sedução
>
>

Vida Aliciada
Albano Epalanga

Escamotearam minha alegria
Precipitando-a no vale
da desolação
agora sou o que não sou
Falo o que não falo
e vivo nos sangrentos dias
de vento
Lamento…
eu já não sou o que sou
desde minha miudagem
já tinha perdido o norte
andava semi-nu nas ruas
de Nova-York
Clamava mendigando resto
de água e pão
invés disso ofertaram-me
por excesso a relatividade
de Newton
Entupiram os meus ouvidos
com água salgada
Mandaram-me nas estradas
de Benguela
para ser pisado por Kupapatas
Agora já não respiro por mim
Já não olho por mim
Já não parto por mim
Sou a escuridão do mar
e as enfermidades diárias
envenenados com cálice
dos deuses
que me tornam sucursal
e cheio de remendo no cabelo
ainda assim assalariam-me água
no estado gasoso?
Não sabia eu a diferença
entre dormir de pé e comer
numa velocidade de 100 km/h.

Abismo Profundo

Albano Epalanga

Sinto minha alma
caindo num abismo profundo
no fundo onde não há mundo
no sonho onde só há escuro
cavei o meu buraco
vivi os anos dos meus dias
e me esqueci daquela poesia
poesia que me salvaria
Volte poesia, gritava eu
a poesia respondeu: "jamais voltarei"
então clamei ao Poeta
leva-me nas tuas veredas
nas astúcias do teu infinito
cobri-me com a tua toalha azeda
deleita-me nos teus labirintos
Os teus labirintos
Há há há malditos, esquisitos, feitos...
Aparecidos com peixe frito
Ó morte, tú chegas e não me avisas
Acorrentas minha alma sem que eu ouça?
Tiras-me os desejos sem que eu perceba?
Hó hó hó minha nossa!
De onde vem a tua força?
Os deuses da terra te temem
Os escravos e patrões gemem
E sentem gemidos Dolores
Quando passas próximo de suas casas
Leva-me contigo
Para bem longe dos amigos
Longe das tristezas
Longe das riquezas
Longe das pobrezas...
Ó venha minha noiva
Venha ó esposa minha
Já preparei a aliança
Já comprei a nossa casa
Venha por favor, não demores
A nossa casa é bonita

Lá viveremos eternamente
Eu e tú, tú e eu
Hó hó mori meu.

Meu Barco De Papel
Evaristo Fernando

Um dia sonhei com um barco
Um barco de papel somente meu
Onde rasgasse oceanos em retalhos
Quem sabe ainda dividisse o mundo
Simplesmente com o vaivém dos remos;

Em minhas súbitas epifanias
De mentalidade infante
Vagava em nenhures mares
Remava milhas e milhas
De asfaltos em sonhos
De partida sem regresso;

Quando os olhos provaram
Da maturidade do corpo,
Meus dedos da mocidade
Traçaram com delicadeza
Cada ripa que continha o sonho;

Assim nascera meu barco
De papel entre soluços
E amarulentos suores,
Tal suor que levou-o em viagem
De volta ao passado onde
Brotou tal sonho de ter:

Um barco de papel somente meu.

Metamorfose Xenófoba!

Evaristo Fernando

Renasce-me a vida,
D'uma vida mal vivida
E ardida ao pó da pólvora
Em verdade já mais tida
Independência já mais valida
Portadores de alcunhas postiças;

A quem pertence a terra onde nasci?
E a vida minha que tanto presei,
Quem intitular-se-á dono de mim?

Renasci do cinzeiro fugaz do chicote
Açoitado no delírio negreiro da tua fatuidade
Minh' alma atiçava ânimos nas mazelas do corpo
À calcanhares e unhas, esculpi a independência
E a liberdade no vácuo da minha ciência mandinga;

E agora?
Para onde vai a quietude das armas?
E as almas que se perdem junto as balas?
A quem pertence a paz das falas da outrora?
E irracionalidade belicosa da juventude,
A quem vamos atribuir a carapuça?

Renasce-me a vida
Transparecendo em meus males
Materializei-me em cinzeiros do açoite
Onde meu eu atiçava nas cercanias da tua fatuidade
Ânimos, abeberando-me da minha ciência mandinga.

Negra

Fabious Benfiquista

Por tua culpa, negra
Hoje vivo sem nenhuma regra

Tu me fazes o que não esperava
A minha mãe tentava
Meu amigo julgava
Meu pai condenava

Fazes o cego ver
O surdo ouvir
O mudo falar
O perplexo dançar

Por tua culpa, negra
Hoje sou mais eu

Posso arder chamas no gelo
Levo frio ao forno
Alegria ao cemitério
E frieza ao inferno

Por tua culpa, negra
Sou mais feliz
Felicidade que me alegra
Do tamanho do meu nariz

Tudo isso…
Por tua culpa, negra!

Angola
Fabious Benfiquista

És tu a minha esposa
O amor dos meus amores
Mais linda que uma rosa
Também rica em sabores e dissabores

Eu sou Angola
Onde sou rico com tanta pobreza.
Tu, Angola, fizeste-me gabarola
Para uma falsa proeza

Tu és Angola
Em ti encontro a minha alegria
Mas, carambolas!
O que por ti não faria?

Nós somos Angola
Onde somos ricos mesmo sem ser
Na inocência do sorriso de um pobre ser
Com esperança na arte do bem viver

Seria Bom
Fabious Benfiquista

Seria bom que fosse bom
Ouvir aquela música sem som
Mesmo em outro tom
Cantar mesmo sem ter dom

Seria bom se eu soubesse
Que só amaria quem tivesse...
Amor de quem mais quisesse
Ser amado e sem stress

Seria bom caminhar no alto
Nesta terra de planalto
Com aquela mulher de salto alto

Seria bom se as crianças soubessem
Que o futuro não existe
E que por mais que a lua e as estrelas desaparecessem
Apenas o presente persiste

Seria bom que não fosse fatal
Que hoje fosse natal
Que o homem não fosse mortal
Que eu fosse chamado o tal.

Voces me tornaram assim

Fernando Paciencia Luteiro Palaia

Voces me tornaram assim:
Nos Génesis da minha criancice comecei a mamar o leite materno
com sabor de guerra...   E aprendi que quando uma ovelha se
transforma em carnívora é porque ja sentiu o sabor amargo da erva.
Voces me tornaram assim   Voces me tornaram assim
me ensinaram que quando o governo inaugura um chafariz é
motivo de alegria   E que quando se constroem escolas é um gesto
de filantropia.
Voces me tornaram assim

Me ensinaram a aplaudir e gritar viva mesmo quando nao entendo
nada...
Pois quando reclamo as minhas heresias sao jogadas a beira da
estrada...

Voces me tornaram assim   Voces me tornaram assim
No lugar de imaculado plantaram em mim uma alma maquiavélica e
perversa.   Todavia eu aprendi o a e i o u sentado numa lata de leite
mesmo sem farnel, pois tudo o que eu tinha era a toalha da mesa.
E o vazio das panelas...   E me ensinaram que so é jovem aquele
que empurra um cigarro na boca e que afoga as suas magoas num
gole de cerveja.

Voces me tornaram assim:

Quando jogaram a minha felicidade numa lista negra   ...
E me ensinaram que quando eu marco um passo com sabor de
victoria é mais um prego que se enverga...
Voces me ensinaram assim
Voces me tornaram assim

Me ensinaram que o melhor massagista é o purete que chicotea sob
o corpo de uma zungueira...   Voces me tornaram numa criança
precoce e perversa
Voces me tornaram assim.

Maus trilhos de África

Guilson Silvano Saxingo

Quando voltares à terra
Ó Rei das ideias!
Bani toda a guerra
      Que hoje é o nosso carrasco
Prostituíram a fraternidade
A solidariedade foi despida
Quebraram a honestidade
E a verdade ao abismo foi lançada

Por influência dos forasteiros
Silenciaram as vozes da discordância
E, de provação, em provação
A opulência tomou conta de muitos
Só ouvem a voz da ganância

Salvemos de toda a demência
Os países que nos conflitos jazem
Enquanto eles se cobrem de mantos estrelados
Nós continuamos a trajar-nos de mwlamba

Enquanto eles vão nascendo em berços de ouros
Nós nascemos em palhotas
E as nossas criancinhas
Sem um teto, nem terraço, só em tocas…

Basta a guerra
Avante a PAZ

Nesta África tão sofrida
Minh'alma tão dolorida
Augura um voto final
Para todos, todos nós
Uma mesa de cristal!

271

Cidade diamante
Guilson Silvano Saxingo

Terra terna matreira
No chilrear dos pássaros
Que entoam hinos em coro sem freio
No manso avesso confesso

Atento aos encantos do teu andar senhoril
Que anuncia a esp´rança
Na ânsia
Do crescimento a porvir
Com verdadeira bonança
Sem mácula a banir

Oh Saurimo!
Cidade diamante
Radiante
Com o gingar cintilante

Te encontro nas quedas do Chihumbwe
Te reencontro na Mwana Pwo sem pejo
Te vejo de Alentejo
Te revejo em Catoca

Terra da cianda e mapopo
Terra da mukanda e matamba
Terra da felicidade…

Minutos Recordes

Ismael Ambrósio Dias Farinha

Segundos, minutes, é o tactear do meu relógio no tic tac da hora
certa em alerta,
O tempo passa, avança me cansa e me abraça.
Não danço salsa nem tango muito menos kuduro, para desanuviar
reflicto no conflito aflito.
Os contractados estão no up and down para que equilibrem a
balança dos minutos recordes.
Assim é a vida incrível, o invisível aprecia os cambalachos dos
humanos na terra cheia de guerra.
Haja calma e paciência para sanarmos os nossos problemas que nos
afligem no dia-a dia nestes minutos records

A morte
Ismael Ambrósio Dias Farinha

A morte é um corte impecável não agradável, momentos bilingues
inéditos, e os anjos cumprem com os seus trabalhos questionando a
nossa vivencia, e o tumulto é tanto que cria espanto.
A morte não tem volta, ninguém deseja morrer porque somos
pecadores, nossos legados falaram por nós, feitos e defeitos
palpitando o aroma do mundo do além.
E o Altissimo lembra nós "o mundo é passageiro e todas coisas
existentes nele"
Ai de nós que se nos deixarmos enganar com as futilidades penosas.
A morte não tem volta.

A carta das lagrimas

Joel Fernandes

Um rosto cheio de lagrimas
Lagrimas de uma criança
Lagrimas de um povo
Lagrimas de sofrimento
Lagrimas de dor
Lagrimas Cai no ocidente
Lagrimas comove o mundo
Da primavera árabe
Levou-me pensar
Levou-me escrever
Levou-me a chorar, porque lá
Levou -me bater as portas lá
Com a carta das lagrimas
Com o propósito da vida.

O contraste da vida
Joel Fernandes

O LHANDO NO MEU ROSTO

CHORO ESPACO DO AMOR DA MINHA VIDA

O LHANDO NO MEU ROSTO

 JÁ NÃO SO MESMO ATRAENTE COMVENCIDO NO MEU
EU,

O LHANDO NO MEU ROSTO

 SINTO O APERTO DA POBREZA DA VIDA.

O LHANDO NO MEU ROSTO

MEU OLHAR ASTUTO SEM LAGRIMA PARA DERRAMÁ-
LA

O LHANDO NO MEU ROSTO

 ONDE AVAIDADE AVELICE UNIRAM TRACOS DA
JUVENTUDE NO MEU BEIRAL

O LHANDO NO MEU ROSTO

A SAUDADE E ANGÚSTIA ASSOLAM O MEU ROSTO SEM
APOIO DOS MEUS FILHOS

O LHANDO NO MEU ROSTO

SINTO O CONTRASTE DA VIDA NO TEMPO DO AMOR
DA MINHA VIDA

Um sorriso no rosto

Levita Estanislau Neto

Eu só quero ver um sorriso
Sorriso no rosto daquela mãe
Um sorriso no rosto daquela irmã
Daquele pai
So quero um sorriso no rosto
Porque cada sorriso no rosto
É mais um ano de vida
Então bota um sorriso no rosto
Um sorriso para alegrar o meu dia
Um sorriso para trazer harmonia
Ofereça um sorriso
e bota um sorriso no rosto
Um sorriso no rosto daquela criança que chora
Bota um sorriso no rosto daquela mãe que ora
Hoje eu so quero um sorriso no rosto
No rosto do adolescente
Que com poucos anos de vida
ja trocou a magia
De uma bela sorrisada
Pela amargura da vida
Eu quero um sorriso no rosto
No rosto Daquela mulher
Que ja trocou o encanto
De um lindo sorriso
Pelas chagas das mágoas
 e apertos das decepções
Eu quero um sorriso no rosto
No rosto daquela mãe que sacrifica a vida para lutar pelos filhos
E que não conhece o poder do sorriso
Por causa das malambas da vida
Eu so quero um sorriso no rosto
No meu
No teu
E no rosto de todos nós
Sorria
Sorria para ti
Sorria para mim
Sorria para o mundo

Bota um sorriso no rosto
Para libertar a dor
Bota um sorriso no rosto
Para sentir o calor
Bota um sorriso no rosto
Porque sinônimo
De sorriso é Amor...

Amar é loucura
Lorna Telma Zita

Tu és a minha maior loucura
É assim que eu me sinto quando te vejo
Sem o teu amor, eu não tenho mais cura
Tu és tudo o que estava a procura
Nessa vida tão triste encontrei-te toda pura
Do amor mais faminto tu és o meu desejo.

Do meu rosto sombreado de lágrimas e amor
Dos dias que fico feito criança sorridente
Nos teus lábios eu ganhei luz e calor
Pois, descobri que o teu amor me tornou dependente.

Tu és o meu maior vício.
Do qual não tenho a cura
Se houver fim irei até ao inicio
Se precisar de mim eu estarei a tua altura.

Eu vejo no teu olhar sem querer me apaixonar por nada
Mas, com a minha teimosia acabo apaixonada
Com o meu robusto medo de que serei abandonada
Mas quem foram os que inventaram o nada?
Se nada nessa vida faz sentindo sem asnada
Só depois de perder é que pensamos e valorizamos o passado.

A prostituta

Lorna Telma Zita

Eu sou a prostituta
Aquela que não tem valor
Aquelas que todas mulheres tem pavor
A destruidora de lares
A que é vista com maus olhares.

Sou eu sim, a dita, a falada
A que vende o corpo para sobreviver.
Sou mãe, sou filha
Mas deixo o meu lado sentimental
Fazer o que ? se o meu lado profissional é que me sustenta.

É por ganância sim, pobreza.
É pelo meu futuro que faço isso.
Mas que futuro?
Cá nas ruas não há futuro.

Apenas dinheiro, sexo sem amor
Mulher de todos os homens,
Que usam, pagam e vão embora
Essa é a vida tão sofrida a que escolhi.

Mas se largo essa vida viverei de que?
Cá nas ruas iluminadas ganho a vida
Ganho desprezo cada vez mais, sou mulher.
Que não se da o respeito.

É difícil me entenderem que meu trabalho
É como um outro qualquer
Não quero que tenham pena de mim
Mas que me respeitem.

Que não seja apontada o dedo.
Nas ruas onde nasci
Nas ruas onde cresci
Peço respeito é o que mais desejo.

Porque querem que eu me cale?

Lorna Telma Zita

Se liberdade não oprime
Se liberdade é cantar, por vezes gritar sem medo
Se liberdade é pensar, falar o que eu sinto sem que seja nenhum
crime
Mas cá no meu pais, sempre soube que a verdade tem sabor azedo.

Oh liberdade, onde é que te escondes
Uivo feito um lobo enfurecido, mas não me respondes
As vezes tento falar, mas alguns fingem que não me entendem
E a pouca liberdade que me resta prendem.

Vivo na escravidão do silencio
Onde a vida tem seu preço
 E me calo porque sei que a justiça cá, não tem nenhum apreço.

Porque querem que eu me cale?
Querem que eu continue sendo esse escravo do silencio?
Não! Não posso mais
Quero liberta-me.

Quero expressar-me sem medo
Onde ninguém possa me apontar o dedo
 Conquistar, viver sem segredo.

Poema I
Magno Domingos

Não vão perceber a tua dor
Ninguém vai compreender as tuas lágrimas
Nem a tua fome será sentida por outras barrigas.
O teu cambalear, ainda será motivo para risadas
O cair das tuas calças, quando a tua cintura já não suportar cinto
algum, aproveitarão para dizer "está bêbado de novo".
O teu falar asilabado, será visto com humor, "ele gosta de fazer rir",
dirão.
Quando gritares "socorro" entenderão como se estivesses a contar
outra história lá dos tempos do mato. "Ele é assim mesmo", dirão.
Mas quando tombares encontrarão culpas em ti. Não haverá outro
culpado do teu tombo.
Porquê que ele não pediu uma bengala? Não sou "aleijado" mas até
tenho duas em casa.
Porquê que ele não segurou aquela parede? Estava proxima.
Porquê que ele não descansou naquela sombra? Era mesmo ja aí.
Ele não me chamou, não me chamou porquê? Eu viria socorrer,
sempre vim.
Sentirão raiva. Mas tanta raiva de ti, por não terem percebido que ja
não aguentavas mais, que a sirga ficou pesada e que estavas a ruir.
Sentirão raiva. Mas tanta raiva de ti, por não terem compreendido a
linguagem do teu bocejar.
E serás o culpado do teu ruir
Culpado dos teus esforços
Culpado das tuas lutas.
Como prémio, por tudo o que significaste
Reunirão condições
E por fim comprarão a melhor das urnas
As mais belas tulipas enfeitarão a tua morte
Farão o melhor e mais sentido funeral,
Desejarão que a tua alma, finalmente
Descanse em paz.

Poema II
Magno Domingos

A madrugada vieram as saudades
Perdi o controlo a procura de novidades
Sem dar conta liguei para ti
Sei lá, me perdi
Não, não liguei
Agudizei.
Coisas que o coração não controla
Tive até miragem
Vim com um truque que tirei da cartola.
Falei atoa
É que na minha mente a tua voz ecoa.
E recordo sempre da lagoa
Aquela aventura
Nós, ninguém segura
... Que loucura!
Mas desculpa
Juro, não se preocupa
Vou saber me controlar agora.
É que desde que foste não sou o mesmo
Até me atirei no misticismo
Pode parecer ilusionismo
Ou ateísmo.
Mas nisso do amorismo
Quem não se ocupa vai no alcoolismo.
E você ia querer me ver bebado?
Terias dito que fiquei juado
Que estou perturbado
Ou que ando magoado.
Epa, é saudade
Que trás ansiedade
Mas não é maldade.
Agora vou evitar a madrugada
Vou preferir a alvorada
Quando a mente estiver ocupada
Para não cometer mais borrada.
Desculpa

Poema III
Magno Domingos

Nasci no tempo em que o poder era popular,
Em que tudo era pelo povo
Em que sem providência cautelar
Se queria formar um homem novo
Nasci meses antes de Maio
No fervor que fez de Nito lacaio
Quando a nação em triste desmaio
Obedeceu ao médico garraio
Com o tempo a aura de um Santo
Levou-nos além do esperanto
E em línguas falamos o pranto
Que agora tornou-se o conquanto
O partido era único
Pensamento era afásico
Sofrimento era utópico
E o sonho perestróikico
De repente caiu o muro
Nós que ja estávamos no escuro
Rápido esquecemos o agouro
E a vida tornou-se um apuro
Partimos atrás do Jaguar
Queríamos nossos males atenuar
A terra apaziguar
E tudo novo conceituar
Nasci no tempo em que o poder era popular,
Em que tudo era pelo povo
Em que sem providência cautelar
Se queria formar um homem novo
Recordam o Santo que tinha aura?
Agora nos faz que nem escrava Isaura
Afinal o mal não era o Jaguar
Era o Santo que queria em nossas mentes madrugar
O solo saqueia saqueia
Dinheiro branqueia branqueia
A vida bloqueia bloqueia
Nos jovens batéia batéia
Frustrado prendeu quinze partes de min
Reuniu mais abutres ao festim

E em coro acusaram-me assim:
Tentativa de promoção
De ações que levariam a uma insurreição
Ou de uma situação
Em que ordem e a tranquilidade publicas seriam seriamente
afectadas, nesta Nação
Nasci no tempo em que o poder era popular

Criatividade

Marcelo Bernardo Maluarte Pedro

Esventrando o sentido das palavras
Perfurando as minas rochosas do carácter
Apercebo-me do reluzir da luz escura
Da permanente intermitência dos sentidos
Da penetrante ingerência dos pensamentos
Na mais fugaz das questões humanas
A inspiração…

Erógeno
Marcelo Bernardo Maluarte Pedro

Perduro em ânsia erótica
De sentidos excitados
Preciso de um bordel inteiro de pensamentos
Preciso a qualquer custo, aliviar minha tesão criativa
Ejacular violentamente poesia volumosa
Para já atrofiado, acomodar os nervos na abstracção
Contemplar a cópula na recordação!

Televivência

Marcelo Bernardo Maluarte Pedro

Orbitávamos imunes aos crimes
Imunes ao vicio
Ao trabalho
Habitávamos imunes ao espaço
Imunes a vizinhança
Ao contacto
Habilitávamo-nos a inércia
A corrupção
A inaptidão
Fechávamo-nos num mundo inelástico
Mundo inflexível
Televisionávamo-nos nos outros
Electroconectados
Televiviamos

Desafoga-Te
Márcia Rosel Chambule

Desafoga-te das lágrimas que ironicamente estupram-te os sorrisos,
Da ira que encharca-te o coração de sentimentos maléficos
Desafoga-te das dolências e consternações que sem escrúpulo
intoxicam-te a alma,
Dos fantasmas que rudemente fuzilam-te esperanças
Chore!
Sorria!
Chore de alegria e Sorria dos problemas
Deixa-te embrulhar pelo som do vento e dance sobre as ondas do
mar
Embriaga-te na inlúcida lucidez da vida
Namore um copo de whisky, de cerveja, de vinho e entrega-te aos
amenos prazeres da vida
Faça sexo suavemente com a vida e dê a ela múltiplos orgasmos
Ame
Abrace
Beije
Ame intensamente, sem porções
Abrace como se o fossem mutilar os braços
Beije com verdade e serenidade
Não deixe que o medo de viver
Tire-te a vontade de viver.

Revolta
Márcia Rosel Chambule

As vezes
Amassada pela insatisfação da dúvida, indago-me:
Mas afinal,q ual é a coerência da nossa existência?
Por quê vivemos
Se somos avassalados, açoitados e adulterados pela dor!
Se somos corroídos, supliciados e monarquiados pela fúria e pelo
rancor!
Que inferno pode ser mais horripilante que este,
Que incedia-nos ainda vivos
Sem rastos de cinzas!
Se partilhamos do mesmo sol
Por quê fulgura-se ele mais para uns e menos para outros!
Se perduramos debaixo do mesmo céu
Por quê para alguns é arco-irisado e para outros amargamente
ofuscante!
Tantos são os inocentes embriagados pelo vinho da culpa
Enquanto os culpados vão afogando-se no mar da inocência.
Não será a morte
O nosso palácio de paz
O refúgio para as nossas agonias e dolências!
Não será a tão idolatrada vida
Nossa madrasta
E a tão temida morte
Nossa mãe!

Entusiasmo
Márcia Rosel Chambule

E qual é que seria a lógica da vida
Se não iventassémos o que gostamos,
O que sacia a insaciável fome da alma.
O que banha de heterogênios prazeres a frigidez cálida do coração!
E de quê anuiria-nos a viver
Se não rebelassémos contra o que em coisa nenhuma nos acresce
E em tudo nos decresce
É primordial divorciar-se do medo
Viver sem metanoia
Deixar-se balear de virgens armas,
Para que não se divise a vida como um fardo
É primordial indenizar aos desejos da alma
Para que em nossas faces maculadas de angústia jorrem gracejos de
ternura,
Para que em nossas mentes não se tricotem filosofias banhadas de
letargias e auto-aniquilamentos.
É primordial desvendar receitas de mandiga para sorrir,
Sorrir sempre
Até que a alma tenha uma parada cardíaca de euforia.
De minguadas minhocas humanas,o mundo já se embriagou!

Sei Que Te Escondes Por Aí

Mohamed "Mociano dos Santos" Canhanga

Na cidade, no jardim
Na floresta, no capim
Na fragrância da jasmim
Aparece
Por mim

Sei que te escondes nalgum lugar
No rio, no mar
Na chuva, no ar
Num simples gotejar
Não tarda
Vou te encontrar

Sei que te escondes por aí
No tempo, no espaço
Num espaço de tempo
No calor, no abraço
De cada momento

Sei que te escondes nalgum lugar
Nas videiras, no vinho
Na árvore, no ninho
Deserto, caminho
No sol, sozinho

Sei que te escondes nalgum lugar
No céu, no paraíso
Ainda lembro
Teu sorriso, preciso
Saudades...

Escritos Libertários
Mohamed "Mociano dos Santos" Canhanga

Deixem passar
Apenas numa folha
Os escritos da liberdade
Será que dissolvem a autoridade?

Deixai-os publicar
Apenas escritos da liberdade

Para um povo que se oprime
É a boca da caneta
Contra a boca dum regime

Folha branca
Mente escrita
Nunca é crime
Apenas escritos de liberdade

Também vós tendes escrito:
"É a boca dum regime
Contra a boca da caneta"

E na mesma folha branca
A mente desperta!
Mostrar mensagem original

Contigo acordo
Bem perto da alvorada
Estás sempre acordada
Nas minhas noites de insónias
Passámos o dia
Vamos além do crepúsculo
Atravessámos barreiras, atravessámos pontes
Bela, de aparência desnuda
És contemporânea exibindo curvas
Contigo renasço
Contigo morro
A ti devo fidelidade
Minha futura esposa

Quinta_Feira
Mohamed "Mociano dos Santos" Canhanga

Chegaste
E contigo chega ela
É sob o teu enredo
Que finalmente posso vê-la
Não se acabe logo
Preciso sentir-la
E com meus própios dedos
Hei-de toca-la

Chegaste quinta
E com a tua chegada
Hei-de beija-la
Abrirei meu coração
Para que a possa amar
Para que não a largue,
Farei laços e nós

Chegaste
Mas no rosto veio a timidez
Teus olhos rasgados descrevem a fluidez
Do olhar mais belo que já enxerguei

Chegaste, quinta-feira
Sim
Chegaste
Mas nunca bastou o tempo de sentir teu cheiro
Por isso, aguardo
A tempo inteiro

Bem, antes de partires,
Já ficam as saudades!

Se eu parar pra pensar
Ngonga Salvador Luciano

Se eu parar pra pensar
De certeza que de ti vou-me lembrar
Se vieres em meu pensamento
De certeza que lembrarei de um lindo momento

Aí começarei a sorrir
Porque sonharei com você mesmo sem dormir
Pois nossas lembranças serão apenas lembranças divertidas
Gravadas em meu coração e jamais serão esquecidas

Se eu parar pra pensar
De certeza que meus olhos vão lagrimar
Se tiver triste o pensamento vai-me animar
Pois só você me enche de alegria ao ponto de me fazer chorar

Então vou querer começar tudo de novo
Te encontrar e viver novas aventuras
Te abraçar e permanecer ao teu lado sem que haja algum estorvo
E deliciar da tua companhia como se desfruta doçuras

Por isso sempre paro para pensar
Para pensar em ti
Porque eu te amo e você me faz bem
E os laços que nos unem vão muito além
Além de superficialidades
Além da falsidade
Aquilo que nos une é a mais pura irmandade!

Até Quando África

Ngonga Salvador Luciano,

Desde os primórdios que é reconhecida a tua beleza
Foste abençoada com uma rica natureza
Roubaste dos outros a atenção por causa da tua riqueza
Teu glamour era uma certeza!

Então vieram os saqueadores e roubaram o que te pertencia
Maltrataram teus filhos e levaram a tua alegria
Sem forças apenas lamentavas enquanto o caos acontecia
Até que uma brisa de mudança trouxe algum tempo de folia
Mas teus próprios filhos te jogaram um balde de água fria
E a suposta folia não passou de utopia!!!

Ganhamos a suposta independência
Mas o continente entrou em decadência
Expulsamos os forasteiros
Mas ainda assim aumentamos a violência
O nosso povo sofre com a carência
E apesar da riqueza ainda vivemos na dependência
Levamos nossa terra a verdadeira falência
Aqui a gente luta pela sobrevivência...

Agora questiono...
Até quando mãe África?
Até quando teus filhos gananciosos destruirão por causa da
ambição
Viverão lutando entre si vivendo em desunião
Levando a própria terra a destruição
Com líderes que acabam por ser sempre uma desilusão
Enquanto muitos continuam mendigando pão
Queria eu encontrar uma solução

Oh África minha!
Será que um dia uma geração verá uma África melhor
Longe da tirania e de todo terror
Sem guerra, fome, e livre do temor

Não sei se isso um dia acontecerá...
Mas carrego em mim a esperança de que um dia um povo verá

297

A solução para um continente alguém encontrará
E uma nova era alguém um dia trará!
Tenho muito orgulho em ser africano
Mas condeno e tenho pavor dos seus actos desumanos!

O Mundo
Obedes Lobadias

O mundo, hoje,
parece mais
um frigorífico
de esfriar
corpos,

e não mais
aquela velha
lareira
de esquentar
 almas.

(Se é que fora um dia)

Já não mais é
um coração
onde vivem
e crescem
os amores.

Folha-Dos-Ventos
Obedes Lobadias

Uma vez
A folha
tão seca de solidão
apaixonou-se pelo vento
e abandonou o seu ramo
e foi deixando de ser folha
em cada pedaço do tempo.
pois o vento só é fiel aos pássaros.
E é tão errante, que deixou a folha namorando o chão
Beijando as pedras e roçando o tempo.

E o chão (foi) desfolhando-a
dos poucos aos nadas
até folha, não mais ser
 - E o ramo,
nunca mais
foi buscar
a sua folha?
Não! Ele ficou receoso.
Com medo de que na sua saída
um rebento, urgisse em seu lugar
e perdesse logo
o aposento.

Ininteligível
Obedes Lobadias

ininteligível
é como nos dá medo a morte.

Se é viver
que nos oferece os maiores perigos.

Um ocidente em mim

Orlando Joaquim Ussaque

Apartai-se das balas
Embriagai sua alma
De santidade que não prolífera
Na metrópole dessa avenida.

Embrulhai de medo
Sua coragem de fracassar,
O tamanho da batalha
É surreal ao medo...
Anónimo a coragem.

Nesta guerrilha utópica
De nada vencer
Sobressai-se
O promotor...

E a escravidão legitima
Esta ausência presente
Em cada alma negra
Multi-facetada ao ocidente
Das bélicas inovações.

Ohh minha mãe…
Diz aos seus filhos:
O sangue negro é inviolável
Mesmo nesta descoberta
De partir
E não voltar a ti.

Resolução

Orlando Joaquim Ussaque

Se ninguém sustentar essa fúria
Então há fome.
Se há fome, não há batalha,
Conflito muito menos multi-opiniões,
Não há nada.
Se não há nada, há paz.

Profetizar
Orlando Joaquim Ussaque

Da insónia que me faz gente
Nasce o indigente
Que vive o mundo,
Cosmo e polita da liberdade
Que guia os prisioneiros.

Uma regra
Dois tabus
Uma ausência
Sua família
E tudo um pouco ausente
No quadrado que lhe chama
A reflexão.
O mundo
(Este círculo)
O palhaço
(eu)
A peça
(Minha pena).
Saudades
(minha gente)
Tempo
(passado que o futuro me reserva)

Esta e outras manias
Forças motrizes
Do condicionalismo
Que obedece a li-ber-da-de.

Gentes contra agentes
A gente contra gentes
Agentes contra a gente

Minha terra
A voz do comando
Que se foi.
Vive a presença
Um novo líder

Nascerá.

Paisagem
Rosa Ribeiro

Um lugar, uma miragem…,
Uma paisagem
Perdida no tempo,
Com o vento
Ou sem tempo,
O teu pensamento
Torna-se talento
Dos teus sentimentos.
Sentimentos que passam
E ficam sem cessar,
Que esmorecem no tempo
De quem os procura,
Na esperança de um dia
Os poder encontrar.
Perdidos e vazios
No fundo do mar,
Guardam em silêncio
O encanto do teu olhar.
Que brilha no tempo
Sem apagar,
Memórias e Historias
De encantar,
Que embalam
Nas ondas do mar,
Perdidas e achadas
Com o vento,
Reclamadas no tempo
Para acalmar,
Um momento
De afectos,
Sem magoar
O tempo e o momento
De quem os guardou…!

Filha do Tempo...
Rosa Ribeiro

Sou filha do tempo, Filha do vento,
Das tempestades frias e quentes
Que assolam o meu coração
Nas frias noites de inverno...
Mas o talento e o alento
Das tuas palavras,
Dão-me calor e alento
Que transformam
No meu único "Ser",
Um sorriso
Estampado no rosto,
Que permanece disposto,
Sem perguntas e impostos...
Só tu sabes,
O que me vai na alma
E na mente.
Muitos cobiçam e não sabem
A verdadeira razão
De um "Ser" quente,
E transparente
Que não sente maldade
Nem bondade
Mesmo quando está a beira do abismo...
Abismo são escuros e fundos
Sem luz
Nem mundo,
Mas a alegria de um ser
Passa somente
Em viver e acreditar
Que a mente
Não morre nem mente,
Quando sente a sede
E a fúria
De viver somente
Um dia cadente e ardente
Que queima por dentro
Quando tu não estás
Para me embalares

E abafares a minha fúria de viver...
Eu grito ao Mundo
E digo sem medo
O quanto Eu gosto de Ti...

Faixa De Gaja
Soberano Canhanga

Entre montanhas e a praia
Apenas savana e secura
Um túnel já sem distância
Ajuda quem por lá relaxa
Mais abaixo, a terra da promessa
Onde morre quem paus arremessa
Na vasta savana de relva escassa
Um bebedouro sedes aguça
Faixa da gaja
Entre montes gémeos e terra prometida
Caminho abaixo, a cova do umbigo
É entre saia e blusa!

Conte(...)São

Soberano Canhanga

Já fui locutor p'ra tua sede de notícias
Em tuas horas cultas fui poeta
Recitei Êça,
Camões e Vigário
Já fiz teatro,
Sátira e Comédia
Até colo emprestei
P'ra lágrimas que não provoquei
Chuva e frio enfrentei
P'ra te ver sorrir
P'ra saciar tuas fomes até exílio tentei
De repente,
Olho atento p'ro espelho,
Do cárcere me liberto
Reencontro-me e grito:
- Jamais!
Chega de patetices
Animador de tuas noites
Não sou mais!

Carta à minha Mãe Angola

Sónia Sousa Robalo

Minha Mãe...
Gosto de ti, como de quem precisa do ar que respira.
Gosto de ti, como de quem precisa da terra e do mar.
Gosto de ti, como de quem precisa de um abraço, como de quem
necessita de um beijo, como de quem almeja o seu espaço.
Como de quem salta o vazio e encontra o teu regaço.
Gosto de ti, porque não tenho medo, porque não minto em
segredo, dizendo que os teus filhos te respeitam.
Sinto uma dor na alma, porque esses filhos te mentem, dizendo que
te defendem...oh...Mãe, mas no fundo eles te agridem.
Os meus irmãos roubam constantemente o meu chão.
E eu sinto-me vazia...oh Mãe...não sei que mais sombras virão!
Não sei se teremos luz amanhã! Não sei o que sobrará!
Mas Mãe, tu deixas tanto de ti em mim.
A estrada ainda é longa, eu sei! Mas sabes...quando a espera não tem
fim, a distância não tem perdão.
Não sei quanto tempo falta, para nos olharmos como irmãos! Nem
sei o que restará de nós! Apenas sei...que me sinto só.
Matam os meus irmãos e eu fico com as mãos mais vazias de ti...
Escrevi o teu nome no Céu. Mostraram-me a promessa da
reconciliação.
E eu, estou aqui ao teu lado para lutar, com a paz no coração e uma
mensagem para contar.
Não sei lutar com armas, mas sei dar amor oh minha Mãe e tu
disseste que por isso seria forte.
Nos meus sonhos, beijas-me e abraças-me como o sol te faz a ti.
Mostras-me que só com amor e compreensão poderei ser útil ao
meu irmão.
E nós...como loucos...lutamos.
Estivemos tão perto e agora estamos tão longe.
De tanto querer, ficámos sem nada.
Oh Mãe Angola, o teu povo está a sofrer.
Tatuei o teu nome na Alma
Senti o teu beijo fiel
E mesmo com os ventos agrestes do sul
Eu estou aqui!
Tens tanto para me contar e os meus irmãos não me deixam ouvir.
Eu sei...deste-nos tudo e ficámos sem nada.

Mas eu...não desisto de ti OH MINHA MÃE ANGOLA.

Nós...

Sónia Sousa Robalo

Eu... Quando sou amplitude, sou a flor que desabrocha, calor que queima, o fogo da paixão. Quando sou a verdade, sou a parte que cabe, a pureza que invade, a fuga da ansiedade. Quando sou coragem, sou a sombra da tarde, a verdadeira liberdade, a força que arde. Quando sou amor, sou a doçura inquietante, da verdade possante, o ser vibrante.

Tu... Quando és amplitude, és a ternura indefinida, a explicação consentida, um sabor a luar na minha vida. Quando és a verdade, és a ternura concreta, da realidade certa, do silencio gritante. Quando és coragem, és o tsunami que varre, furacão valente, força envolvente. Quando és amor, és a melodia Angelical, o aconchego letal, uma verdade incondicional.

Nós... Quando somos amplitude, somos uma multidão, juntos na oração, presentes na solidão. Quando somos verdade, somos sentido coerente, de atitudes incandescentes, do certo e não do ligeiramente. Quando somos coragem, somos heróis de verdade, com força na saudade, impossível de travar na verdade. Quando somos amor, somos uma espécie de céu, estrelas ao léu... Verdades de mim, certezas de ti... Luz da noite, escuridão do dia... Somos a coerente incoerência da nossa verdade, onde mais ninguém cabe... Somos a vontade, a garra e a saudade... Somos o que é puro, forte e inseparável... Dois corações ligados, duas Almas numa, duas pessoas apaixonadas!!

Retrato Imortal

Tony Kunsevi

Pautei no meu coração
A alma nobre do seu amor de pai
Ultrapassei dificuldades
Lamentando os lamentos
Obstinados nos mais obscuros momentos

Kuduro das espectativas marcou
Ultimo momento da nossa vivência
Nasceu entre mim e a vida… o desespero
Sempre vagando no alheio com
Esperança tatuada de dor
Vida pintada no escalonar da alma malfada
Íntimo é o som que penetra os meus ouvidos.

Artista

Tony Kunsevi

Nascem talentos
No firmamento das artes
Para registarmos momentos
Com letras
Imagens
Sons
Movimentos.

Artista cria mundos
De seres irreais
Realizados num panorama místico
Onde se concretizam sonhos
Dançantes nas emoções
Impressões
Sensações.

O artista
erguer –se
bem alto das colinas do universo
E brilhar entre as estrelas

Porção Mágica Da Vida

Tony Kunsevi

Mulher assemelhas –te
Com a frisa fria
Que embala o amanhecer
Inocente dos Olimpo

Onde os deus
Cansados com a imortalidade
Buscam –te nos orvalhos
Grudados na orla das folhas
Caídas no leito
que a musa descansa

És o despertador
que desperta os sentimentos
ao longos das noites caladas por tormentos

Ardonas vidas
Com cintilantes sorrisos
No declive das palavras tidas
Como provérbios

És a porção mágica
Existente entre as nuvens
Que cobrem os seios
Da palavra mátria

És a actriz
E a sua ventre a matriz

Meu Pai, Meu País

Victor de Viriato

- Oh meu pai tenho medo!
- Luta meu filho, luta...

Aprendi o valor da CORAGEM,
Mas meu país a roubou.
Deixou meu corpo a tremer
Sem saber o que fazer.
Medo entrou no meu ser
De forma a comer
O pouco que restou.
E aqui estou com a coragem entre as pernas.

- Oh meu pai tenho medo!
- Luta meu filho, luta...

HONESTIDADE não tem preço,
Mas meu país a comprou.
Deixou meu coração na rua
Sem conhecer a cura.
Fome chorou na minha mente
De olho para beber
O pouco que restou.
E aqui estou com a honestidade no bolso.

- Oh meu pai tenho medo!
- Luta meu filho, luta...

Saber AMAR o meu,
Mas meu país a esqueceu.
Deixou meu sono as escuras
Sem sonho de ajuda.
Sede cantou na minha alma
De boca aberta a pensar
O pouco que restou.
e aqui estou com o amor por um fio.

- Oh meu pai tenho medo!
- Luta, Luta meu filho, que nem daqui a 50 os meus netos têm vinho.

Foi ontem, que teu olhar deixou de lutar
Victor de Viriato

Foi a noite…
Lágrimas percorreram o caminho do rosto
Em forma de gotas, que lentamente caíram.
Molhaste e provocaste um dilúvio de dor.
Mostraste que ainda existe esperança
Mas teu olhar molhado deixou de lutar.
Nasceste com uma missão de união
Num lar, que o destino queria acabar.
Tarefa difícil foste capaz de aceitar.
Escolheste Novembro para começar a lutar.
Tempo de chuva, para abençoar a tristeza do conto.
Fizeste com classe, para que a linha não rebentasse.
Ensinaste a valorizar a defesa, em nome do amor.
No momento certo a mais bela mudou o destino do lar.
Solitária de nome, com o destino bem riscado
Deste o brilho bondoso, com o olhar da íris.
Chamaste os anjos, com o poder da salvação.
Três batalharam, numa luta de valorização.
Mas só a natureza olhou sem vendar a visão.
A cor se foi transparente inundar a solidão.
Olhaste para o anjo, que ensinou a voar.
Perdeu as asas, porque andaste sozinha.
Assim foi a noite…
Aqueles por quem lutaste, aprenderam a ver
Mas não aprenderam a lutar, pelo que importa
Porque perder é a melhor solução
Por isso que ontem teu olhar deixou de lutar.

Tenho a pátria rasgada no peito
Victor de Viriato

Milhares tombados pela pátria
Lutaram de coração e mãos vazias
De palavras duras a boca enchia
A espera de lúcidas carícias
Mas inferno entornou sua raiva
Nos poucos que lhe puseram a prova.

Quem da raiva dorme dela morre
Porque o tempo é relógio maldito
Bandido da fala agora corre
Veneno no sangue já era dito
Mas morte de líder fica poema
Na esperança sagrada o ama.

Escolhido do poema mais novo
Numa visão duradoura de paz
Futuro arquitecto o nativo
No encanto de um bom capataz
Mas nomeado com tempo finito
Na morte a esperança o aceito.

Setenta e quatro dias depois nasci
Nação de medo deixa aflito
Bonita terra enquanto cresci
Tenho a pátria rasgada no peito
Mas acredito na fala do tempo
Nos gritos da caneta que limpo.

Renúncia
Virgílio Henrique Chilaule

Nesta terra
Que nem os céus brancos
Cabem para os santos,
Nem os santos entregarão
As suas almas aos ventos

Aos olhos teus,
Nascente de todas as correntes
E em minhas palmas
Doloridas de todas as dores
Desinteiro-lhes!

Se em poesia faz-se combate,
Em vida faz-se a arte!

Sala Mana
Virgílio Henrique Chilaule

Do mesmo Jeito que me trousse ao mundo,
Eu vou-me embora
Não vejo a hora
De rasgar a tua linha alba
Com as minhas garras frias e sujas
De regresso ao ventre
Que outrora me aconchegara

É nítida e lúcida a escuridão do teu interior
Do que a lúz do dia que se Despoja
Na disputa entre o sol e a lua,
Segando os meus olhos de criança

Não importa o tamanho da minha cabeça
Nem as gorduras que fazem do meu corpo
Um porco de gente

Estou de regresso a ti,
Como quem volta às origens,
Para que sintas os meus punhos e chutos
E renoves o nosso contacto placentário
Que permite a partilha da água que bebes
E dos alimentos que comes

Assim, terás a necessidade urgente
De me nascer novamente
E ouvirás pela segunda vez
Os gritos recem chegados
Aos teus ouvidos ensurdecidos
De tanto me ouvirem chorar

Mesmo assim, vou me embora
Para que me possas nascer
Numa nova terra.

Geração alagada
Virgílio Henrique Chilaule

Pedimos boleia nessa longa travessia
Onde a nossa imagem de gente
Prende-se na miragem dos que pilotam
O barco a vela chamado Moçambique

Pedimos boleia para outra margem
Nem que para isso,
Tenhamos que pagar portagem

Estamos inundados
Pelos mares libertados
Pelos nossos próprios poros

Nossas sombras túrgidas
Desconhecem a osmose
Dos nossos corpos
Flácidos e saturados de sal

Irmãos!
Afinal de contas,
Em qual dos mandatos
Virá o barco vazio para nos buscar?

Pedimos boleia...

Ânsia
Daniel Da Purificação

i se fosse a primeira vez que te visse...

i se fosse a primeira vez que te visse
passar pela rua...

te assobiaria
te olharia com lascividade
nao duvidaria em falar contigo
com a clara intenção
de
sussurrar-te palavras bonitas ao ouvido

mas

que te convidassem a indecências no meu leito
pois
sabemos que a tua figura estimula os meus sentidos
somente
que
pela
teimosia que me caracteriza
eu
me
desafiaria a mim mesmo
a
medir a proporcionalidade da tua bunda
com
a
capacidade do teu cerebro
para
desejar que o momento nao seja efímero

mas

como quebrar as correntes do passado?
de facto
insisto perguntando
seria isto possível?

Ai…

Aqui está o perturbado momento de querer que esta a primeira vez
a
primeira vez que te visse
por isso mesmo
demonstra que tens magia
i
eu sei que tens magia
i
eu sei que és dona do tempo
i
eu sei que fazes as coisas acontecer
como
se fosse a primeira vez…

Poema
Daniel Da Purificação

Esta
é
a poesia que conhece i desconhece as metáforas que encontra
ironias nos desencontros
é
a poesia do silêncio proíbido dos passos no caminho da fome alheia
é
a poesia de ninguém porque não se escreve e não se fala
é
a poesia que nunca carregou nem sentimentos que nunca nasceu
mas só teve o nome que a puseram
é
a poesia que não tem ódio mas tem olhos a que não dói nem se
sente a que sempre duvida mesmo nas suas certezas a que nada quer
mas que tem desejos de si mesma e em si mesma
Esta
é
a poesia que nao teve gosto que nunca teve cor
é
a poesia que mataram quando a rasgaram e a despedaçaram os que
sempre entenderam da vida do homem a mulher a natureza e seus
mistérios
é
a poesia que nunca existiu e que nunca se escreveu
Esta
é
a poesia do nada estas são as palavras do vazio esta POESIA é a
voz do caos esta POESIA é a indiferença ao medo esta POESIA é a
olhada ao tempo que chegará...

Part 11: French Poems

1°)
Sami Tchak

Ici, avant ta naissance, coulait une rivière fougueuse et poissonneuse. Aujourd'hui, l'herbe en a effacé jusqu'au lit. Écoute ! Écoute les murmures du ruisseau à jamais tari ! Regarde ! Regarde au loin, comme des mirages, la danse de ton passé !

2°)
Sami Tchak

Durant des années, mes nuits furent peuplées par l'image d'une femme nue, m'adressant de tous les espaces intérieurs et extérieurs de sa vie, de larges sourires qui disaient toute la profondeur de son âme, avant, parfois, de se métamorphoser en une tourterelle ou en un corbeau et de s'éloigner en me promettant de revenir, sans jamais préciser l'heure de ce rendez-vous mystérieux. Parfois, dans un demi-sommeil, je la voyais sensuelle sous la douche, l'eau en jets puissants sur son corps, la vapeur créant comme un halo érotique qui l'enveloppait d'une pudeur que j'eusse voulu ôter d'un geste impatient comme on lève le voile. Il me fallut du temps pour comprendre qu'en vérité remontait ainsi de mon inconscient l'univers de mon enfance là-bas au village, qu'il s'agissait donc d'un succube qui charmait l'incube que j'étais devenu. Je me laissai alors gagner par une nostalgie transformée en une lumière crue sur mon âge. Me convaincre qu'en vivant chez soi ou ailleurs, l'on habite toujours le pays de son enfance, cela ne me suffisait plus pour panser ma blessure, celle née de la certitude que, sans y avoir été forcé, j'avais perdu ma patrie.

3°)
Sami Tchak

Sentier qui, au village, de notre concession, nous conduisais à nos champs, dis-moi : combien sont-ils déjà, celles et ceux qui, aujourd'hui tous morts, t'avaient, avant et après moi, emprunté pour aller quêter auprès de la terre de quoi se sustenter ? Peut-être de l'homme que je suis devenu, tu ne gardes point de souvenir. Il est probable que mon odeur ait disparu de ta mémoire. Vois-tu ? Moi non plus je ne me reconnais pas. C'est pourquoi je tente de me recréer dans mes livres.

Untitled

À ma mère

Armel Fernand Mbida Ebo'o

Je suis né dans ton sein mere,
J'ai grandi a l'ombre de ton amour
Petit creature je fus ta joie et celle des tiens
Mes premiers refuges furent ton sein
Je me souviens de tes sourires, de tes mains,
Qui me couvaient, je me souviens de leur parfum
Il etait celui d'une mere qui suais sans relache,
Une ouvriere infatigable qui se tuais a la tache.
Je me souviens de ton sourire ;qui de tous les sourires au monde
etait le plus doux.
Tes coleres pour nous etaient du miel,
Et pour rien au monde nous n'aurions manqué ce bout de ciel.
Mais en toi gisais un lourd secret,
Jusqu'a la fin tu as lutté, mais jamais,
Tu n'as montré de signe de faiblesse face au mal qui allait
t'emporter, tu t'es eteins comme une sainte
Le visage radieux, tu as simplement fermé les yeux,
Un chapelet dans la main, comme une image peinte
Tu n'as pas voulu que tes enfants, tes oeufs
Voient comme Elizé, ton ame monter aux cieux
Femme, noire, mama, femme au coeur d'ivoire
Tu a été rappellé au Pere,et quitté ce monde noire
Me laissant tes sourires qui au monde patient les plus doux
Et cet amour manquera a jamais a tes enfants et a ton epoux.

Untitled

Armel Fernand Mbida Ebo'o

Je suis jugé a cause de ma couleur de peau,
Noire,je suis,comme une feve de cacao.
A longueur de journee je porte ce fardeau.
Des siecles de traite,ou,capturé,enchainé
Arraché aux miens,vendu tel du betail
Nous etions au plus bas du regne animal
Plus de cent ans a maculer les champs
De canne à sucre,de blé, coton et nos enfants
Etaient pour les leurs des animaux de compagnie
Notre sang repandu sur la fleur de coton
Nous recevions pour salaire, fouet et coup de baton
Alors quand au ciel nous elevions nos voix
Naquit du gospel a l'intention du Dieu sur la Croix
Peuple interdit du reste des hommes
Vivant toujours de leur aumone,
Viennent les jours ou, l'homme noir Accablé par tant de souffrance
Se levera de et portera en lui l'espoir
De tout un peuple exploité par la blanche
Quand viendront donc les excuses des colons
Les memes encore chez nous, tiennent le baton
Vous etes libre,vous etes independant
Mais toujours vous tirez les ficelles et renversez nos
gouvernements
Cessez de creer la division chez l'homme.
Nous sommes tous freres et pas des betes, en somme,
Laissez nous respirer cet air frais et leger
Qui rassemble les peuples et a pour nom liberté.

330

Untitled

À Rocío
Armel Fernand Mbida Ebo'o

Je me sens si fragile mon amie
Je me sens si las.
Cette fleur qui se meurt.
A besoin d'etre nourrie, une liqueur
Qu' elle s'abreuvre aux sources de Eros
Pour renaitre tel le phoenix, des cendres de Milo
J'aime une femme qui est a l'autre
Bout du monde
Sa voix est pareille a une ode
Chantée pour nous les hommes
Ô belle nymphe des forets azteques
Fille du serpent a plume, dieu meteque
Couvre mon corps de ta chaleur
Et mon coeur de tes baisers.
Donne moi de vivre pour tes sourires
Parle moi de toi, de ce qui te fais plaisir,
Je t'aime est si facile a dire
Mais aimer, est si merveilleux a vivre.
Tu vis en moi bel oiseau, pose toi sur mon coeur et rend le plus
beau.

Marine par temps calme, 1646

Samira Negrouche

De ciel à voile
le vent qui tend et froisse
l'un attend patiemment
le retour du voyage
l'autre scrute telle roche
dénudée
tel éclat de nuage
à heure ascendante
des verres tintent
dans ce pays-là
les gens
cultivent la mer.

Cours d'eau, effet du matin, 1824

Samira Negrouche

Il y a un instant
dans l'aube qui pointe
ce on ne sait quoi
qui se fige
et retient son souffle
rien ne frémit à l'horizon
ni les ondulations de l'eau
ni même l'ombre naissante
il y a dans cet instant-là
le désir furtif
d'une éternité.

Ménerbes, 1954

Samira Negrouche

Ouvre un petit coin blanc
et construis un ciel
vertical si tu veux
estival et hivernal à la fois
qu'importe
creuse ton champ
cultive-le sur du sable
ocre et chaux s'épousent bien
hors saison
et pour les pentes ?
hachées ou granulées
saupoudrées miel
mais surtout
surtout
n'oublie pas de tailler
une barque à ta mesure
un souffle d'horizon.

Part 12: Best "New" African Poets 2015 Collaborations

Peaceful Conflict in the Land of Utopia
19 poets

Dawn hit me * *Charles Orji Nonso*
with its usual gifts of cinnamon fragrance
Abandoning its call, I tow the unfamiliar trail of arrogance
Ignoring the way of my instructors
I set about to justify my dark cravings
Defiant and daring in my focused quest
Rejecting all desperate pleas for a retrace
In a land where conflict is alien
I want to pioneer what my fathers never did
In this state of ideals, my ideas must be idealized

Oh! The perfection of ideals * *Chuma Mmeka*
where we wield words not wars
Restrained in our fraternity
One people in mien, in mentality
We are one another's keeper-
The strong lives for the weaker
And none is the other's reaper;
We're free and that's truly better
Enjoying a world of inventions,
With no guns, spears nor arrows

The sun is hung and cannot be returned * *Archie Swanson*
the river has run its course
There is blood crusted dust
Between our toes
And the cry of the infant child in our ears
But there is also music
The clapping
The dance
The smile
The fragrance of approaching rain
Swelling our lungs again

Because I write * *Christine Coates*
to elephants and trees, and to stars
And to the oceans of fish
My heart no longer beats rough and ready

The river and stars fill the valley
And I am in it
A hymn some days

To be sung in every lip and clime *Godswill Chigbu*
to be known in every land and time
Write to the tendrils and to the root
The hymn Agu Dube sung
The thoughts the sages' thought
The cause our father fought
That one day in Mandela's land
Where Achebe grew in story kind
We shall be free even in our mind

Eyes are mirrors of hope we want to see * *Chenjerai Mhondera*
that mankind is not in war again!
I see peace like a sea permanent still
The cries of civil wars and rebels cursed by
Conscience of mankind saying no
To stabbing one another
Maybe tomorrow is our celebrations;
Today cymbals and tambourines
Loud being tasted, are brought together
As we march through greens of imaginations
Shall it be a myth or reality, after all?
It's not yet time for answers. Let's all think!

And in this land of utopia * *Christopher Kudyahakudadirwe*
we shall never forget
Those who get angry
On behalf of our leaders
And end up lashing out at us
The innocent, the poor and the voters
On their shiny black boots
Our teary faces we shall see
While they trample and kick "sense"
Into our brainwashed brains

Tearing bones from our flesh of patriotism * *Osinachi*
wielding hammers of words, hours of threats
Bound in the love-lacking blue constitution-

Constituting a colony that is only theirs
Where human rights are a whistle in their mouths
Yet smoke in our hands:
They stifle love by placing loud words in adult's bedrooms
They cause wars by spraying religious words like insecticide,
Seeking to crush the new lovers like mosquitoes,
Saying they suck away their forefather's morality

The genesis of this nemesis, * *Akinlade Oluwaseyifunmi*
on our leaders' we placed
Our heroes' past isn't past
If in one accord we speak
Form into the void;
And reform our thoughts
We are the leaders,
The future of this world.
It's not fictional, Utopia's conflict
Should be for peace....

Darkness washed over us * *Sheril Guzha*
sending a cold chill down our spines
Fear and doubt curled inside us and clung in our ribs setting
Uncomfortably in our chest
Large pillows of clouds were forming
Blotting out the old-gold colour of the sun
Heavy raindrops, nectar of the gods
Fell on the sun parched earth and
Lightening lit the sky like a heavenly photographer
Each second seemed to last an eternity,
As we trudged out of the gates of the past
We bit our lips, pleading with anxiety not to deter us
from becoming angels of our better nature
The elders bound the chains of the iron gates, finally and
The raindrops faded into musical chime
We dared not to look back, waving our flags,
singing our anthems and ready to start anew

As we plant our feet on the ground * *Cláudia Cassoma*
as we leave our footprints in the past and enter the land
As we get ready to finally stand

To finally enjoy the years of cultivation
Feel the damp earth by the sweat of our people
As we starve off segregation
This time with no complication
As we feel it burn from inside
The sun of this awaited utopic land
Happiness where we spent our toil
Fortune, finally on our soil

I see generations * *Jackson Matimba*
drowning in a river of gushing honey
As they traverse to beg for food in the neighbouring country
The river originating in our land
But overloading over the frontier
Our people expiring from hunger
Because fruit trees are too lofty to reach
The land is strewn with festering fruit the flies and monkeys
The bee hives have screens of bees armed with riffles
When shall we construct a dam to harness our honey river?
We don't have to chop the fruit trees to obtain our dinner
The kingdom is full of honey, fruit and every nutriment
But how shall we end these muted contentions rocking the
paradise?

Remember how days were familiar * *Emily Achieng*
the pleasure of tracing steps,
we do not really choose our thoughts
or where memories fall
for they come, but all at once
To study hours and deeply retain the focus
through the line that cuts beyond infinity
beyond the swirl of an empty glass, beyond ebony darkness
Time feels strange.

Yes, the story unfolds * *Edward Dzonze*
we can endure nights longer than our sleep
but we cannot endure sleep longer than the nights upon us
We grope, we fall but that's not all
We rise to go but sometimes we fall again
We might not see but we sure know
Africa will someday conquer its miseries,

It shall dawn in Africa as it dawned in America
and the lines will be read to the children of Africa
Yes, the story will be read to this end

I dare to dream * *Kariuki wa Nyamu*
of a world where we'll embrace sobriety in politics
of a world where tribalism will be extraterrestrial
of a world where we'll abhor religious fundamentalism
of a world where civil clashes will be affably resolved
I dare to dream.

We like broken glass   * *Taijhet Nyobi*
and bitten nails,
we discarded ourselves as such,
one big pile of multi-stained glass
dripping liquor and our parents'
tears we dared drink,
that mountainous and jagged heap
of convictions we were,
cutting anyone who dared to mount us
of all this toughness gathered,
of teeth split on the backs of curses
for what now?
how do we hold this new tranquility
we knew would come?
I am wading through the ruin looking for all the shattered pieces,
but I have become so unlike myself,
we have become so alike in this way.
I cannot tell which of the hurt parts are mine.
maybe some of us are to be an artifact of the past.
guardians of an historical perspective,
protectors of sacred burial sites.
In our utopia we can't forget our ancestors
let us weave all the names we lost to injustice
in the fabric of our town making.
Street names, parks, the second names of our children…
Utopia is not an undoing or a forgetting!
It is to graciously and intentionally step into a righteousness,
understanding the ever present incompatibility of selves and
identities. —

I hear * *Tendai R. Mwanaka*
the call of light in the paternal delights,
Maternal delights of grandmothers and grandfathers
The joys of motherhood and fatherhood
The wild mix of love and fear in daughters and sons
The scenes of family love in brothers, sisters, cousins, aunts,
uncles, friends, in-laws. As we buzz through the remaining
yards like rumour. Let us arrive in this land of utopia
with all our babies, teens, adults, our hopes, our dreams.
Let us arrive in this land of utopia with our pride, our stories,
our laughter, our songs. Let us arrive in this land of utopia....
With trust in our hearts to again allow the song

Utopia's rein shall prevail forever, * *Yolanda kumalo*
from bone to bone, flesh to flesh,
Blood to blood and generation to generation.

Arranged by Christopher Kudyahakudadirwe and Tendai R. Mwanaka

342

I Can Still See
Cláudia Cassoma, Sheril Guzha and Tendai R. Mwanaka

Even with my better half, with less melanin
Because of my peevish hair
My reality is still one I can't bare
And since I chose not to multiply
He thinks his bullets can now fly
He hides his truth as he ends ours
Giving reasons for dry flowers * *Cláudia Cassoma*
One hundred and two times
One hundred and two times
One hundred and two prides

Many of my friends' lives were cut short
A few made it back home, lost in foreign lands
An eternal soldier who fought with all his might
The tiny piece of torn flag that I kept in my pocket * *Sheril Guzha*
Gave me hope, a hope in a child's heart
Not yet turned into stone
They promised that a banquet
Would be thrown at our arrival
My lover's fears were fulfilled as she embraced me in her arms
Fickle fate knows no God

And my voice is now horse from all I have delivered
In darkness they have chosen to live
Preaching Satan's controversial teachings
Sufficient, insufficient knowledge, they boast of *Tendai R. Mwanaka*
And remain to the call deaf, dumb, blind…
And insinuate your wise teachings
Opposing to their own destruction the truth
A people now destined to an everlasting death
What would the dust take back to the endower?
They consume alcohols like they do to water
And survive from drugs as if it's the sages' words

It's been decades since they gave me plastic medals
I am aging now; I cannot march together with the angry crowds
Or flee from the blood thirsty beasts that await
To devour us on the command of their masters *Sheril Guzha*

343

"Voestek! Go back to your homes."
As the bitter and dismal pack pushes and shoves
Its way past the armed peace enforcers
As I sit by the window like a wingless bird
I cannot fly in mad fits and rages

Despite what it took me to get here
Illusions aside: I still can see
Across the Atlantic, the bellies empty * *Cláudia Cassoma*
Tears are plenty. Giant sables trying to flee
Blood and missiles in the Mediterranean Sea
Poverty all over its horn
No rose, just thorns
I see more sinners than one god can save

I can still see the persecution
Why are young innocent people being slayed?
In the Sudan(s), the Congos, CAR, Burundi, Libya…
There is nothing they have done slyly
Nation upon nation, uprising * *Tendai R. Mwanaka*
Tribe on tribe, the massacre
People against a people, throttling
Unproductive violence and retaliation
Young infants dying from old people's wars
Living a life so horrible and traumatic
What have they done to deserve this life they live?
Demoniac, immoral, transgressive

My child sits next to me frail and sick
Nibbling the bread crumb that would serve * *Sheril Guzha*
As the sole meal for the day
Look closely into the blood shot eyes
And I hope you see what I still see

Spirit mediums, faith healers, witches
In your name they now caste and thieve
And lie to your people of plagues not there
On your people they sow and reap without kindness * *Tendai R. Mwanaka*
Honey dripping from their fat lying lips
Sacrificing you everyday, all their lives

344

Pockets now full of Judas' sweat

I am living to see the day when
Political religious, educational leaders
Passionately strive to attain the virtuous elements of Justice * *Sheril Guzha*
Equality, freedom and tolerance
Towards stability and mutual gain
For now I can still see the society rot

A leader now parasitic and corruptive
Milking people's trust and sweat
Fattening their pockets without a care
They trod upon the poor mercilessly
A man in dire distress, ceaselessly
Gazing into the void
This godlessness of our own age is now despair *Tendai R. Mwanaka*
Unimaginable brutality
A sickening depravity
Murder and robbery out for enrichment
Murder and robbery for pleasure's sake
From no one, from nothing, never shrinking
Spits and pollutes and puts to dire peril
The goodness society has toiled painfully to build
You think I don't see, do you?
No, I can still see
The wrongs you with a shameless ordour for wronging
Everyday to your fellows, do again and again.

Of Love & Sex In Africa

Akinlade Oluwaseyifunmi and Chenjerai Mhondera

He wrote her off.
Like bad writings,
Her opinions don't count..
The society grades her lower than she's worth, the man ranges over her, placing her under
When they ought to be
In one accord.
I have seen scenes of separation,
Regarding gender discrimination.
Like an anthem,
Every Nation sings hers.
Shouldn't there be solutions
To this fraction?
Tell me what to make of this song,
That women should hide on hides,
That those who woo them
Should equally rule them.
Isn't she the sweetest before they tied the knot,
How come she now taste sour?
I shudder in laughter
Your honesty isn't constrained,
And I love your twist and tales.
True Negs are hard
Today's Negros are only known by their skin.
The mathematical differentiation of the human gender,
Places the woman as the figure 8,
Whilst the man is simultaneously 1.
Akin,
I'm keen to know about that world yonder,
Where you said freedom on sex has to go a long way in Africa.
Were you talking about man over woman,
And man refusing to lay under woman?
Of course no!
You cried that Peter married James in the Land of Negroes.
And there I feared to disagree to agree in the valley of morality,
Far near god where even gods have goddesses,
Dogs and doggess alike.
Akin,

There's this woman, I always call aunt by day,
And sneak to make love with when night falls,
She is one or two years less mama.
Am I saying I'm hypocrite?
Oh no. I guess you got me right!
That if man be ashamed of making love to opposite sex of twice or
thrice older than him,
What more if man and man marry,
And woman and woman kiss & dance in shadows of romance?
I hate riddles,
But it is true I can't love and marry a dog,
And scream in sounds of romance!
I am a true Negro;
To sodomise is of Sodom and Gomorrah?
Unless I'm lesbian, gay or animalistic,
I am no billed break routes and be West in sex;
Making sounds of making love,
Cupping my manhood!
Tell me the chemistry of attraction & fusion of feelings in absence
of opposite sex,
And 'll laugh at the myth of man disgracing universe;
Male and female created alike....

Part 13: Best "New" African Poets 2015 Reviews And Poetics

A Cocktail of Verse: An appreciation of *Best "New" African Poets 2015 Anthology*

Christopher Kudyahakudadirwe

During an interview with Flora Veit-Wild, one of the most celebrated Zimbabwean poets, Dambudzo Marechera was asked the question: *what is poetry?* In his answer he chose to borrow an idea from T.S. Eliot and said 'poetry is an attempt to put into words what is inside a person emotionally, intellectually, imaginatively. The poet's job is to find the equivalent, the verbal correlative of a particular feeling'.* This is what the reader will discover when he/she picks up *Best "New" African Poets 2015 Anthology*. It is a cocktail of verse as varied as the backgrounds from which the poets have emerged from. The anthology has 214 poems written by 79 poets from over 23 African countries and the diasporas in three languages; English, French and Portuguese. These poems feature a myriad themes and styles. The result took the form of a big African beer-pot frothing with portent offerings that have left this reviewer spoiled for choice as to which poems to include in this review. However, the heartening thing is that most poets zeroed more on politics, gender, sexuality and life in general.

The first poet who deserves discussion is Lekpele M Nyamalon. In his poem entitled 'Dig the graves', Nyamalon evokes the spirits of some of the great leaders who have come out of Africa. This is a free verse poem that rebukes death for taking away true sons of the continent. The persona in the poem says, 'I want to … burst the graves/and hold the bones of our fathers'. He/she is regretting why great leaders such as Lumumba, Sankara, Cabral, Nkrumah, Nyerere and others died before solving Africa's problems. Simply put the speaker is inviting Africans to embrace and share the spirit that these leaders had for the success of the continent. Such lines as 'Tell Nkrumah and Toure the table is set/oh Nyerere your seat is kept' remind the reader of how wistful the poet is about the leadership that has gone forth. The poem resonates with Pan-Africanism which, however, seems to elude most African leaders today.

351

Mike Kantey in 'A Vision of Peace' prompts the reader to consider the prospect of a peaceful existence in 'the Promised land'. He uses the motif of the Israelites to ferment a yearning for peace. The persona says that the people to whom peace has been promised find themselves 'caught between sleeping and waking' and this is reminiscent of the political malaise that is currently being experienced in African countries such as Zimbabwe, Somalia and Libya where those who find themselves at the political front do not have the political impetus to allow peace to prevail for the benefit of the people they govern. Thus people are left hanging failing to enjoy the peace and freedom that was fought for. This poem speaks to other poems in the anthology, for example, 'Relegation' by the same poet. 'Relegation' is an indictment of African leaders who cling to power and do not want others to take over even when they are incapacitated. The narrator urges such leaders to 'watch from the stands' while others pick up from where they left. In this poem the poet employs rhyme and therefore it is presented as a fixed verse.

In the poem 'Born to nothing' Tulile Siguca bemoans how Africans were brought up. In other words he is against the idea of welcoming all visitors with open hands as this has resulted in the visitors taking advantage of locals. One such way of welcoming that the persona castigates is 'to greet all visitors with a smile'. Thus he/she insinuates that this upbringing was detrimental to the well-being of Africans on their fathers' land hence they were 'bred with struggle as our daily bread'. In this piece the poet blames the forefathers who did not see how the cunning settlers were doing to them. This is a powerful poem that plays on alliteration to lyricise some of the lines; for example, 'the force that taught us to forge forth'. The 'f' sound underlines the force in the line. His references to the visitors as 'savages' shows how the settlers have behaved in the foreign lands that they appropriated as theirs. This poem, therefore, can be categorised as a revolutionary poem recording how the black people were dispossessed by the white people. They enjoy life in Africa while the black people suffer in the land of their forefathers. Thus any self-conscious son/daughter of Africa who wants to understand his/her predicament should take up this anthology and conscientise themselves.

Taijhet Nyobi challenges sexuality, gender differences and preferences as well as misogyny in her poem 'Bold Fade'. In it she portrays men as people who want to dictate how women should conduct themselves in their lives. The persona or narrator 'enter(s) the space meant for men' – a barber shop - for a haircut. This takes the men who were there by surprise especially when she asks for a bald cut and not just a trim. They therefore deride her and the reader is exposed to misogyny but the persona is not moved a bit. Her women's professor seems to have prepared her for this when she taught her the power of her sexuality. It is from her encounter with the professor that she became aware that 'my body belonged to me'. This poem takes the fight to the doorstep of masculinity. Africa, being the home of pronounced patriarchy, should embrace this poem if it is to cleanse itself of this mentality.

From just the few poems that have been discussed above, it can be surmised that *Best "New" African Poets 2015 Anthology* is a rich volume that can be used to emancipate the African people from the social, economic and political ills that, for decades since the dawn of independence, have impeded Africans to enjoy *uhuru*. It is hoped that this collection will not be the last of its kind. Such anthologies should be published annually to give voice to the voiceless on the continent.

Marechera, D (1992) Cemetery of Mind, Baobab Books, Harare.

A Translator and Educator of Cultures, Heritages, Traditions...: An appreciation of *Best "New" African Poets 2015 Anthology*

Delia Watterson

Best "New" African Poets 2015 Anthology is an encyclopaedia of learning. I anticipated an education; but nothing like the education it gives. At the beginning, is a struggle of ancestors fighting to achieve an Africa that is free. An African now corrupted; discarded, chained and enslaved by dictators and greed, are the lessons given by *Lekpele M Nyamalon*. The silent suffering that young African girls are subjected to, bodies and minds encumbered by worldly responsibility before childhood has ended. Childhood's stolen by poverty, by rape and cruelty, and the desperate need for these young girls to be heard, to be unyoked from this existence, is cried out by *Handson Chikowore*. Teaching us to strive for greater, to reach higher, to better our fathers that have gone before us, to be more than we think we can be, more than is expected of us, to soar, to fly farther than the sun, is what we learn from *Ohioleh Osadebey*. I could list all the contributors, as I was moved by and learnt from each one.

Before reading *Best "New" African Poets 2015 Anthology*; I am embarrassed to say, I thought I knew our African history, that I understood the words; heritage, tradition, culture, legislation, governance, individuality, sexuality, memory, and I believed that African meant born in Africa. And since reading *Best "New' African Poets 2015 Anthology*, I now know; I am no more than an embryo in this land, in this cradle of life, and my education borders on illiteracy. What I thought I knew versus what I learnt, I can only express and explain in metaphors. "...We talk, We laugh, Like nothing ever happened, Like the knives we threatened to kill each other with, Were never sharpened..." -Orimoloye Moyosore- "...Yet time and time again, we are told of a free press, a free state, free will, freedom of speech, freedom to write what we like, to preach, what we like, freedom to make a mess..." - John Eppel- "...So Love, kindly appreciate this extraordinary love poem, for

ours is totally out-of-the-ordinary love...”- Kariuki wa Nyamu-
“...Like Icarus, Did you not say that to fly too near the sun was to
overreach?...” -Ohioleh Osadebey.

At times I had to get up from my laptop, and walk outside and
recompose myself; because of the goose bumps, the hair rising all
over my body, the frog in my throat, the rage that balled hands into
fists, and to wipe the tears in my eyes. Just to be summoned back by
the call for insurrection in the words of *Lekpele M. Nyamalon*, in *Dig
the Graves*, “Where are we now Africa? Sometimes I ask, The truck
is stuck. Where are the men? Sometimes, I want to grasp the diggers
and burst the graves. And hold the bones of our fathers. And tell
them to come back...”

Asking the reader how far have we really come, what has
happened to progress, what happened to the warriors and the great
leaders of this land? Reminding us of the men that have bled into
African soil, that have fought for those incarcerated, fought for
freedom from injustice, and that Africa needs men like them again.
The writer’s desire for the resurrection or the reincarnation of these
leaders, in an Africa that has regressed is made clear. As well as the
anger and the sorrow that these leaders would feel should they still
be alive in this Africa, that has lost sight of the original goals; goals
of democracy, equality, a fair constitution and the upholding of
legislation and human rights. In the words of the writer, “....Ay
Madiba your strength is needed...Dig the graves...the heroes please
live again, or breathe through your sons”

Asking for a leader, a descendent of an African hero to save
Africa from its current state. Words that demand of the reader;
“Where is our courage”, save our African land from those that seek
to destroy what was fought for, and not to allow their deaths, their
sacrifices, their suffering to have been for nothing.

I heard clearly the voice of *Taijhet Nyobi* in *Bold Fade*, expressing
sexuality and the prejudice she has faced as a lesbian within African
culture; “I enter into the space meant for men, the heads don’t turn
but the eyes strain at the corners.” Illustrating to the reader the lack
of acknowledgment, the disrespect, and the scrutiny she receives in
a homophobic and misogynistic world, unwilling to respect her
choices, her body, herself. The intimidation felt at the hands of men

that have made her feel powerless and insignificant because of her sexuality and her appearance. How she has been discredited by those close to her, made to feel immoral by men of religion who are meant to be accepting and without judgment. "My down there, the space between my legs, the open wound became a mouth that could talk back." The writer's discovery of her inner strength and the powerful authority she finds in herself. Sharing the ridiculous, the incredulousness she encounters, and her response to them; "I'm queer because I am beautiful and I have a right to say what I do with my body, how I dress it, and what I call it."

I found myself searching with *Badradeen Mohammed*, "When the eyes look at the eyes, it is always a normal look, but when yours look at mine, it is definitely something else" Hoping to find the answers he looks for in *Your Eyes*. He takes the reader through the uncontrollable physical responses of his body to the eyes that invoke his feelings; "My blood pressure goes up and suddenly down, with no signs of balance". Feelings he cannot explain away with reason or logic, feelings he cannot master. The writer expresses his uncertainty and his doubt over this love, not trusting what the eyes is communicating to him. "I see scattered messages all over the space of your eyes, I try to collect them, open them, read them, or even translate them into love signs, but I seem to always draw blanks".

Trying to solve the questions in the eyes which bring him closer to frustration, how his doubt grows surrounded by other suitors perusing the eyes. The writer experiencing elation and depression whilst looking and waiting for reciprocation of his feelings, waiting for the validation he yearns for, but unable to discern the signals due to a past of hurtful transgressions, that have marked him. "And I used to be a damn romance but time has played me roughly so, I can't distinguish your romance from your being nice". Leading him to delve into his subconscious self in an attempt to find the answers. Relaying to the reader the experience of a love that to him is never certain, never sure, and that his quest for answers from the "adorable eyes" has only taken him deeper into doubt and confusion, and although he tries to escape the eyes, he is constantly drawn back in, because of his love for them, and the eyes' pull on him.

Best "New "African Poets 2015 Anthology, is a translator and educator of Cultures, Heritages, Traditions. A collaboration of brave voices and fearless pens, sharing Memories, Individuality, Sexuality, Political views, from over 23 African countries, 79 contributors, 214 poems, edited by *Tendai R Mwanaka* and *Daniel da Purifacacção.* This is a collaboration I could read again and again, never tiring of the powerful messages within it, you find yourself discovering something new each time, and it leaves you wondering profound thoughts on an African history. You find yourself as the reader transposed into the pages of this book, becoming one with the sand and the rocks of Africa, hearing the African voices cry out, and witnessing the strength and will of our Africa.

For more critical reviews on the anthology please visit these links and several others online:

https://africainwords.com/2016/05/30/review-best-new-african-poets-2015-anthology/

http://www.wordgathering.com/issue37/reviews/mwanaka.html

On being a pen-guine: An interview with Fiona Mahomed Khan

Interviewed by Tendai R Mwanaka

My literary meandering started in 1992. It was my first poem published in America entitled *The Cheetah and the Antelope*. It was the start of many successes. These successes came from a very painful backdrop of domestic violence, emotional and mental abuse. There was only one thing that could save my sanity and that was one thing I was born with. My writing! Being gifted was something my teachers discovered when I entered school. They groomed and nurtured that talent through much toil and encouragement because I guess I always broke the conventions. I made and lived by my own rules and restrictions. My appetite and thirst for writing and reading was and still is voracious. I feel bereft or lost without it. Having a lonely childhood with very much older brothers and sisters my only companions were music and books. I am a fantastic singer from opera to pop. I wrote on everything. Toilet paper, tissues, newspapers, walls, books, pages ….

There were many poems published internationally in many magazines and anthologies. In 1995 I had my first children's book published called *I Am What I Am* in five languages. It set me on a path that has been an adrenalin rush and I marvelled and cherished every moment.

What sets me apart from other poets is that I was raised and taught classics in literature. So I write with an excellent vocabulary and many feel that it makes me too bourgeoisie. It was a harsh lesson to tone down. I started spoken word poetry in 1995 and even converted it into a dramatic art form on stage with *Windows of a Women's Mind*. I know how to teach students and children to write and perform poetry using rap, musical instruments and drama. I can write immediately on any topic and that's versatility. I don't need prompts. I have not been promoted much because of racism. Writing and publishing in South Africa has always been white and elitist and sadly I stood alone all these years fighting the system. Now we have young black yuppies who have taken up the fight and

I am glad. I was really ostracised for speaking out against the system.

I am a bookaholic and invented the word 'únputdownable' in 1982. I live, breathe and write books. I am listless if I do not read. I have become more sophisticated now with the social media where I receive all my news, reviews and the latest on everything. I have quirkiness like I must read a new book or the daily paper that is untouched. I love the fresh smell and the crispness of the pages.

My favourite books started at three years old. I was raised on fairy tales and there was one story that was edged in my mind as it was used to scare or control my waywardness. It was called *The Hobbiyas and little Dog Turpy*. At 4 years old I was an avid reader. At 5 the librarian used to keep all the *Noddy* books for me. I revelled in Enid Blyton and Beatrix Potter and read them voraciously. I was fluent at 5 years of age. My appetite for books was unstoppable. Even the librarian and my family couldn't cope. As I grew as an orphan it became my only solace. I was captivated by Shakespeare at the age of 12 and Thomas Hardy and Dickens, then the Iliad and the Odyssey, I read Lady Chatterley's Lover at 12 years. It was a banned book in South Africa. My brother brought history alive with his vivid narratives of Egypt and Rome and those books filled my imagination with Helen of Troy, Cleopatra and Julius Ceaser. I loved French books from Napoleon and Three Musketeers, then Jules Verne and his Science Fiction, Wilbur Smith because being a South African he never supported the SA government and apartheid. Unlike other authors who cried apartheid but forced us to study their hardcore narratives at school and were supported financially by the education department. I loved the Orientalists in Ghalib, Tagore and Khalil Gibran. Gibran inspired my love for poetry until I found that he was very inspired and indirectly copied the styles of Indian Poets and writers. *To Sir with Love* was my first introduction into African literature, then *Things Fall Apart*. Bessie Head and the American writers.

I am presently working on a youth novel, a collection of essays on a gender issue, and my novels, two of them actually. I break this up with poetry and indeed I work so I have a full day. My social life is my writing and my followers or my colleagues. I am the project manager of the *Minara Aziz Hassim Literary Award* that focuses on debut and published writers. We kick started the project last year to a resounding success. I am presently completing my MBA and I am loving it. It's my dabbling in the corporate world and it's exciting.

I write every day even if its dabbling, doodling or just toying with ideas. I start at 4 am till 6am then again at 6pm until 10pm. I am flexible with time. My greatest distraction is procrastination. I do get a bit lazy. Sometimes I ponder both sides of a story or thought or idea. It takes a few days to reach a resolution. Then I get back to the writing process. I have had many challenges to divert my attention and time is not my best buddy *write* now. There is too much to do and too little time.

Everything inspires me. From a bee on a flower, to prayer, to the weather. I see beauty in all of God's creation. Because I am a spiritual being, everything is viewed on a metaphysical level. Everything is for a reason or a choice or a motivation. Nothing is incidental. The Universe I view as a relative creation. It's a source of transient energy and is binary. Our lives here are just a passage, a passing or a crossing. There is no permanency of anything.

Food for me has no value anymore as it has become too genetically modified and engineered. As a third world country we have become the dumping ground for the rest of the world. I am an award winning environmentalist. I firmly believe in permaculture and organic grown foods. The effects of climate change is devastating and has created a world -wide compromise on food, water and survival. It's the catalyst for future wars and civil unrest. So I eat organic with a balanced diet and keep living simple. My vice is chocolate.

I am most cautious in everything I do. I know what's my destination and I don't allow people to deter me. If they do deter me it's through scheming and conniving. And I do believe that karma is a bitch scorned. It comes back ten-fold to bite you in the ass and how.

The Leaf did not Fall is based on my observations of last Winter and is an allegory for our political restlessness. I watched a tree shed its leaves but this one leaf, grey and shrivelled, refused to fall. For 4 months it bobbed and twirled and sung to and fro but would not fall. I thought of our President. Tenacious and indefatigable in keeping his position. No matter how hard his opposers and political foes dig up the evidence against him, he rises above them and does not fall. Almost like a weed. I included this line which is very biblical and a metaphor, 'Shaded by the Leaven'. In the Gospel of Luke, they speak of leavened bread. Leaven is a raising agent like yeast used to make the bread rise. But it also speaks of the work Jesus did in the community for which few people valued, most never appreciated was his prophethood. And it refers to women being domesticated. When one looks at the president, it is the women who are his strongest supporters, they who keep the home fires burning. So the humble beginnings of our President have now become infected and he has grown and has become too large for his own good and that of his country. 'The parched thirst of African soil . . .' Are the people of SA. They are tired of being raped and ripped. Then will come the successions after the elections. People are fickle and feeble with minds that change all the time. If they are not in favour of a leader , they will be vocal by the way they vote. A typical comparison to *Animal Farm* by Orwell.

BNAP is innovative in this continent in its strategy. It was researched and targeted well, looking for a niche market. This concept is only found in America but has been adapted to suit the African market and expand the opportunities in publishing. The strategic marketing via social media and using the poet's websites and social media site to promote the book in fact encouraged the self -awareness and sales of the book. Publishing of poetry is limited to an elite few in Africa. BNAP has created a platform for emerging poets and a jump for established poets. At cost free the exposure and marketing of the talent and profiles related in making the poets a commodity and improved their profiles and saleability. With BNAP on their CV's they are on the move. BNAP is the springboard for success for emerging poets. My suggestion is that the poems be converted to a spoken word poetry slam at relevant venues. Its art. Its performance, its poetry.

Thabo Mbeki's dream of an African Renaissance: An interview with Christine Coates

Interviewed by Tariro Ndoro

Christine Coates is a Cape Town based poet who has a great interest in preserving personal history and poetry is her chosen platform for expressing thoughts. Christine talks about her love for telling one's unique story through poetry and how the BNAP anthology takes her back to former South African president, Thabo Mbeki's dream of an African Renaissance.

'I've always loved reading stories and poetry, says Christine Coates, whose poetry has been featured in the *Best New African Poets* (BNAP) *2015 Anthology*, "I have a creative urge and this led me, together with my love of reading, books and art, to wanting to express myself in poetry and story. I wanted to tell my story, write about the world I inhabit.' Influenced by many writers, Christine learnt that she needed to make time and space for herself as a writer. 'Emily Dickinson's unique and secret voice urged me – doing what she had to do or she would die. Mary Oliver's nature poetry inspires me, Anjtjie Krog teaches me to express my anger, my rage boldly. I love some of the newer American writers like Rae Armantrout, or a Danish poet like Inger Christensen. I love discovering new (to me) poets. Doing a Masters in Creative Writing gave me structure and the encouragement to tell my story my way. Reading is what changes my writing most – I began to find my own voice, began to trust my own story, began writing from what I know. I believe we all have a creative urge but we need to find an outlet for it. Everyone has a unique story – it's all we really have. I love widely reading other poets and I study all the time.'

'We have really only our unique story – and the BNAP anthology is a lovely gathering of unique voices. There are stories here – sad, hopeful, angry, disappointed, happy stories. We must tell our stories if we are to recover. Collectively, telling our stories helps us meet each other over the stretch of the continent. As they say Africa is a continent not a country, but it is a country too. This anthology makes me feel that – one with my countrymen and

362

women. *Poets are witnesses and voices* – sometimes we are lone voices that cry out in the desert, but I believe we can affect change. There are many wonderful poems and poets in this anthology. "Inside Timbuktu" by Lekpele M Nyamalon struck me as it echoed what I said about stories. Timbuktu is mentioned elsewhere in the anthology. It resonates with South Africa's ex-President Mbeki's dream for an African Renaissance and his vision to save the Timbuktu manuscripts. Now they are destroyed and, as the poet says, "Timbuktu – we need you". We need poetry and stories to save us. I also loved Idara Idemeko's idea of memory and the Diaspora; "I could not remember not because I forgot,/but because I was a stranger in my mother's land./And yet I was home". And her "Filing Cabinets and Smoked Peppers" – a beautiful and sad portrait, "a song for the broken". I loved the litany of the "I am" in Ohioleh Osadebey's "I Have Learned to Boast like My Fathers", and his "The Thing I'd Love to Tell My Father". I loved the images in Aaron Brown's "N'Djamena Morning" – the sun shining in patches through the trees – "the trees with needle-thin leaves/and Moussa tuning the radio". Also his poem "Twin" struck me deeply. I loved the bravery of Taijbet Nyobi's "Bold Fade" – "...the open wound/became a mouth that could talk back/became a shelled muscle that spilled pearls/became oceanic enough to hold rage and sadness/became mine". There are many other gifted poets and strong voices.'

Entrevista com o Sonia Robalo

Interviewed by Tariro Ndoro

Há quanto tempo você está no jogo para a poesia?
Tenho, uma relação muito especial com os livros, desde que me recordo de ser "gente". Tive a sorte de ter uns pais que sempre me incentivaram a ler. Levavam-me a bibliotecas e às melhores livrarias com muita frequência. Escrevo poesia, como escrevo prosa...tudo depende ao que me proponho fazer e ao meu estado de espírito no momento. Existem duas razões básicas para eu escrever poesia: ou por excesso de felicidade ou por excesso de tristeza (risos).

As Almas infelizes são capazes de criar as maiores obras literárias. Talvez porque o ser humano aprecie um bom drama. Sempre li poesia, mas senti-la na sua verdadeira essência?!... Talvez tenha despoletado a minha veia poética criativa com o meu primeiro desgosto de amor (risos).

Que tipo de poesia/ storytelling tradição existe na sua cultura/país e que isso teve qualquer influência na sua escrita?
A minha Alma é Angolana e o meu Coração é Português. Sinto-me assim. Essa mistura influenciou não só o meu DNA, mas acima de tudo a minha visão das coisas. As duas culturas influenciam constantemente a forma como percepciono o que me rodeia e por conseguinte a forma como escrevo. A poesia Angolana é o espelho da sociedade Angolana. Os poetas tentam, com esta arte, chamar a atenção do que se passa à sua volta. É uma poesia que "arranha" constantemente a situação socio-politica que o país vive. A poesia Portuguesa transporta-nos para uma realidade um pouco diferente. O panorama socio-politico é diferente, pelo que a tónica de quem escreve poesia é diferente de um poeta Angolano. Embora se possam de alguma forma cruzar em certos âmbitos. A poesia Portuguesa é muito virada para o amor e tudo o que este transporta enquanto sentimento. Obviamente, que a forma como escrevo, tem influência directa destas duas culturas.

Que influências (por exemplo HipHop, batida da poesia) urbano influenciaram sua escrita?

Todos os acontecimentos que me rodeiam têm uma influência relevante naquilo que escrevo. Seja na prosa ou na poesia. Escrevo sobre o que vejo à minha volta, o que sinto, o que percepciono. Gosto de escrever sobre sentimentos, vivências. Gosto de escrever sobre o amor.

Qual estilo de escrita (verso livre, lírica etc) você inclinar-se para?

Tenho uma predição por versos livres. Os chamados versos irregulares, que não possuem restrição métrica. Prefiro não me basear em critérios pré - definidos, mas sim em decisões intuitivas ou em normas criadas por mim. Talvez isso aconteça pela afinidade que tenho com a prosa.

Quais escritores que influenciaram a sua escrita?

São muitos os Escritores/ Poetas que me influenciam; Florbela Espanca, Carlos Drummond de Andrade, Martha Medeiros, Clarice Lispector, Pablo Neruda, Mia Couto, Alda Lara, Ernesto Lara... Inspiram-me fortemente.

Como é que o status de imigrante/ expatriado/ refugiados influenciado você está escrevendo?

Claro que as minhas raízes estão sempre presentes no que escrevo. Não só na poesia, mas nos livros que escrevo, nos artigos para jornais, nas crónicas...em tudo. Não posso fugir do que sou, e isso, influência a minha forma de ver os factos. Não me perco nos mitos do tempo, porque nunca me esqueço de onde vim.As minhas origens estão sempre na minha memória...e nos meus horizontes também. Transporto a saudade do que vivi e do que fui para o agora. Essa transição, entre duas culturas diferentes, marcou-me, mas nem por isso de uma forma negativa. Sinto-me filha de duas"mães" e aproveito essa mais valia a meu favor.

Conte-nos sobre os seus poemas em BNAP e se você já leu a antologia em tudo, o que você golpeou sobre ele?

The Best " New" African Poets 2015 Anthology enche-me de orgulho. Primeiro, por mostrar o talento Africano. Pessoas diferentes, com vivências diferentes, mas com algo em comum...o gosto pela escrita. Incorporamos o espírito Africano que nos une às diferenças que também nos acabam por unir...SOBERBO. Existem lugares no mundo cuja história ficou marcada por largos períodos de luta e sofrimento. Que continuam a viver nesse registo até hoje. Um desses lugares chama-se África. E nós...os seus filhos, fomos chamados para que de alguma forma acendêssemos a chama do espírito humano colectivo. E não é para esse despertar que serve também a poesia? Desenvolveu-se uma forma de expressão artística de excelente qualidade, que ficará registada como uma herança que perdurará no tempo. Muito nossa. Muito Africana, mas com a globalização bem presente em cada um de nós. Os meus poemas, são a minha pequena contribuição para esta grandiosa obra que envaidece a todos nós que amamos a nossa África.

I am a simple farmer, poet, and writer: An interview with Fayssal Chafaki, the Poet from the Kingdom Of Morocco

Interviewed by Tendai R. Mwanaka

Who is Fayssal Chafaki

Whenever I am being, respectively, asked this question, my answer reveals itself this way. I am a simple farmer, poet, and writer. This humble answer summarizes a great deal of the poet's life, as it also sheds light upon who Fayssal Chafaki, the Poet of the Kingdom of Morocco, is. I am a farmer because this is what I have chosen to be. I am a poet because this is my nature, my inner self, and the reason of my existence. I am a writer because my modest academic background has granted me, alongside the composition of poetry since childhood, the ability to write prose in terms of short stories, articles, novel-attempts, books, and research papers related to the study of Phonology. My writings in prose are only in English. Fayssal Chafaki, in a sum of words, is a Moroccan Arab poet, whose poetic style still preserves the norms and conventions of Classical Poetry, both in Arabic and English, in form and content, but delivers conventionally and conveys faithfully a modern and contemporary message to a multi-cultural literary audience. Fayssal Chafaki, the farmer, the poet, and the writer, lives now in the Western country-side of the Kingdom of Morocco, where he leads a normal life, yet full of struggle, and where he has devoted himself to revive poetry and literature which, seemingly, have ceased to play their great and important role in his country.

Tell us what inspires you to create

To be frank with you, the one and only thing that inspires me the most will have to be the last thing I mention to you. I can almost be inspired by anything that surrounds me. Nature and the farm come first. Then, the fact of being away from the noises of the city-life is what constantly pushes me to create. I can also compose under any circumstances and, above all, when I am faced with stress. When I sense danger, mainly danger that threatens faith, ethics, my homeland, human-being existence as a whole, or any kind of danger that may menace all of us, I use my pen. I compose for war, as I compose for peace. Many of my Arabic and English poems are triggered either by a global, or social, or political event that necessitates the interference of poetry. Sometimes I can be inspired by a simple post on social-media sites, an article I've read, a video I have watched, a comment that made me happy or upset, a kind message or a provoking insult, an old poem, a beautiful lady, a flower, a bird, an insect, an idea, simple or complex, a piece of art, a constellation of the stars, the rising sun, the moon and the clouds, the rain and the winds, the movement of the seasons, calm and solitude, my adorable spouse, my beloved little daughter, my dear mother, and even a friend or a person who may request a certain poem for himself or herself. At the end, the one and only thing that inspires me the most, and which I always consider the source and power of my Arabic and English poems, is the Holy Qur'an.

Above being a poet you are also a farmer and academic, tell us how you balance these three

I have mentioned the fact of combining poetry, writing, and farming into one of my Arabic poems stating that "By day, my work, a hoe in my hand; and when night comes, it is my pen."In truth, farming has never appeared to hinder me from composing my poems, reading, writing, or conducting research. The farm is not that big enough, so the work there is easily planned and done. Usually my work in the farm starts early in the morning and ends with sunset. After the kids go to bed I isolate myself in a room and begin either to compose a poem, or read, or deal with my writings. I always find the appropriate moment to be in the company of books, papers, and pen. I also find time, occasionally, to be on-line and post some of my poems. Conducting academic research as a farmer and a poet, though demanding, is given a share of my time, and has never been a heavy task for me. Mainly my academic research is conducted independently after facing major obstacles from some university professors. The main focus of my research papers evolves around the study of sounds in Arabic and Old languages. The life of a farmer is very simple, and so the life of a poet, or a writer. To balance between these three, I always feel the need to exert mental effort besides physical one. You may not recognize me as a poet and a humbly educated person when I am wearing my boots and ploughing the land for crops, but when I compose and write you will.

Tell us about your work as a farmer, what crops you grow or animals you keep etc

The farm, as I mentioned above, is not that big enough, four acres land, situated in a plain zone in the West of the Kingdom of Morocco. The main agriculture we deal with is seasonal. We grow wheat, corn, beans, carrots, onions, clover, and different types of vegetables in a system of rotation. In the past ten years and more, we used to find difficulties with irrigation. In the present day we have been able to set a small system of drip irrigation that really saves time and effort. As to animals we keep, for the time being there is only some chicken and few sheep, as we witnessed a period of drought and lack of cattle feed. During this actual season, we are planting yellow melon. We are also planning to innovate our small farming agriculture techniques and methods. The whole work in the farm is done and managed by my brother and I, and our two small families.

Tell us about the Moroccan poetry and literary scene, both performance and written

Very recently, the Moroccan Prime Minister announced that the Kingdom in the future will not be in need of poets, writers, philosophers, and Men of Letters, but rather will be in need of people who produce wealth. This is encouraging and dis-encouraging at the same time. Encouraging in the sense that poets in the Kingdom of Morocco will have to be more creative than they may happen to be, and of course dis-encouraging in the sense that poetry and literature are endangered in my country. This leads us to tackle the issue of Moroccan poetry and the literary scene in brief. Moroccan poetry possesses a rich poetic and literary heritage. Poets of the twentieth century like Al Halwi, Al Balghiti, and Bin Brahim will always be the same great modern poetry figures who have lit the path for many other poets. Today, unfortunately, there is very few poets like these great ones, if not even a single one. The reason lies behind the fact that great poets like Al Halwi, Al Balghiti, and Bin Brahim belong to the Arabic Prosodic Poetry school, also called Classical Poetry. After these poets and their likes have gone, Free-verse "poets" have taken the literary scene for a period of three to four decades with the claim that Moroccan Arabic Classical Poetry is not fit for the modern world, and, therefore, is dead. As a result to this kind of literary "conflict" between Free-verse and Classical poetry schools in their Moroccan Arab context, Moroccan poetry, and Arabic poetry in general, degraded. Poetry lost huge audiences of ordinary and educated people alike. This made the literary scene vulnerable to low culture interference, where commercial singing and dancing festivals, for instance, replaced poetry and literary gatherings. People's artistic taste in Morocco have deteriorated towards consumable and ready-made low types of art, leaving poetry and literature into a dark corner face to face with oblivion. There are of course contemporary Moroccan poets who also belong to the same prosodic Arabic poetry school but are seldom active in the literary scene, and if there is any, they do not happen to gather their efforts and collaborate with each other to bring back poetry on stage. Some Moroccan poets secure themselves into closed groups and organize their own events without taking the pain to open their arms to other poets. Some others are timid. Some are fake. Journalists, critics, university professors, the Ministry of Culture, and media are also responsible for such grave and dire situation poetry and literature has reached in the Kingdom of Morocco. Media platforms and newspapers are for sale. Critics are blocked. University professors do not care very often. The Ministry of Culture supports everything but poets' creative work. This is in brief the harsh reality behind the literary scene in my country. To measure how much does a nation value its poets, it would be enough to see how many of them are honored by that nation. My country, I am sorry to say it, values the more all that would help spread ignorance, not what would enlighten brains. The burden is still upon us, poets, to bring poetry's fame back.

If you were to be reborn, what form would you like to return in

If I were to be born again, I would like to return into nothing but the same Servant of Creator, the same human being, the same simple poet. I would like some change, yes, but a change in time and probably in space. I would like to return in time when bards used to be listened to, respected, counseled, and regarded with high esteem. As to place, it does not matter. Everywhere there is the High Creator, and everywhere there is Him, we have a chance to be reborn.

Tell us about your poem, "No Wise Man" in BNAP 2015

Talking about my poem "No Wise Man", or any other poem of mine, is always done with some reservation. I prefer to leave room for readers, critics, audiences, and potential researchers to study the poem, or poems, without the interference of the poet, fearing that my opinion, somehow, about the meaning, the structure, or the whole essence of the poem would be taken for granted and considered as a final judgment. Yet, I can always talk about the circumstances under which this particular poem has seen light and the reason behind composing it. "No Wise Man" is a poem about a very old so-called political conflict in the North of Africa. The poem is one among a series of English poems defending the Issue of Moroccan Sahara. "No Wise Man" points to the issue of the Moroccan Sahara and is considered very critical for the poet. The Moroccan Sahara for him is an issue of existence, and in his poem "No Wise Man" he provides evidence to support his right. This poem, and all the other poems that fall under the title of "Defending the Moroccan Sahara" explain to what extent the poet is related and linked to this desert part of his homeland. The poem indicates that the Moroccan Sahara is the poet's mother and place of birth, mentions the poet's origins as connected to his Moroccan Sahrawi nomad grandfather, and informs the reader smoothly about the reality and truth of this so-called conflict. The poet in this poem, "No Wise Man", refuses to break his historical ties and bonds with his grandfathers who constantly live in the Moroccan Sahara. The poet respects the past, lives in the present, and looks for a peaceful tomorrow in the region, as reflected in his poem. What really triggers the poet to compose poems defending the

371

Moroccan Sahara is that the poet is born six months before this so-called conflict started. Prior to 1975 there has been no such dispute and no one has claimed that the Moroccan Sahara is another nation. During that period the whole Kingdom of Morocco had been suffering from colonization. The North and the South was colonized by Spain while the rest was colonized by France. French colonizers left the country in 1956 and the Spanish kept the Moroccan Sahara under their control until later. We have been colonized, and so many African countries, and still today there are greedy persons who want to divide our country. The same tribes that lived in the Moroccan Sahara are living all around the Kingdom today. All these reasons above, and many other ones, are behind the composition of "No Wise Man". The poem at the end makes it clear that only a fool will keep fighting for something that does not belong to him or her, and that the earth will only be owned by the creator.

What does BNAP represent for you and the continent at large and what improvements do you want to see in the next BNAP

BNAP is home for me and the best and unique adobe for African poets. BNAP is a torch of enlightenment the continent really needs. It has succeeded into bringing African poets together and presenting them to the world. By this, BNAP has carved a honorable mark in the field of poetry and literature. BNAP is a new African literary movement able to carry the universal message of poetry and give Africa a strong voice among other continents. I will always be happy to see BNAP supporting African poets and leading them towards success. I certainly hope that future series of BNAP would welcome more African poets, especially young ones, and would one day, if possible, include poems in Arabic and Hausa. BNAP is always that heart that speaks for Africa.

Let's begin at the grassroots: An interview with John Attah Ojonugwa

Interviewed by Tendai R Mwanaka

Tell us about yourself

My name is Ojonugwa John Attah. I am a Nigerian poet and short story writer. I also write football reviews and compose text messages. I teach English Language and literature. I have a poem in the *Best New African Poets 2015 Anthology* and I have been published on notable literary platforms in Nigeria, Uganda, The USA amongst others.

Tell us about the poetry scene in your country

Poetry is a large genre in my country. These days, people get involved unlike in the past when only those involved were the poets and those who loved poetry events. The promotion of poetry is something that has been done gradually since many persons in the past believed only prose was the thing and if you weren't writing prose, you were never read. Right now, poetry is gaining ground with the number of poetry festivals, poetry workshops, award ceremonies and seminars organized for children and adults alike. The spoken word is also gaining ground as well.

What influences your creativity?

My creativity is influenced by a lot of things. One of them is nature. Whenever I see trees, the sun, the moon, animals, the birds and feel the general movement of nature, I pick up something. These days, I take photographs of nature with my phone until I get a camera as a birthday gift! Secondly, people, situations and events influence my creativity. There is a part on social media and then there is a daily interaction with the tea man somewhere, the tout on the road, the tomato seller and all others. This is why I love meeting people and experiencing several situations which are likely to develop the innate part of me that tends to keep those experiences for future use. Another influencing factor on my creativity is music. It just does not matter the genre. Sometimes, it depends on what I am doing or on what I am thinking about. The music could be hip hop, blues, jazz, gospel, reggae or pop. It depends on what I listen to at a moment or what I am doing at the moment. Sometimes, I love it quiet or alone to help me think more, to create.

How do you get around life and your creativity, how do you achieve balance between these, living and creativity?

Combining life and creativity can be so interesting. One thing that improves my creativity is my daily interaction with all that life consists of. It is not good enough to disengage both from each other and feel alright. Life goes with creativity and that is what I feel. One thing for me is to live my life daily interacting with those I meet and with the animals or things I encounter and to an extent, bring them into my writing.

What do you think is lacking in writing, or poetry-making in the continent and how do you think we can solve this?

I will choose to speak about the problem of poetry-making in the African continent because it is very important. Prose and drama took early centre stage in and around the continent. Poetry was initially seen by many as a genre filled with complexities in language, imageries and all. Many refused to dedicate their time to interpreting in their own words, the content of poems they come across. This withdrawal led to a lot more problems. Although the continent keeps rising in this area, a lot still needs to be done. One problem I feel needs to be addressed is that of an early contact with poetry from childhood for many school children. At the primary or basic level, nursery rhymes like "Twinkle, twinkle little star" and "Old Roger" could be taught before other poems from poets around the continent and beyond are taught at intermediate and tertiary education levels. At that point, the learners would have encountered the poems and works of old poets like William Shakespeare, John Milton, Robert Burns, William Wordsworth, John Keats, Ralph Waldo Emerson, PB Shelley and co while kicking on with modern poets like Chimalum Nwankwo, Tendai Rinos Mwanaka, Shittu Fowora, Jumoke Verissimo, Damian Opata, Daniel Chikwuemeka, Chuma Mmeka, Ejiofor Ugwu and the numerous poets brought to the limelight through the publication of various anthologies of poetry in and around the world. If we begin from the grassroots, poetry will become more than a national or continental genre and not be limited to only those who read, write or critique it. This is the type of transformation the continent needs. Poets are as well not properly recognized, promoted and awarded. This has to change but we must start somewhere.

If you were a poem, what type of form will you be in and why?

Waoh! That is a tough one there. If I were a poem? Well, I do not have a particular form which I love. When I initially started poetry, I loved the sonnets of Shakespeare and the pattern as well but I prefer the nature of poems these days. They barely follow a certain pattern as each person tries to develop something beautiful instead of being limited to a particular form or content.

What type of sports are you into?

I love football. Although I am a Chelsea fan, I love football without borders. I prefer people discussing or arguing about football with some bit of sense and not negativity, taking in the truth no matter how painful and learning further by listening to the opinion of others whether favourable or not. I also love volleyball and basketball but I love watching and playing football more!

Tell us about your poem(s) in BNAP

I have a solitary poem in BNAP. It is titled "I Have Been Watching You." The poem is written from the point of view of a young man whose lover has done something terrible and wants to own up but remains silent. This silence makes the poetic persona to speak in these words to his lover: "I have been watching you/I know you want to say something/But you don't want to or are afraid to do so…" The lover concludes by saying "But I will keep watching you!" It is a poem I love and for it to appear in the anthology is an achievement.

What do you think can be done to improve BNAP anthology in the future editions, marketing, editorial etc?

First of, I would like to register my gratitude to Tendai Rinos Mwanaka and Daniel da Purificação for the consistent efforts in searching for good poets as well as good poems from the continent and beyond and creating a melting pot out of our varied creativity in all its forms and themes. There were challenges no doubt but the successes recorded thus far have been amazing. Although there are successes all around, there are places the anthology can still improve. One of them is in the area of promotion both of the BNAP anthology and the contributing poets. As I speak, a lot of the contributors in certain parts of the continent are yet to hold the anthology in their hands which should have been before other readers and reviewers did. The marketing as well needs to be improved upon. Besides Amazon, if there are other retail outlets, there should be co-opted into the distribution of the anthology. If possible as well, let there be publishers in at least four to five African countries so that the production and marketing stress will reduce and the anthology get to the contributors and other readers in time. All the best to all the contributing poets for the future. I am happy to have featured in this wonderful anthology!

Thank you for the interview.

Entrevista com o Soberano Canhanga

Interviewed by Tariro Ndoro

Há quanto tempo você está no jogo para a poesia

Escrevo poesia desde principios da década de noventa do século pasado. Porém, o lado artístico surge mais tarde quando passo a usá-la como forma de expressão das minhas captações sociais que não encontravam espaço na prosa jornalística que é a minha profissão.

Que tipo de poesia / storytelling tradição existe na sua cultura / país e que isso teve qualquer influência na sua escrita?

Os verdadeiros poetas de todo o mundo são livres na sentir e no dizer. Assim é em Angola. Marcou o meu período de afirmaçao intelectual a poesia épica de exaltação aos feitos patrióticos bem como a lírica com as suas "canções" à esperança por dias melhores. O Amor e a Pátria juntavam-se num mesmo gérero. Isso foi fundamental para despertar o meu lado artístico que andava incubado.

Que influências (por exemplo, hip hop , batida da poesia) urbano influenciaram sua escrita?

Os versos e as estrofes da poesia dos anos oitenta e noventa do sáculo passado davam corpo à música mais difundida pela Rádio. Era o que formava a nossa consciência de novos cidadãos do país ainda emprionário. Os versos cantados forjaram homens que travaram ventos...

Qual estilo de escrita (verso livre , lírica etc) você inclinar-se para?

Embora tente nalguns textos exprimir-me de forma conservadora, seguido a harmonia e a rítmica que marcou a poesia do século XX, é na liberdade do verso que mais me encontro. Para mim, a poesia nada mais é sena°ao a conituidade da prosa e, sobretudo da crónica. Sou um cronista. A poesia serve para dizer, às vezes, em poucas palavras o muito que não cabe numa crónica. É o refúgio silencioso de quem tem muito por dizer.

Quais escritores influenciaram sua escrita?

Sou um leitor heterodoxo, tendo lido Textos de Camões, Fernando Pessoa, Alda Lara, Noémia do Espirito Santo, Agostinho Neto, Alexandre Dáskalos, Aires de Almeida Santos, entre outros lusófonos. É essa imensidão do secular verso lusófono que me influencia e vai continuar a fazê-lo.

Como é que o status de imigrante / expatriado / refugiados influenciado você está escrevendo?

Não taxativamente o estatuto de imigrante ou refugiado. É a condiçao de ter chegado à grande cidade de Luanda na condição de deslocado (emigrante interno)que despertou em mim a necessidade do registo das captaçoes sensoriais e emocionais. Tornei'me um coleccionador de cenas do quotidiano e, à certa altura, senti a necessidade de ir registando em versos ou prosa, aquilo que era o país do meu tempo. É também uma forma de fazer história.

Conte-nos sobre seus poemas em BNAP e Se você já leu a antologia em tudo, o que você golpeou sobre ele

Ainda não li o livro. Lembro-me ter remetido três textosversificados que acabaram aprovados. Se bem me lembro, um é Mano Décimo e o outro é À hora do grito. Mas há um terceiro de que já não me lembro o título.

For more links on interviews, facebook features, photos, videos, audio recordings etc.., visit these links:
http://bestnewafricanpoets.blogspot.com/
https://www.facebook.com/BestNewAfricanPoets2015/

Impressions of the South African Launch of BNAP 2015

Archie Swanson

Marcia Raymond is a retired librarian who has for years been hosting a poetry event at the Cape Town Central Library on the last Saturday afternoon of each month called Poetry Circle on behalf of *Friends of Central Library*. There is an opportunity for open mike and each month there are guest poets. Marcia very graciously agreed to the launch of BNAP2015 in South Africa at the Poetry Circle event on 27 February 2016.

The Central Library is housed in the Old Drill Hall; a colonial building right next door to the Cape Town City Hall where Nelson Mandela gave his first speech to tens of thousands of people on the

Grand Parade on the day he was released from Victor Vester Prison. The library is a busy place with plenty of young students doing research. The poetry reading space is in a central well surrounded by elevated galleries holding the tall stacks of bookshelves several levels high. Normally during reading random visitors lean over the railings to listen to the poems.

First up was Christine Coates who has an MA in Creative Writing from the University of Cape Town and whose debut collection of poems *Homegrown* was published in 2014. She read her own poems "Mapungubwe" and "House of Kolmanskop". Each poet also represented an absent poet and read one of their poems. Christine read Aaron Brown's poem "Twin". Aaron grew up in Chad and currently lives in the US where he teaches at Stirling College. Helen Walne read Chaun Ballard's poem "Chrysaora Achlyos", and Tendai Mwanaka's poem, "Body". Chaun was raised in Missouri and California and now lives in Ghana. Mwanaka, one of the editors of BNAP 2015, is a multi-disciplinary Zimbabwean artist with a host of publications. Troydon Wainwright, a Cape Town poet with a popular poetry blog, read his own poems "Ideals" and "It Only Took a Moment". He followed this by reading Sierra Leonean poet Ostia Kabba's poem "The Realm of the Men with Broken Wings".

Cathy Abrahams represented Lekpele Nyamalon and read "Inside Timbuktu" as well as Idara Idemeko's "Black Water". Archie Swanson, published in the *McGregor Poetry Anthology, Stanza, New Contrast and the Spanish newspaper, El Mundo*, read his two poems "Non" and "Suleiman" and Maakomele Manaka's "At the Foot of Uhuru". The award-winning novelist Jade Gibson who recently published her novel "Glowfly Dance", read "In my Country" by Nigerian poet Daniel Chukwuemka and Sowetan poet Maakomele Manaka's "Leono on My Mind".

Finally, Zimbabwean poet, Christopher Kudyahakudadirwe, who has a Masters in Creative Writing from the University of Western Cape, shared his poems "The Passage" and "My heart Packed a Suitcase". He closed with Maakomele Manaka's "At the Foot of Uhuru". The 50 attendees participated in lively discussions on all the poems and left enriched with the various perspectives of our Africaness.

Christine Coates

The Cape Town launch of BNAP at the Central Library was well attended. The audience packed the central well of the beautiful space in the historic Old Drill Hall which was converted by renowned architect, John Rennie, into the library. I, Christine Coates, opened the event by reminding the audience that we have an anthology of unique voices. There are stories here – sad, hopeful, angry, disappointed, happy stories. This anthology makes me feel one with my continent. Poets are witnesses and voices sometimes we are lone voices that cry out in the desert, but I believe we can affect change. I had invited friends who are artists and writers to represent poets who were absent from this reading. I chose to read Aaron Brown's "Twin" as well as two of my own poems. It was a beautiful afternoon in a spectacular space. As the other poets read, I watched as library users leaned over the balcony railings to listen to the poetry. Words filled the space, lifted to the rafters. Everything was wrapped in words.

Troydon Wainwright

I entered Cape Town Central Library for the first time. The building itself was over a hundred years old. Inside I could literally smell its history along with the rows of books, which offered up their usual scent that at once made me feel at home. In the centre of the library, I found chairs set out in rows facing a table, with a mezzanine level looking down on the area. Yup, I am here, I thought. I loitered for a while, waiting for others to show up, before I took a seat in the front row and started talking to the gentleman to my right. He turned out to be Christopher Kudyahakudadirwe, another poet also featured in the *Best "New" African Poets 2015 Anthology*. Next I met Archie Swanson, a fellow BNAP and the guy who had done most of the corresponding in getting us all together for the event. When I first saw Archie, he was talking to Marcia Raymond, the librarian who organizes and hosts the monthly readings at the library and had done so for over a decade. I cannot voice my gratitude enough to her and likes of her, who give of their time and effort to provide us poets with a stage on which to sing.

Christine Coates was the final Best New African Poet who was attending the event. She was friendly and had a sparkling sense of humor. She was also first up on stage. Her poems *Mapangupwe* and *House of Kolmanskop* were brilliant as was the Aaron Brown poem, *Twin*, which she read and which (like all the poems read before the open mic session) featured in the Best "New" African Poets 2015 Anthology. Her reading was followed by Helen Walne who read Chaun Ballard's poem, *Chrysaora Achlyos*, and Tendai Mwanaka's poem, *Body*. Again the quality of the poems impressed me. Christopher, meanwhile, was filming the entire event. I had learnt through the group e-mails leading up to the event that aside from being one of Africa's best new poets, he was also a cameraman.

I was up next and I felt my heart flutter as I always do when I am called up onto stage. There were roughly fifty souls in the crowd and also all of their eyes were suddenly on me. I read Ostia Kabba's breathtaking poem *The Realm of the Men with Broken Wings* then my own two poems, *Ideals* and *It Only Took a Moment*. Afterwards, I took my seat both elated and relieved that my part was over. Cathy Abrahams then stood up and read Lekpele Nyamalon's Inside *Timbuktu* and Idara Idemeko's *Black Water*. Both of which blew my mind.

383

Now, it was Archie's turn. He read Maakomele Manaka's *At the foot of Uhuru* and his two poems, *Non* and *Suleiman*. All three of which I enjoyed immensely. Jade Gibson, an outstanding poet in her own right, read Daniel Chukwuemka's *In My Country* and *Leono On My Mind* by Maakomele Manaka. They went over very well. At last, Christopher handed his camera over to someone else to film, while he took the stage. He read his poems *The Passage* and *My Heart Packed in a Suitcase* which were exceptional. His poems were made all the more impressive by the fact that English is his second language. Christopher closed the show with Maakomele Manaka's *At the foot of Uhuru*, which maintained the high standards set by the rest of the work. After the Best New African Poets' Presentation there was an open mic session. Voices young and old spoke their hearts. Who knows perhaps one of those voices will one day be among Africa's best new poets.

I was deeply honored to simply be a part of the event and the anthology. May Africa keep singing and may its voice be heard the world over.

Lightning Source UK Ltd.
Milton Keynes UK
UKOW03f2235210417
299617UK00003B/78/P

9 789956 764891